MODERN LEGAL STUDIES

NATURAL JUSTICE

AUSTRALIA
The Law Book Company Ltd.
Sydney: Melbourne: Brisbane

CANADA AND U.S.A.
The Carswell Company Ltd.
Agincourt, Ontario

INDIA
N.M. Tripathi Private Ltd.
Bombay
and
Eastern Law House Private Ltd.
Calcutta
M.P.P. House
Bangalore

ISRAEL
Steimatzky's Agency Ltd.
Jerusalem : Tel Aviv : Haifa

MALAYSIA : SINGAPORE : BRUNEI
Malayan Law Journal (Pte.) Ltd.
Singapore

NEW ZEALAND
Sweet and Maxwell (N.Z.) Ltd.
Auckland

PAKISTAN
Pakistan Law House
Karachi

MODERN LEGAL STUDIES

NATURAL JUSTICE

by
PAUL JACKSON, LL.B. (Lpool), B.C.L. (Oxon.), M.A. (Dubl.)
of Grays Inn, Barrister
Professor of Law, University of Reading

SECOND EDITION

LONDON
SWEET & MAXWELL
1979

First edition 1973
Second edition 1979

Published in 1979 by
Sweet & Maxwell Limited of
11 New Fetter Lane, London
and printed in Great Britain
by Northumberland Press Limited
Gateshead, Tyne and Wear

ISBN Hardback 0 421 24780 0
Paperback 0 421 24790 8

"The fundamental human right is not
to a legal system that is infallible
but to one that is fair."

(*Maharaj* v. *Attorney-General of Trinidad and Tobago* (No. 2) [1978] 1 W.L.R. 902, 911 *per* Lord Diplock)

GENERAL PREFACE

Modern Legal Studies is a series written for students of law in Universities, Polytechnics, and other institutions of higher education. It originated in the belief that law students need a series of short, scholarly monographs in different areas of the law, resembling those now being produced in other fields of social science.

The Series has five principal aims. First, it aims to supplement traditional textbooks by providing opportunity both for new topics to be written about and introduced into the syllabus of traditional courses, and for older topics to be given deeper consideration than they receive in the standard texts. Secondly, as the series progresses, it aims to provide a possible alternative to the one-textbook-per-course approach of many law courses; a set of several short books in, for instance Property Law, could be used as substitutes for the present all-purpose texts. This would enable the student to become acquainted with a variety of views and approaches to the subject. Thirdly, the existence of a series of small, relatively cheap, legal monographs will, it is hoped, facilitate the breaking of boundaries between traditional courses—*e.g.* Contract and Tort—and the creation of new courses built upon monographs in the Series.

Fourthly, the Series aims to promote greater consideration on the part of other social scientists of the legal aspects of social political and economic problems who are too often discouraged from considering the law on a whole range of matters because of the daunting nature of legal textbooks. Without compromising on the standards of legal scholarship, a smaller monograph should prove less formidable and therefore more useable. Fifthly, and by no means least in importance, the Series offers an outlet to legal scholars in the United Kingdom and elsewhere. The Editorial Board hopes that, where they have something worth saying to a wider audience than their own students, but which does not fit the length of either a law review article or a full-length book, they will be stimulated to prepare a monograph for the Series.

Modern Legal Studies then has ambitious aims, which will be realised only with time. But it is very much a co-operative venture, between the authors, who have written or are writing for the Series, the Editorial Board, and the wider community of legal scholars, teachers and students who are both the consumers now and, it is hoped the producers of the future.

J. P. W. B. McAuslan
University of Warwick

CONTENTS

OTHER BOOKS IN THE SERIES

Human Rights and Europe, by R. Beddard
Economic Torts (Second Edition), by D. Heydon
Settlements of Land, by B. Harvey
Administrative Procedures, by G. Ganz
Law Reform and the Law Commission, by J. H. Farrar
Variation of Trusts, by J. W. Harris
Mortgages, by P. B. Fairest
Industrial Tribunals, by Keith Whitesides and Geoffrey Hawker
Anatomy of International Law, by J. G. Merrills
The Regulation of Takeovers and Mergers, by Paul Davies
Small Businesses, by Michael Chesterman
Immigration Law, by J. M. Evans
Compensation for Unemployment, by John Mesher
Registered Land (Second Edition), by David Hayton
The Court of Justice of the European Communities, by L. Neville Brown and Francis G. Jacobs
Exclusion Clauses in Contracts, by David Yates
Council Housing, by David Hoath
Constructive Trusts, by A. J. Oakley
Development Control, by John Alder

TABLE OF CASES

TABLE OF STATUTES

CHAPTER 1

INTRODUCTION AND HISTORY

I. TWO MEANINGS OF NATURAL JUSTICE

IN this century, as in the past, judges and others have used the phrase natural justice in a way which implies the existence of moral principles of self-evident and unarguable truth. To justify the adoption, or continued existence, of a rule of law on the ground of its conformity to natural justice in this sense conceals the extent to which a judge is making a subjective moral judgment and suggests, on the contrary, an objective inevitability. Natural justice, used in this way, is another name for natural law although devoid of some at least of the theological and philosophical overtones and implications of that concept. This essential similarity is clearly demonstrated by Lord Esher M.R.'s definition of natural justice as "the natural sense of what is right and wrong"; *Voinet* v. *Barrett* (1885) 55 L.J.Q.B. 39, 41. Examples of judicial use of natural justice in this sense occur in many areas of the law. In *Thornborough* v. *Baker* (1675) 3 Swans. 628, 630 Lord Nottingham explained the rule that the mortgagee's interest in mortgaged land is confined to security for the money loaned as attributable to "natural justice and equity." Lord Mansfield founded liability to repay money had and received on "natural justice and equity"; *Moses* v. *Macferlan* (1760) 2 Burr. 1005, 1012. Some years later Lord Kenyon declared that "It is a principle of natural justice and of our laws that *actus non facit reum nisi mens sit rea*"; *Fowler* v. *Padget* (1798) 7 T.R. 509, 514. In the nineteenth century the right of support which one landowner enjoys against his neighbours for his land, unencumbered by buildings, was ascribed by Lord Campbell C.J. to natural justice; *Humphries* v. *Brogden* (1850) 12 Q.B. 739, 744. Kindersley V.-C. invoked natural justice in *Rice* v. *Rice* (1853) 2 Drew. 73, 79 to help determine the conflicting priorities of two equitable interests. Lord Watson, in discussing the right of a mortgagee to tack (*i.e.* to claim for subsequent advances to the mortgagor the same priority, as against other mortgagees, as his original loan enjoyed[1]) said of an earlier English decision (*Hopkinson* v. *Rolt* (1861) 9 H.L.C. 514) which, it was argued, was inapplicable to Scotland, "the principle of that decision does not rest upon any rule or practice of English conveyancing but upon principles of natural justice"; *Union Bank of Scotland Ltd.* v. *National Bank of Scotland* (1886) 14 R.(H.L.) 1, 5. In *Dalton* v. *Angus* (1881) 6 App.Cas. 740, 818, Lord Blackburn explained the wide variation between the laws of prescription in different legal systems on the ground that "Prescription is not one of those laws which are derived from natural justice." Where the rules of equity and common law differed on a matter of procedure relating to awarding costs Sir George Jessel M.R. followed "the common law practice [which] in this case is founded in natural justice"; *Newbiggin Gas Co.* v. *Armstrong* (1879) 13 Ch.D. 310, 311. Examining the origin of the right of a cargo owner to general average contribution Brett M.R. said in *Burton & Co.* v. *English & Co.* (1883) 49 L.T. 768, 769;

> "... It seems to me that the right arose at the time of the making of the Rhodian laws, it is a consequence of the peculiarity of sea danger and has become incorporated into the municipal law of England as a law of the ocean and of marine risk, because when two parties were jointly in danger of the same misfortune, natural justice required that any loss falling upon one party for the safety of the whole adventure should be recouped by the other party in proportion."

Despite the "strong and general" words of the Infants' Relief Act 1874 the Divisional Court held, in *Valentini* v. *Canali* (1889) 24 Q.B.D. 166, that an infant could not recover monies paid for something consumed or used; to allow him to recover in such circumstances would, according to Lord Coleridge C.J., be contrary to natural justice. The American Supreme Court, in *Brown* v. *Walker* 161 U.S. 591, 600 (1896) described the first eight amendments to the Constitution as incorporating "into the fundamental law of the land certain principles of natural justice which had become permanently fixed in the jurisprudence of the mother country." Thus the court included within the phrase such various provisions as those recognising the right to free speech and the right to speedy and public trial of criminal charges; those prohibiting double jeopardy, excessive bail and cruel and unusual punishments; and those protecting the security of homes from searches or billeting of troops, the right of citizens to bear arms and the right to trial by jury.

In this century natural justice has been invoked in discussions of parental rights arising from "guardianship by nature and nurture"; *Re Carroll* [1931] 1 K.B. 317, 354 *per* Slesser L.J. and as a factor to be taken into account by a court when considering whether to exercise its discretion to set aside a voidable decree of divorce; *Wiseman* v. *Wiseman* [1953] P. 79, 92 *per* Lord Denning M.R. In the House of Lords natural justice in this wide sense has been used in cases involving the right of the Crown to destroy property in wartime, *Burmah Oil* v. *Lord Advocate* [1965] A.C. 75, 149 *per* Lord Pearce, and the defence of drunkenness in criminal law; *D.P.P.* v. *Majewski* [1977] A.C. 443, 474 *per* Lord Elwyn-Jones L.C. Despite the existence since the time of James I of Statutes of Limitation which, in effect, allow the acquisition of title to land by dispossession of the former holder, Lord Denning M.R. in *Wallis's Ltd.* v. *Shell Mex* [1975] Q.B. 94, 103, described the taking advantage of one's own wrong to acquire title to land as "contrary to equity and natural justice."[2] In *Davis* v. *Whitby* [1973] 1 W.L.R. 629, 631, affirmed [1974] Ch. 186, Burgess V.-C. rejected an unmeritorious defence to a claim under the Prescription Act 1832 on the ground that

> "It would be contrary to common sense and natural justice if a friendly agreement ... concurred in by all interested parties, was to deprive the plaintiffs of the rights they were in the course of acquiring."

In *S.* v. *S.* [1978] Fam. Law 57 the Court of Appeal had to interpret section 14(5) of the Legal Aid Act 1974 which provides that, where a party begins to receive legal aid in connection with any proceedings after those proceedings have been instituted, the right of an unassisted party to be paid his costs from the legal aid fund shall be limited to "so much of those costs as is attributable to that part." The court, in holding that costs incurred by the unassisted party in the course of proceedings before the granting of the legal aid certificate were not "attributable" to the subsequent part of the proceedings, justified its interpretation of the statute as one which did not "produce an anomalous or unfair result or one which was in any way contrary to any conception of natural justice"; *per* Stamp L.J. at p. 58.

Finally, it should be noted that in territories under British rule natural justice was invoked, often in conjunction with a reference to "equity and good conscience," to justify the adoption of a rule where the local legal system lacked one or the rejection of a rule which was regarded as repugnant to British ideas of civilised behaviour.[3]

The use of natural justice as a standard by which to judge the content of rules as well as the procedural safeguards necessary to their fair application is equally attested to by cases where the courts have rejected litigants' attempts to impugn rules as contrary to natural justice. In *Phillips* v. *Eyre* (1870) 6 Q.B. 1, for example, the argument was advanced that a retrospective colonial law was contrary to natural justice. Willes J., however, rejected the contention: "Allowing the general inexpediency of retrospective legislation, it cannot be pronounced naturally or necessarily unjust" (p. 27).[4] In *Semtex Ltd.* v. *Gladstone* [1954] 1 W.L.R. 945 it appears from the judgment of Finnemore J. that counsel had tried to argue that natural justice required that a term be implied into contracts of employment to the effect that employers would not require servants to indemnify them for losses caused by the servants' negligent acts committed in the course of their employments. A novel attempt to invoke natural justice was made in *R.* v. *Gravesend Justices, ex p. Doodney* [1971] 1 W.L.R. 818. Affiliation orders were made against D in favour of the mother of two children who later went to live in Yugoslavia. When D fell into arrears a complaint was laid at the mother's request; the magistrates adjourned the complaint *sine die* on condition that D paid off the arrears at 5s. per week. D later applied to vary the orders but the magistrates held that they had no jurisdiction because the mother resided abroad. D then sought certiorari to quash the order requiring him to pay the arrears on the ground that natural justice forbade the enforcement of the order at the instance of a party who was not prepared to submit to the jurisdiction of the court in proceedings for variation or revocation. The Divisional Court dismissed D's application. It pointed out that the magistrates had statutory powers to remit arrears wholly or in part which could be used to alleviate any hardship arising from lack of jurisdiction to vary or revoke an affiliation order. The court was not prepared to accept "the broad proposition of natural justice" entailed by D's argument; "the requirements of natural justice are best considered in the light of the facts of each individual case"; *per* Cooke J. at p. 822.

Natural justice may, however, be used not as a standard for criticising the content of legal rules but to refer to the principles which must be followed in the *application* of rules, whatever their content, to particular cases. In this sense natural justice may be said to relate to formal as opposed to substantive justice. However just the substance of a rule, injustice will occur unless the rule is applied impartially, treating like cases alike and different cases differently.[5]

"Formal" must not, however, be confused with "procedural" in the sense in which that word is used to describe the rules governing the initiation and progress of litigation in the courts or the admissibility of evidence. A litigant may be entitled to complain of any breach of such rules, however trivial, but, as Kerr J. pointed out in *Lake District Special Planning Board* v. *Secretary of State for the Environment, The Times*, February 18, 1975, there cannot be a "technical" breach of the rules of natural justice since that concept relates to matters of substance, not technicalities. The so-called rules are, in fact, "principles of substantial justice"; *L.G.B.* v. *Arlidge* [1915] A.C. 120, 142 *per* Lord Parmoor. The courts have often contrasted these principles with their own detailed rules of evidence and procedure which are helpful but not essential to the doing of justice. In the words of Diplock L.J. the "technical rules of evidence" lie outside the scope of natural justice; *R.* v. *Deputy Industrial Injuries Commissioner, ex p. Moore* [1965] 1 Q.B. 456, 488.[6]

Natural justice, used to refer to formal justice, may be contrasted with natural law, used to refer to substantive justice. This may have been the sense in which Lord Reid meant to use the two phrases when he referred to the belief of lawyers of earlier generations that Parliament could not legislate in a manner contrary "to the law of God or the law of nature or natural justice"; *British Railways Board* v. *Pickin* [1974] A.C. 765, 782. The lawyers of those earlier generations would not, however, have drawn that distinction themselves for they regarded the two concepts as one. In *Day* v. *Savadge* (1614)

Hob. 85, for example, the rule that no man should be a judge in his own cause was described as "natural equity" and as an instance of those *"iura naturae"* which were immutable. In modern times, the ancient connection between the two concepts has been neatly expressed by the definition of natural justice as "that part of natural law which relates to the administration of justice."[7]

The two principles which, pre-eminently, are generally thought to be necessary to guarantee that the law, or any body of rules, is applied impartially and objectively—and hence justly—are that no man should be judged without a hearing and that every judge must be free from bias, or, as they are often cited in the form of latin tags, *audi alteram partem*[8] and *nemo iudex in re sua*.[9] It is not possible to produce an exhaustive list of the rules of natural justice in this formal sense, or of the requirements of the rules, because the rules of natural justice are means to an end and not an end in themselves; *Official Solicitor* v. *K.* [1965] A.C. 201. In the words of Tucker L.J.:

> "The requirements of natural justice must depend on the circumstances of the case, the nature of the inquiry, the rules under which the tribunal is acting, the subject matter that is being dealt with and so forth" (*Russell* v. *Duke of Norfolk* [1949] 1 All E.R. 109, 113).

The New South Wales Court of Appeal emphasised the flexibility of the phrase when it defined natural justice as "the basic concepts of justice which in any particular day and age offend the sensibilities of the judges"; *Ex p. Brown*; *Re Tunstall* [1966] 1 N.S.W.R. 770, 775. The defendant, a man of nine stones, with one arm in plaster, was accused of assaulting three policemen, two of whom weighed 12 stones each, the third 20 stones. The Crown refused to produce certain documents, including statements made by the defendant to doctors, although he had been cross-examined on those statements by the prosecution. This refusal was held to amount to a breach of natural justice. In an equally wide-ranging approach Bagnall J. was prepared to equate the rules of natural justice with "the settled practice of the court"; *Mayes* v. *Mayes* [1971] 1 W.L.R. 679, 680.

Whatever the uncertainty inherent in the phrase natural justice, it connotes, above all, the maxims *audi alteram partem* and *nemo iudex in re sua* because they "are so vital and essential to the due performance of the office of the judge that without them the judge is no judge at all."[10] However, in certain circumstances, natural justice may seem to require the recognition of the fundamental importance of other rules such as that a court should sit in public; that reasons should be given for decisions; that decisions should be based on evidence of probative value and that defendants are entitled to legal representation and, possibly, legal aid. These rules, themselves, are sometimes discussed in connection with the maxim that justice must not only be done but be seen to be done. Whether natural justice should indeed be regarded as extending beyond the two, admittedly basic, principles of a right to a hearing and a right to an impartial judge will be discussed later.[11]

The widespread recognition, in many civilisations and over many centuries, of the importance of the two fundamental maxims of natural justice is strikingly expressed by one author who says that they "belong rather to the common consciousness of mankind than to juridical science."[12] In the ancient world, the requirement of hearing both sides before reaching a conclusion was enshrined in a proverb, often quoted or referred to in Greek literature, and formed part of the Athenian judicial oath.[13] Seneca referred in *Medea* to the injustice of reaching a decision without a full hearing[14] and the *Digest* contained a prohibition on a *paterfamilias* killing his son without a hearing.[15] The need for a judge to be impartial and the danger of bias arising from a personal interest in the case before him was recognised by the Romans in both legal[16] and non-legal writings.[17] A number of legal texts dealt with the problem of the judge *"qui litem suam fecit."*[18] The exact meaning of this phrase is unsettled but it can be assumed to have included, at least, instances of partiality.[19] The recognition given to the two maxims by the common law in the middle ages and successive centuries will be discussed later in this chapter. In the modern world international tribunals have recognised them as "general principles of law common to civilised communities."[20] They are enshrined in Article 10 of the Universal Declaration of Human Rights, Article 14 of the International Covenant on Civil and Political Rights and Article 6 of the European Convention on Human Rights.[21] In *Transocean Marine*

Paint Association v. *E.C.C.* [1974] E.C.R. 1063 Warner A.-G. demonstrated the general acceptance of *audi alteram partem* among the Member States of the European Communities and the court held that it applied to decisions of the organs of the Communities.

II. Fair Play and Fairness

Judges[22] and writers[23] have criticised the use of the phrase natural justice to describe the essential requirements of a fair hearing. Lord Shaw thought the expression "harmless," "high-sounding," and, in some contexts, "vacuous"; *L.G.B.* v. *Arlidge* [1915] A.C. 120, 138. Black J. thought "Natural Justice means no more than justice without any epithet"; *Green* v. *Blake* [1948] I.R. 242, 268. Maugham J. in a comment reflecting both insularity[24] and cynicism said,

> "The phrase [natural justice] is, of course, used only in a popular sense and must not be taken to mean that there is any justice natural among men. Amongst most savages there is no such thing as justice in the modern sense. The phrase 'the principles of natural justice' can only mean, in this connection, the principles of fair play so deeply rooted in the minds of modern Englishmen that a provision for an inquiry necessarily imparts that the accused should be given his chance of defence and explanation" (*Maclean* v. *The Workers Union* [1929] 1 Ch. 602, 624).

Ormrod L.J. has complained that

> "the phrase 'the requirements of natural justice' seems to be mesmerising people at the moment. This must, I think, be due to the apposition of the words 'natural' and 'justice.' It has been pointed out many times that the word 'natural' adds nothing except perhaps a hint of nostalgia for the good old days when nasty things did not happen" (*Norwest Holst Ltd.* v. *Department of Trade* [1978] Ch. 201, 227).

The same learned lord justice has warned that the phrase is "highly attractive and potent and as such ... must be used very carefully";

Lewis v. *Heffer* [1978] 1 W.L.R. 1061, 1076. In *Transocean Marine Paint Association* v. *E.C.C.* (*supra*) the Advocate-General, Warner, described the phrase "natural justice" as "somewhat flamboyant" and expressed a preference for the French phrase *"les principes generaux du droit."*[25]

No doubt a charge of flamboyance might also be levelled at such similar phrases as "the first principles of justice" (*Harvey* v. *Shelton* (1884) 7 Beav. 455, 462 *per* Lord Langdale M.R.); "the principles of universal justice" (*Drew* v. *Drew* (1855) 2 Macq. 1, 8 *per* Lord Cranworth); "the substantial requirements of justice ... the essence of justice" (*Spackman* v. *Plumstead District Board of Works* (1885) 10 App.Cas. 229, 240 *per* Earl of Selborne L.C.); "the essential principles of justice" (*Tameshwar* v. *The Queen* [1957] A.C. 476, 487 *per* Lord Denning M.R.); "the elementary principles of justice" (*Geraghty* v. *Minister for Local Government* [1976] I.R. 153, 160 *per* O'Higgins J.) or "fundamental justice" (Canadian Bill of Rights 1960, s. 2(e)).[26]

The use of the phrase natural justice, or of some similarly qualified reference to justice, may be defended as being hallowed by custom. It may also claim statutory approval, since the Foreign Compensation Act 1969, s. 3(10), recognised a right to question determinations of the Foreign Compensation Commission on the ground that they are "contrary to natural justice." (The Trade Union and Labour Relations Act 1974 similarly referred to natural justice, in a provision (s. 6(13)) which was, however, repealed by the Trade Union and Labour Relations (Amendment) Act 1976, s. 1.) Such a term emphasises the vagueness and uncertainty inherent in the concept and the importance attached to it by the courts. Although it is no longer believed as it was formerly (*Day* v. *Savadge* (1614) Hob. 85, 87) that Parliament cannot legislate so as to violate the basic principles of a fair hearing, nonetheless, in the words of Lord Reid—

> "It is now well recognised that the court has power to expand procedure laid down by statute if that is necessary to prevent infringement of natural justice and is not plainly contrary to the intention of Parliament" (*Atkinson* v. *United States Government* [1971] A.C. 197, 232).

The only objection to such usage is if it leads to a belief that natural justice must be confined to those basic rules which might be thought appropriate to some imaginary society living in a state of nature. Such, with respect, was the mistake of Lyell J. in *Pett* v. *Greyhound Racing Association* (*No. 2*) [1970] 1 Q.B. 46, when he was considering the right to legal representation as part of natural justice. The learned judge referred to *University of Ceylon* v. *Fernando* [1960] 1 W.L.R. 223, 233, where Lord Jenkins had equated natural justice with "elementary and essential principles of 'fairness' " and went on to say:

> "I find it difficult to say that legal representation before a tribunal is an elementary feature of the fair dispensation of justice. It seems to me that it arises only in a society which has reached some degree of sophistication in its affairs" (p. 65).

Natural justice may, however, vary in its requirements as the views of society change. A preferable approach to that of Lyell J. is to be found in the decision of the Irish Supreme Court in *The State* (*Healy*) v. *Donoghue* [1976] I.R. 325 where the court took into account the development of ideas of justice and held that young prisoners, charged with serious crimes, were entitled not merely to legal representation but also, in order to make that right a reality, to legal aid and to be informed of their rights. In criticising the approach exemplified by Lyell J. in *Pett's* case it is not, of course, intended to suggest that natural justice necessarily implies a right to legal representation, still less legal aid, in all cases.

Critics of "natural justice" may wish that English courts, like the American, had retained the usage of Coke and referred to the minimum of necessary procedural safeguards required to ensure that a decision is reached justly as "due process." The connection between this phrase and the right to a fair trial stems from Chapter 39 of Magna Carta which provided that a free man should not be condemned *"nisi per legale judicium parium suorum vel per legem terrae."* The statute 25 Edw. 3, c. 4 (1350) referred to Magna Carta and went on to provide that no-one should be condemned except "in due manner, or by process made by writ original at the common law." Four years later, 28 Edw. 3, c. 3 provided "That no man of what estate or condition that he be, shall be put out of land or tenement, nor taken nor imprisoned, nor disinherited, nor put to death, without being brought in answer by due process of the law." Coke himself used the phrase "due process of the common law"; *e.g.* 2 Inst. 50. Both Magna Carta and the statute of 1354 were quoted in the Petition of Right 1628 which used the phrase "due process of law." In the United States "due process" has been ensured enduring currency by its adoption in the Fifth and Fourteenth Amendment to the Constitution. For evidence of judicial recognition of its ancestry in Magna Carta it is only necessary to look at *Re Gault* 387 U.S. 1, 62, (1967). In the English law reports, however, it makes only fleeting appearances in appeals before the Privy Council from territories whose written constitutions similarly refer to due process as, for example, in *Maharaj* v. *Att.-Gen. of Trinidad* (*No. 2*) [1978] 2 W.L.R. 902.

The English courts, on the other hand, resort increasingly frequently to such alternatives to natural justice as "fair play in action,"[27] "common fairness,"[28] "fairness of procedure,"[29] "the fundamental principles of a fair trial";[30] "a fair crack of the whip."[31] These phrases have the advantage of emphasising that requirements of natural justice vary with the circumstances of individual cases. Lawton L.J. has justified their use as helping to discourage a tendency to subject hearings to "legal strait-jackets" and ensuring that the courts will not be led "into the trap of legalism."[32]

Such phrases may sometimes be used to refer not to the obligation to observe the principles of natural justice but, on the contrary, to refer to a standard of behaviour which, increasingly, the courts require to be followed even in circumstances where the duty to observe natural justice is inapplicable. The distinction between the two concepts is clearly shown in the following extract from the speech of Lord Pearson in *Pearlberg* v. *Varty* [1972] 1 W.L.R. 534, 547:

> "A tribunal to whom judicial or quasi-judicial functions are entrusted is held to be required to apply those principles [*i.e.* the rules of natural justice] in performing those functions unless there is a provision to the contrary. But where some person or body is entrusted by Parliament with administrative or executive functions there is no presumption that compliance with the principles of natural justice is required, although, as 'Parliament

> is not to be presumed to act unfairly,' the courts may be able in suitable cases (perhaps always) to imply an obligation to act with fairness."[33]

The procedural standards which are implied by the duty to act fairly, in the sense in which Lord Pearson used that phrase, will be discussed later.[34] It will be seen that they are analogous to those required by natural justice but not necessarily identical. In particular a procedure may be fair although there has not been a hearing of the kind normally required by natural justice. Conversely fairness may sometimes impose a higher standard than that required by natural justice. Thus the giving of reasons for decisions is probably not required by natural justice but, it has been said, may be required by fairness because "the giving of reasons is one of the fundamentals of good administration"; *Breen* v. *A.E.U.* [1971] 2 Q.B. 175, 191 *per* Lord Denning M.R.

Fairness, however, is not only used as a synonym for natural justice, or to describe the minimal form of that concept as it applies to administrative bodies, but also as a standard to guide the courts in many situations which cannot be described as raising questions of natural justice, unless the meaning of that term is to be stretched far beyond any rules related to the right to be heard before an impartial tribunal. To attempt to illustrate this use exhaustively would be inappropriate in this book. A striking example is provided by the speeches of the members of the House of Lords in *Connelly* v. *D.P.P.* [1964] A.C. 1254. The House held that the prisoner, who had been acquitted of murder, could properly be charged with robbery arising out of the same set of facts. Lord Reid saw "nothing unfair in holding that the plea of autrefois acquit must be given a limited scope" (p. 1295); Lord Morris referred to reliance on the test of fairness which, in this context, he described as "somewhat vague and imprecise" (p. 1299). Lord Devlin was, on the other hand, prepared to accept fairness as a test of general applicability to guide judges in exercising their control over the courts:

> "The judges of the High Court have in their inherent jurisdiction ... power to make and enforce rules of practice in order to ensure that the court's process is used fairly and conveniently by both sides" (p. 1347).[35]

Other examples are provided by a number of recent cases dealing with the power of the courts to dismiss an action on the ground of the plaintiff's delay in prosecuting his claim. In *Sweeney* v. *Sir Robert McAlpine & Sons Ltd.* [1974] 1 W.L.R. 200 Stamp L.J. said a position had been reached "when in fairness to the defendant this action ought to be stayed." Although the House of Lords, in *Birkett* v. *James* [1978] A.C. 297, differed from the Court of Appeal as to the appropriate principle to be applied in cases of delay, Lord Diplock, in a speech with which the other Law Lords agreed, said that the court has an inherent jurisdiction to dismiss an action for want of prosecution if the delay was such as to "involve a substantial risk that a fair trial of the issues would not be possible" (p. 318). Fairness has also been invoked in cases dealing with the right of a plaintiff who has been required to undergo a medical examination at the request of the defendant to see the medical report produced for the defendant. Bean J., for example, in *McGinley* v. *Burke* [1973] 1 W.L.R. 990, 993 referred to the necessity of "fairness between the parties." Lord Denning M.R. similarly referred to acting fairly and fairness in *Clarke* v. *Martlew* [1973] Q.B. 58, 63 and in *Causton* v. *Mann Egerton (Johnstone) Ltd.* [1974] 1 W.L.R. 162, 167 and 168.

III. The Development of the Modern English Law

From the time of the Year Books English law has recognised the importance of a hearing[36] and an impartial judge.[37] Coke described the rule against bias as according with "the reason of the common law,"[38] while he emphasised the importance of a hearing by comparing unfavourably the behaviour of Rhadamanthus, as described by Virgil,[39] with that of the Christian God; "*Castigatque auditque dolos, subigitque fateri.* First, he punished before he heard and when he had heard his denial he compelled the party accused by torture to confesse it. But far otherwise doth Almighty God proceed postquam reus diffamatus est. *1. Vocat 2. Interrogat 3. Judicat.*"[40] (Coke himself is here guilty of condemning Rhadamanthus unheard. Classical scholars cite this line of the *Aeneid* as an example of a favourite mannerism of Virgil who often reversed the temporal order of events, adding emphasis by describing first the event which, in fact, occurred last.) Divine support for the right to a hearing was later claimed in *R.* v. *Chancellor of the University of Cambridge* (*Dr. Bentley's Case*) (1723) 1 Str. 557, 567 where the events in the Garden of Eden were relied on; "Even God himself did not pass sentence upon Adam before he was called upon to make his defence." However, as Professor Heuston has pointed out,[41] divine punishment may on occasions be administered without a preliminary hearing: *Belshazzar's Feast*, Dan. *v*. Later in the century Lord Kenyon said it was "an invariable maxim in our law that no man shall be punished before he has had an opportunity of being heard"; *R.* v. *Benn and Church* (1795) 6 T.R. 198.[42] Blackstone referred in his *Commentaries* to the rule that no man should be a judge in his own cause and quoted the cautionary tale of the pope who, judging himself, condemned himself to be burned to death; Comm.iii.299, quoting Y.B. M. 8 Hen. 6, 20: a fable which illustrates that the objection to a judge with an interest in the outcome of litigation is not based only on the fear that he will be influenced in favour of that interest but also that he may do injustice by leaning too far the other way in an attempt to demonstrate his impartiality.

The importance attached to the rules of natural justice is clearly illustrated by a number of decisions from the seventeenth century onwards concerning the validity of the alleged custom of "foreign attachment." This was a procedure claimed to exist by virtue of local custom in a number of leading mercantile centres. Under the custom A, who was owed a debt by B, was entitled, without informing B, to enforce payment against C to the extent that C was indebted to B. The first B might know of the proceedings was when he sued C and was met by way of defence with the plea that C, by court order, had discharged the debt by payment to A. Such a procedure meant that B had no chance to challenge A's claim that B was indebted to him. In *Fisher* v. *Lane* (1772) 3 Wils.K.B. 297, 302, Lord de Grey C.J. said, of the alleged custom, "Customs of particular cities may deviate from the course of the common law, but a custom contrary to the first principles of justice can never be good." That view was followed later in *Bruce* v. *Wait* (1840) 1 Man & G.1, and approved by Willes J. advising the House of Lords, in *Mayor etc. of London* v. *Cox* (1867) L.R. 2 H.L. 239, 265.[43]

While the right to a hearing and to an unbiased judge have, from the earliest days, been recognised by the common law, the willingness of the courts to interfere with decisions on the ground of breach of these principles has varied from generation to generation. Throughout the nineteenth century the courts freely imputed an obligation to observe the rules of natural justice. In *R.* v. *Justices of West Riding of Yorkshire, ex p. Thornton* (1837) 7 Ad. & E. 583, 589 Lord Denman said, "No rule is more invariable than that a person shall not be prejudiced in any manner without being heard." The same learned judge also said that, "It is implied by natural justice in the construction of all laws, that no one ought to suffer any prejudice thereby without having first an opportunity of defending himself"; *R.* v. *Wilson* (1835) 3 Ad. & E. 817, 826. Thus magistrates were required to grant a hearing even when acting under statutory provisions which made no reference to such a right in cases such as *Painter* v. *Liverpool Oil Gas Light Co.* (1836) 3 Ad. & E. 433 and *Hammond* v. *Bendyshe* (1849) 13 Q.B. 869 where Williams J. said, "I never heard the proposition doubted that a party is not to suffer in person or in purse without an opportunity of being heard" (p. 448).

In *Cooper* v. *Wandsworth Board of Works* (1863) 14 C.B.(N.S.) 180, the Court of Common Pleas held that the Board of Works could not demolish property without giving the owner a hearing, despite the fact that the relevant statute did not expressly confer such a right. Willes J. said: "A tribunal which is by law invested with power to affect the property of one of Her Majesty's subjects is bound to give such subject an opportunity of being heard before it proceeds" (p. 190). Similarly Byles J. said, "Although there are no positive words in a statute requiring that the party shall be heard, yet the justice of the common law will supply the omission of the legislature" (p. 194).[44]

A series of cases which established the right of office holders to be heard before dismissal show particularly clearly the importance attached to the maxim *audi alteram partem* in the nineteenth century. In *Doe* d. *Thanet (Earl)* v. *Gartham* (1823) 1 Bing. 357 this right was linked to the existence of a freehold estate in the office in question. In other cases it arose from the interpretation of the deed, or the implication of the right into the deed, under which an office holder was appointed. In *Willis* v. *Childe* (1851) 13 Beav. 117, for example, where trustees of a school had the power to dismiss teachers "upon such grounds as they shall at their discretion, in the due exercise and execution of the powers and trusts reposed in them, deem just," Lord Langdale M.R. held that the trustees could not dismiss teachers under this provision without giving them a full hearing.[45] He distinguished, on what have subsequently been called "narrow grounds,"[46] *R.* v. *Darlington Free Grammar School Governors* (1844) 6 Q.B. 682. In that case the governors of a school who were entitled to remove masters "according to their sound discretion" were held by the Court of Exchequer Chamber to be entitled to dismiss a master without a hearing. Lord Hatherley L.C. cast further doubt on the *Darlington* case in *Dean* v. *Bennett* (1870) 6 Ch.App. 487. In the twentieth century, however, the *Darlington* case has sometimes been accepted as establishing that there is no right to a hearing where an office holder can be dismissed at will without the need to show cause.[47] In some decisions the courts, as in *Cooper* v. *Wandsworth Board of Works* (*supra*) implied the right to a hearing into a silent statute. In *Capel* v. *Child* (1832) 2 Cr. & J. 558, a bishop was entitled, by statute, to appoint a curate, to be paid by the vicar, when satisfied "either of his own knowledge or by affidavit" that the vicar had neglected his duties. The Court of Exchequer held that before making such an appointment the bishop must afford the vicar a hearing. In *Bonaker* v. *Evans* (1851) 16 Q.B.D. 162 a bishop sequestrated the profits of a benefice on the ground of the incumbent's non-residence. Lengthy and acrimonious correspondence had passed between the bishop and the incumbent who objected to being required to reside in what he described as "my said damp and uncomfortable hole of a vicarage house." The statute in question provided that in the event of failure to reside after warning "It shall be lawful for the Bishop to sequester the profits." The Court of Exchequer Chamber held that sequestration without a hearing was void. Parke B. said:

> "No proposition can be more clearly established than that a man cannot incur the loss of liberty or property for an offence by a judicial proceeding until he has had a fair opportunity of answering the charge against him, unless the legislature had expressly or impliedly given an authority to act without that necessary preliminary" (p. 171).

Arbitrators were required to observe "the first principles of justice" in *Harvey* v. *Shelton* (1844) 7 Beav. 455, 462 where Lord Langdale M.R. said, "I wholly deny the difference which is alleged to exist between mercantile arbitrations and legal arbitrations." In *Re Brook and Delcomyn* (1864) 16 C.B.(N.S.) 403, 416, Erle C.J., in holding that arbitrators must not take into account evidence known to one only of the parties, said,

> "It is one of the first principles in the administration of justice, that the tribunal which is to decide must hear both sides and give both an opportunity of hearing the evidence upon which the decision is to turn. I am not by any means deciding this case on a point of form, but upon a matter of substance, and one of the last and deepest importance. It may be said that in doing this I am setting up my own individual and imperfect sense of right against the opinions and the usages of mercantile men on a purely mercantile question. But I find the master minds of every century are consentaneous in holding it to be an indispensable requirement of justice that the party who has to decide shall hear both sides, giving each an opportunity of hearing what is urged against him."

Other cases applied the rule to the decisions of domestic and statutory tribunals. In *Wood* v. *Woad* (1874) L.R. 9 Ex. 190 Wood challenged the validity of his expulsion from the Goole Marine Insurance Society, a body which provided mutual insurance and indemnity for its members. Kelly C.B. said the rule expressed in the maxim *audi alteram partem* "is not confined to the conduct of strictly legal tribunals but is applicable to every tribunal or body of persons invested with authority to adjudicate upon matters involving civil consequences to individuals" (p. 196). The application of the rule to social clubs is illustrated by *Innis* v. *Wylie* (1844) 1 Car. & K. 257 (The Caledonian Society of London), and by *Fisher* v. *Keane* (1878) 11 Ch.D. 353 (the Army and Navy Club),[48] and to statutory tribunals controlling professional standards by *Leeson* v. *General Medical Council* (1889) 43 Ch.D. 366.

The right to an impartial judge was equally recognised and applied widely; to the superior courts themselves in the famous case, discussed later in Chapter 2, of *Dimes* v. *Grand Junction Canal* (1852)

3 H.L.Cas. 759; to magistrates in *R.* v. *Rand* (1866) L.R. 1 Q.B. 230; to statutory tribunals controlling professional standards in *Leeson* v. *General Medical Council* (*supra*) and *Allinson* v. *General Medical Council* [1894] 1 Q.B. 750; and to administrative authorities in cases such as *R.* v. *London County Council, ex p. Akkersdyk* [1892] 1 Q.B. 190.

Nor, as will be seen in Chapter 7, Part IV, was the obligation to observe the rules of natural justice confined to English courts. Foreign tribunals, too, had to be impartial and grant a hearing if their decrees were to be enforced by the common law courts. In the words of the Irish judge, Pigot C.B., in a case concerned with the recognition of a judgment of a French court, "The maxim *'audi alteram partem'* is not a mere technical rule of English law. Its foundation is laid in the general principles of all jurisprudence which deserves the name"; *Maubourquet* v. *Wyse* (1867) I.R. 1 C.L. 471, 481.

The twentieth century saw a change in judicial attitudes which, by the 1950s, made it possible for a writer to entitle an article "The Twilight of Natural Justice."[49] The twilight proved, however, to be short-lived and the courts, since the important House of Lords case of *Ridge* v. *Baldwin* [1964] A.C. 40, have been extending the scope of the rules of natural justice so that the position has now been reached where a judge has felt impelled to sound a warning:

> "the principles of natural justice are of wide application and great importance but they must be confined within proper limits and not allowed to run wild" (*per* Megarry J. in *Hounslow L.B.C.* v. *Twickenham Garden Developments* [1971] Ch. 233, 258).

The law, at present, is indeed probably best expressed in the words of the same judge in *Gaiman* v. *National Association for Mental Health* [1971] Ch. 317, 333: "It may be that there is no simple test, but that there is a tendency for the Court to apply the principles to all powers of decision unless the circumstances suffice to exclude them."

The steps by which the courts retreated from the wide approach of the nineteenth century were analysed by Lord Reid in *Ridge* v. *Baldwin*. The analysis, despite the clear change in judicial policy after

Ridge's case, remains of interest both as an example of courts becoming entangled in their own conceptual reasoning and as the best means of ensuring that the mistakes of the past are not repeated. Lord Loreburn in *Board of Education* v. *Rice* [1911] A.C. 179, 182 had said quite generally that to "act in good faith and fairly listen to both sides ... is a duty lying upon everyone who decides anything." However, as Lord Reid pointed out in *Ridge* v. *Baldwin*, the courts from the 1920s onward tended to define the duty to observe the rules of natural justice in terms of a narrow definition of the duty to act judicially. Whether a body is acting judicially is a question which may be asked for various reasons; the definitions of "judicially" vary with the context and have in common only their vagueness and unsatisfactoriness.[50] Unfortunately, in relation to natural justice the courts invoked a dictum of Atkin L.J. in *R.* v. *Electricity Commissioners* [1924] 1 K.B. 171, 205, which spoke of "any body of persons having legal authority to determine questions affecting the rights of subjects and having the duty to act judicially." This dictum, as Lord Reid pointed out in *Ridge's* case, was interpreted to mean that a duty to act judicially was not to be inferred only from the nature of the power conferred on a body: there had also to be a superadded duty to act judicially. But one may wonder whether the restrictive interpretation was not evidence of the court's attitude rather than the cause. That the judges generally were unfavourably disposed to upsetting decisions for breach of natural justice is suggested by the distinctions drawn between exercising judicial and disciplinary powers[51]—in the latter case the rules of natural justice did not need to be observed—and between rights and privileges[52]—in which latter case again there was no right to a hearing—and by judgments such as that of Maugham J. in *Maclean* v. *The Workers Union* [1929] 1 Ch. 602 which expressed clearly a reluctance to interfere with the decisions of domestic tribunals. At no time was a satisfactory definition of "acting judicially" propounded, even in the most restrictive sense. Parker J., as he then was, summarised the case law when he said:

> "The duty to act judicially may arise in widely different circumstances which it would be impossible and indeed inadvisable to attempt to define exhaustively" (*R.* v. *Manchester Legal Aid Committee, ex p. Brand* [1952] 2 Q.B. 413, 428).

Uncertainty was further increased by resort to the concept of "quasi-judicial" functions, a phrase which one writer, perhaps optimistically, described as having "the advantage of obscurity of meaning."[53] The value attached to the concept by one judge at least was shown by his ironical comment that since the phrase merely means a tribunal or official, in some respects, acts like a judge, "even a town clerk when he attends a meeting of his council might be said to exercise 'quasi-judicial' functions; like a judge he wears a wig" (*per* Diplock L.J. in *Wednesbury Corporation* v. *Ministry of Housing and Local Government* (*No. 2*) [1966] 2 Q.B. 275, 305).

The significance of *Ridge* v. *Baldwin* is not that it removed the uncertainty from this area of the law but that it clearly indicated and inaugurated a reversal in judicial attitudes, the litigation itself in its progress through the courts showing the restrictive and liberal approaches. A chief constable had been dismissed without a hearing by his watch committee after his conduct had been the subject of adverse comment by a judge in the course of a trial which concluded with the conviction of a number of members of his force on charges of corruption. The chief constable himself was acquitted of the charges against him. In considering Ridge's claim that the committee's decision was invalid the courts were faced with two questions. First, should an obligation to give a hearing be read into the statutory provisions which empowered the committee to dismiss the constable when no reference was made in the statute to a hearing[54]; secondly, had later statutory provisions provided a right to a hearing irrespective of the meaning of the 1882 Act. Only the former question is relevant here. At first instance Streatfeild J. held that a right to a hearing ought to be read into the statute:

> "It is not merely an administrative matter, as a result of which some person may be prejudiced or may be deprived of the right of property, and so on; what the committee were doing here was to take a very serious step under an Act of Parliament which, of itself, gave no right to appeal—they were exercising the right to dismiss a man, to deprive him of his accumulated pension rights."

However, the judge held, natural justice had been complied with since the committee was entitled to reach its decision on the evidence which the chief constable himself had given in the course of the trial. The plaintiff had convicted himself out of his own mouth. Upholding Streatfeild J.'s decision the Court of Appeal chose to go further than the learned judge. It held that the watch committee was not under a duty to give Ridge a hearing. Harman L.J., for example, said:

> "The defendants were not deciding a question between two opposing parties. There was no lis and nothing to decide. The defendants were acting in exercise of their administrative functions just as they were when they made the appointment under section 191(1) [of the Act of 1882]"; ([1963] 1 Q.B. 539, 577).

The House of Lords held that the committee was under an obligation to observe the rules of natural justice and that, on the facts, the chief constable had not had a proper hearing. Lord Reid regarded the facts of the case as falling within the category of dismissal from an office where there must be something against a man to warrant his dismissal. It was well-established that a right to a hearing existed in such a case and the old authorities were not affected by more recent decisions holding that natural justice has only a limited application to the wider duties imposed on Ministers and other organs of government by modern legislation. Nor was there anything in Atkin L.J.'s dictum quoted above, page 19 to justify the courts in refusing to apply natural justice where in the nineteenth century they would have done so. Lord Reid's speech did not, however, perhaps wisely, attempt to lay down any general principle. It revived natural justice by rescuing old authorities but said nothing about new fact situations which did not fall squarely within established categories. Lord Morris, similarly, founded himself on cases involving property rights and provided no general guide for the future. Lord Hodson referred to cases such as *Capel* v. *Child* and concluded that "where the power to be exercised involves a charge of misconduct made against the person who is dismissed . . . the principles of natural justice have to be observed."

Later cases, while extending the scope of natural justice, have made no attempt to define "judicial" or "quasi-judicial." Resort has been made instead to the idea of acting fairly in the circumstances of the particular case; a notion not unknown in earlier case law but one given special prominence since the dictum of Lord Parker C.J. in *Re H.K. (an Infant)* [1967] 2 Q.B. 617, 630: "[It] is not, as I see it, a question of acting or being required to act judicially, but of being required to act fairly."

In the following chapters it is intended to discuss first, what the rules of natural justice require and, secondly, when they apply and how they relate to the duty to act fairly. In discussing all these questions it will be well to bear in mind the warning of Ungoed-Thomas J. in *Lawlor* v. *Union of Post Office Workers* [1965] Ch. 712, 718:

> "The law on natural justice is not in a satisfactory state and the authorities disclose some differences of view. It is somewhat lacking in precision on the occasions on which it should apply and what it requires to be done on those occasions."

Notes

[1] See Sir R. E. Megarry and H. W. R. Wade, *The Law of Real Property* (4th ed., 1975), pp. 981 *et seq.*

[2] For a criticism of the judicial attitude evinced in this and other cases see P. F. Smith, "A check on *Leigh* v. *Jack*?" (1978) 41 M.L.R. 204.

[3] K. Roberts Wray, *Commonwealth and Colonial Law* (1966), pp. 575 *et seq*; N. Anderson, *Liberty, Law and Justice* (1978), pp. 21 *et seq.*

[4] The same argument was raised more recently, with equal lack of success, in *Liyanage* v. *R.* [1967] 1 A.C. 259, when Lord Pearce refused to hold that the Ceylonese legislature was subject to "a fetter of repugnancy to some vague, unspecified law of natural justice" (p. 284). For a suggestion that non-retroactivity of criminal law is a principle of natural justice see J. M. Kelly, *Fundamental Rights in the Irish Law and Constitution* (2nd ed., 1967), p. 307. L. Fuller, *The Morality of Law* (1964) includes non-retroactivity of legislation among his eight elements of the "inner morality" of law but admits that in certain circumstances "granting retroactive effect to legal rules not only becomes tolerable, but may actually be essential to advance the cause of legality" (p. 53).

[5] H. L. A. Hart, *Concept of Law* (1961) Oxford University Press, p. 155; M. Ginsberg, *On Justice in Society* (1965) Pelican, p. 10; C. Perelman, *The Idea of Justice* (1963) Routledge & Kegan Paul, *passim*; J. Rawls, *A Theory of Justice* (1972) Oxford University Press, pp. 238 *et seq.;* J. Raz, "The Rule of Law and its Virtue" (1977) 93 L.Q.R. 195, 201.

[6] Quoted by Lord Widgery C.J., *Kavanagh* v. *Chief Constable of Devon and Cornwall* [1974] Q.B. 624, 630. See also *Green* v. *Blake* [1948] I.R. 242, 268 *per* Black J.; *University of Ceylon* v. *Fernando* [1960] 1 W.L.R. 223, 236 *per* Lord Jenkins. In *Disher* v. *Disher* [1965] P. 31, 36, Cairns J. distinguished between a "mere irregularity" and a breach of a fundamental rule which nullifies a judicial proceeding. And see

Briscoe v. *Briscoe* [1968] P. 501; *Barnes* v. *BPC* (*Business Forms*) *Ltd.* [1975] I.C.R. 390.

[7] H. H. Marshall, *Natural Justice* (1959), p. 184.

[8] Sometimes expressed in the form "*Audietur et altera pars.*"

[9] Coke used the form "*Aliquis non debet esse iudex in propria causa*"; Co.Litt. 141a.

[10] H. H. Marshall, *loc. cit.*

[11] *Infra*, Chap. 4 and Chap. 9.

[12] Del Vecchio, *Justice*, ed. A. H. Campbell (1952), p. 172.

[13] Aristophanes, *The Wasps*, 725 and 919. Euripides, *Heracleidae*, 180; *Andromache*, 957; Demonsthenes, *De Corona*, 1.

[14] *Medea* 195; quoted in *Boswel's Case* (1606) 6 Co. Rep. 48b, 52; *Bagg's Case* (1615) 11 Co.Rep. 936.

[15] D.48.8.2. See further J. M. Kelly, "*Audi alteram partem*" (1964) 9 Nat. Law Forum 103.

[16] D.5.1.17; C.3.51.

[17] Tacitus, *Dialogus*, 5.

[18] D.5.1.15–17; J.4.5. pr.

[19] J. M. Kelly, *Roman Litigation* (1966), Chap. 5; Pugsley, "*Litem suam facere*" (1969) 4 *Irish Jurist* 351.

[20] Bin Cheng, *General Principles of Law as applied by International Courts and Tribunals* (1953) Stevens, Chaps. 13 and 14.

[21] See F. G. Jacobs, *The European Convention on Human Rights* (1975), pp. 76 *et seq.* On the position of the Convention in the United Kingdom see O. Hood Phillips and Paul Jackson, *Constitutional and Administrative Law* (6th ed., 1978), p. 440.

[22] Scrutton L.J. is often quoted as having described the use of the phrase as showing "well-meaning sloppiness of thought" (*Holt* v. *Markham* [1923] 1 K.B. 504, 513) but that criticism was directed at Lord Mansfield's resort to the phrase in the context of the action for money had and received.

[23] *e.g.* F. E. Dowrick, *Justice according to the English Common Lawyers* (1961), pp. 41–42. The two maxims, he suggests, are no more than two of 11 principles recognised in the superior courts in the 19th century as involved in the concept of a fair trial: (i) judges must be absolutely independent of the government; (ii) judges must be impartial; (iii) no one must be condemned unheard; (iv) judges must act only on the evidence and arguments adduced before them; (v) reasons must be given for decisions; (vi) judges' own characters must be beyond reproach; (vii) each side should state its case as strongly as it can; (viii) parties before the court should be treated as equals; (ix) cases should be heard in public; (x) the judge should be identified and personally responsible for his decision; (xi) to ensure the observance of the preceding rules, parties should have a right of appeal to a higher judicial tribunal; *op. cit.* pp. 31–32.

[24] The Report of the Committee on Ministers' Powers (Donoughmore Committee), Cmd. 4060 (1932), p. 76, similarly linked natural justice and "our natural sense of justice."

[25] See further, Waline, *Droit Administratif* (9th ed., 1963), pp. 465 *et seq.*

[26] See further, W. S. Tarnopolsky, *The Canadian Bill of Rights* (2nd ed., 1975), pp. 264–274.

[27] *Ridge* v. *Baldwin* [1963] 1 Q.B. 530, 578 *per* Harman L.J.; *Edwards* v. *SOGAT* [1971] Ch. 354, 382 *per* Sachs L.J.; *Wiseman* v. *Borneman* [1971] A.C. 297, 309 *per* Lord Morris. Cf. Branson J.'s reference to the "rules of fair play" in *Re Manchester* (*Ringway Airport*) *Compulsory Purchase Order* (1935) 153 L.T.R. 219, 222.

[28] *R.* v. *Secretary of State for the Home Department, ex p. Hosenball* [1977] 1 W.L.R. 766, 784 *per* Geoffrey Lane L.J.

[29] *Re Pergamon Press* [1971] Ch. 388, 403 *per* Sachs L.J.

[30] *Tameshwar* v. *The Queen* [1957] A.C. 476, 486 *per* Lord Denning.

[31] *Fairmount Investments* v. *Secretary of State for the Environment* [1976] 1 W.L.R. 1255, 1266 *per* Lord Russell.

[32] *Maxwell* v. *Department of Trade and Industry* [1974] Q.B. 523, 539; *R.* v. *Race Relations Board, ex p. Selvarajan* [1975] 1 W.L.R. 1686, 1697.

[33] See also *Re H.K. (an Infant)* [1967] 2 Q.B. 617, 630 *per* Lord Parker C.J.; *R.* v. *Secretary of State for the Home Department, ex p. Mughal* [1974] Q.B. 313, 325 *per* Lord Denning M.R.; *R.* v. *National Insurance Commissioner, ex p. Viscusi* [1974] 1 W.L.R. 646, 653 *per* Lord Denning M.R.; *R.* v. *Secretary of State for the Home Department, ex p. Phansopkar* [1976] Q.B. 606, 611 *per* Lord Widgery C.J.

[34] *Infra*, pp. 101 *et seq.*

[35] The maxim invoked in *Connelly*, *nemo debet bis vexari pro eadem causa*, and its variant *nemo debet bis punari pro uno delicto* are also discussed in *D.P.P.* v. *Humphrys* [1977] A.C. 1; noted (1977) 40 M.L.R. 83 (K. J. M. Smith); (1977) 8 Syd.L.R. 505 (I. Parsonage). See also *Wilhelm* v. *Bundeskartellamt* [1969] C.M.L.R. 100; *Re Boehringer Mannheim* (1972) 11 C.M.L.R. D121. Both principles are referred to and included in the common abbreviation, *non bis in idem*. For a full discussion see M. L. Friedland, *Double Jeopardy* (1969) Oxford University Press and J. A. Sigler, *Double Jeopardy* (1969) Cornell University Press. Friedland regards some instances, at least, of double jeopardy as being properly described as breaches of natural justice; *op. cit.* p. 321.

[36] *e.g.* 9 Edw. 4, 14.

[37] See D. E. C. Yale, "*Iudex propria causa*—an historical excursus" (1974) 33 C.L.J. 80.

[38] *Earl of Derby's Case* (1613) 12 Co.Rep. 114. See also *Day* v. *Savadge* (1614) Hob. 85; *Anon.* (1698) 1 Salk. 396.

[39] *Aeneid*, vi. 567.

[40] Co.Inst. 3.35.

[41] R. F. V. Heuston, *Essays in Constitutional Law* (2nd ed., 1964), p. 185.

[42] In *Harper* v. *Carr* (1797) 7 T.R. 271, 275 Lord Kenyon said, "It is an essential rule in the administration of justice that no man shall be punished without being heard in his defence." In *R.* v. *Gaskin* (1799) 8 T.R. 209, 210 the same judge spoke of "one of the first principles of justice, audi alteram partem.... It is to be found at the head of our criminal law that every man ought to have an opportunity of being heard before he is condemned."

[43] See also *Turbill's Case* (1668) 1 Wms.Saund. 67.

[44] See also *Masters* v. *Pontypool L.G.B.* (1878) 9 Ch.D. 677. Contrast *Cheetham* v. *Mayor of Manchester* (1875) L.R. 10 C.P. 249 where a statute authorised the corporation to order demolition "without any presentment, notice or other formality." The Court of Common Pleas held that the owner of property had no right to a hearing before an order for demolition was made: *Cooper* v. *Wandsworth Board of Works* was distinguished; the language in the earlier case was "not nearly so strong"; *per* Lord Coleridge C.J., p. 265.

[45] *Fisher* v. *Jackson* [1891] 2 Ch. 84.

[46] *Ridge* v. *Baldwin* [1964] A.C. 40, 66 *per* Lord Reid.

[47] *Ibid.* See *Infra*, p. 138.

[48] Similarly *Labouchere* v. *Earl of Wharncliffe* (1879) 13 Ch.D. 346.

[49] H. W. R. Wade (1951) 67 L.Q.R. 103.

[50] de Smith, *Judicial Review of Administrative Action* (3rd ed., 1973) Stevens & Sons Ltd., pp. 64 *et seq.*

[51] *R.* v. *Metropolitan Police Commissioner, ex p. Parker* [1953] 1 W.L.R. 1150. But see now *R.* v. *Board of Visitors of Hull Prison, ex. p. St. Germain* [1979] 2 W.L.R. 42; *infra*, p. 128.

[52] *Nakkuda Ali* v. *Jayaratne* [1951] A.C. 66—a distinction which has survived *Ridge* v. *Baldwin*; see *R.* v. *Gaming Board of Great Britain, ex p. Benaim and Khaida* [1970] 2 Q.B. 417, discussed later at p. 119.

[53] H. W. R. Wade, *Administrative Law* (3rd ed., 1971) Oxford University Press, p. 190.

[54] Municipal Corporations Act 1882, s. 191(4). "The Watch Committee, or any two justices having jurisdiction in the borough, may at any time suspend, and the watch committee may at any time dismiss, any borough constable whom they think negligent in the discharge of his duty, or otherwise unfit for the same."

CHAPTER 2

NEMO IUDEX IN RE SUA: BIAS

I. INTRODUCTION

THE maxim *nemo iudex in re sua*, translated literally, prohibits a man from being a judge in his own cause. By extension, however, it is often cited when referring to the allied, but distinct, rule that a judge must be impartial. That the two rules are distinct was recognised by Hobbes in Chapter 15 of *Leviathan*. The eleventh law of nature was, he said,

> "If, 'a man be trusted to judge between man and man,' it is a precept of the law of Nature, 'that he deal equally between them.' For without that, the controversies of men cannot be determined but by war. He therefore that is partial in judgment, doth what in him lies, to deter men from the use of judges and arbitrators; and consequently, against the fundamental law of Nature, is the cause of war."

The fifteenth and sixteenth laws, he described as follows:

> "And because, though men be never so willing to observe these laws, there may nevertheless arise questions concerning a man's action; first whether it were done, or not done; secondly, if done, whether against the law, or not against the law ... therefore unless the parties to the question covenant mutually to stand to the sentence of another, they are as far from peace as ever. This other to whose sentence they submit is called an 'arbitrator.' And therefore it is of the law of Nature, 'that they that are at controversy, submit their right to the judgment of an arbitrator.'
>
> And seeing every man is presumed to do all things in order to his own benefit, no man is a fit arbitrator in his own cause; and if he were never so fit; yet equity allowing to each party

equal benefit, if one be admitted to be judge, the other is to be admitted also; and so the controversy, that is the cause of war, remains against the law of Nature."

Lord Mansfield, when he prevented the justices of Berwick from hearing charges against someone whom they had already sought to disenfranchise because of his alleged misconduct, said:

> "A man may judge impartially even in his own cause. However, we must go upon general principles. I do not speak this with the least imputation upon the magistrates of Berwick: but it is not fit that they should be judges in their own cause and after having already gone so far as they have done" (*R.* v. *Cowle* (1759) 2 Burr. 834, 863).

At least until the time of Coke, the common law was concerned mainly with the maxim in its first sense.[1] The existence of feudal courts and the numerous royal grants of franchises under which the grantees were entitled to hold their own courts meant that powerful magnates were frequently in a position to seek to adjudicate in disputes to which they themselves were parties. In the *Earl of Derby's Case* (1614) 12 Co.Rep. 114 for example, the Earl of Derby claimed to be entitled to decide himself in his own court in Chester, a dispute between himself and Sir John Egerton. Coke reports that it was decided

> "that the Chamberlain of Chester, being sole Judge of Equity, cannot decree anything wherein himself is party, for he cannot be judge in propria causa, but in such case where he is party, the suit shall be heard in the Chancery coram domino Rege."

(Quite apart from the development of natural justice, such decisions were important in the field of constitutional law. They provided the justification for denying the king the right to sit in his own courts to administer justice. Although the courts were, and are, royal courts, if justice is to be dispensed impartially it must be done by independent judges to whom the power of determining disputes has been delegated.[2]) Unlike the Earl of Derby, Holt C.J. ostentatiously refrained from taking part in deciding in his own court the question whether the right to appoint to the office of chief clerk belonged to the Crown or to the Chief Justice; when the case was argued the great judge sat "near the Defendant's counsel upon a chair uncovered"; *Bridgman* v. *Holt* (1693) Shower P.C. 111. An eighteenth-century example of the prohibition of a man being a judge in his own cause is provided by *R.* v. *Bishop of Chester* (1791) 2 Str. 797. The Bishop was both warden and also visitor of a college. It was held that the Bishop could not, in the latter capacity, exercise the normal visitorial jurisdiction and hear appeals from his own decisions taken as warden.

In this sense the maxim has not entirely been forgotten in modern case law. In *Burkett Sharp* v. *Eastcheap Dried Fruit Co.* [1961] 2 Lloyd's Rep. 80; [1962] 1 Lloyd's Rep. 267 the Eastcheap Company had appointed as arbitrator in a dispute with Burkett Sharp someone who was "closely associated" with the company and "wholly or partially managing its business." The Court of Appeal upheld the decision of Diplock J., as he then was, that the award must be set aside, apart from any other reason, on the ground that the arbitrator was acting in his own cause.[3] In *Hannam* v. *Bradford C.C.* [1970] 1 W.L.R. 937, H, a schoolmaster, had been dismissed by the school governors. This decision was confirmed by the staff sub-committee of the local education committee. The chairman of the sub-committee was a governor of H's school and two other governors were members of the sub-committee; none of the three had attended the governors' meeting at which the decision to dismiss H had been taken. Although the court held that H failed in his claim for damages all three judges agreed that the decision of the sub-committee could have been successfully attacked for bias if the appropriate procedure had been used.[4] While Widgery and Cross L.JJ. merely spoke in general terms of bias Sachs L.J. (at p. 942) distinguished between "bias" and

> "a slightly different ground on which it was abundantly clear that the staff sub-committee decision could not stand. No man can be judge of his own cause. The governors did not, on donning their sub-committee hats, cease to be an integral part of the body whose action was being impugned and it made no difference that they did not personally attend the [relevant] governors' meeting."

Whether in a particular case a judge should be described as disqualified from sitting because of bias or because he is judging his own cause may, as will be seen later in the chapter, be of practical significance.

The importance with which the principle that a judge should be impartial has always been viewed could hardly be more clearly illustrated than by the dictum in *Day* v. *Savadge* (1615) Hob. 85, 87, which was quoted earlier: "Even an Act of Parliament made against natural equity as to make a man judge in his own cause is void in itself for iura naturae sunt immutabilia and they are leges legum." Although the belief in the existence of this limit to the power of Parliament may no longer survive (see Blackstone, Comm.i,91), it is still believed to be of fundamental importance that judges and tribunals are free from bias, or, at least, from those biases which society regards as undesirable in a judge.

> "Society demands that its judges be biased in certain directions no less insistently than it demands that they shall be unbiased in others. A man who had not a standard of moral values which approximated broadly to the accepted opinions of the day, who had no beliefs as to what is harmful to society and what beneficial, who had no bias in favour of marriage as against promiscuous sexual relations, honesty as against deceit, truthfulness as against lying; who did not think wealth better than poverty, orthodox religion preferable to atheism, courage better than cowardice, constitutional government more desirable than anarchy would not be tolerated as a judge on the bench of any Western country."[5]

Mutatis mutandis these words apply to everybody who decides anything.

However, at a time when the views of society are changing rapidly questions may arise as to which biases society wishes its judges to have.[6] Judicial comments which cast doubt, or seem to cast doubt, on the wisdom of controversial legislation in social and moral fields inevitably give rise to comment and, to some extent, to concern about the ability or willingness of particular judges—or the judiciary generally—to deal fairly with cases arising under such legislation.[7] At the same time the attention such judicial indiscretions receive is evidence of their rarity and the public assumption that the law is, normally, fairly and impartially administered. It is salutary too for judges and laymen to be reminded from time to time that "Men who make their way to the Bench sometimes exhibit vanity, irascibility, narrowness, arrogance and other weaknesses to which human flesh is heir" (*Sacher* v. *U.S.* 341 U.S. 1, 12 (1952) *per* Jackson J.).[8]

Before proceeding to examine the common law rules relating to bias two general points should be made. First, the law is concerned with the individual "bias" of a particular judge which may result in his failing to give the parties a fair hearing. There is a clear distinction between being prejudiced—or biased—against, say, alleged thieves of a particular race and on the other hand, being "biased" against—in the sense of disapproving of—theft. It is in the latter sense that bias was used in the above quotation. Thus, views in the abstract as to the relative truthfulness or untruthfulness of policemen as opposed to motorists accused of speeding do not constitute "bias" in the improper sense: it *is* "bias" in the improper sense of prejudice for a particular magistrate to say that wherever the evidence of a policeman conflicts with that of a member of the public "my principle in such cases has always been to believe the evidence of the police officer"; *R.* v. *Bingham Justices, ex p. Jowitt, The Times*, July 3, 1974. There is also no doubt that the courts will pay little regard to any suggestion by a litigant that the judiciary as a whole is biased against him. In *Rothermere* v. *The Times* [1973] 1 W.L.R. 448 where it was suggested that such bias might arise from articles written by one of the parties criticising particular judges, Cairns L.J. said,

> "In any case where a well-known writer or other public figure is involved a judge may have private feelings, favourable or unfavourable, towards him. If the judge had been the subject of some individual criticism or had had some private disagreement with the litigant he obviously would not hear the case, although even in those circumstances I think the risk of prejudice would be more apparent than real. Every judge by his training is used to putting out of his mind any knowledge or feelings that he has had about a party before he came into court" (p. 456).

In *Williams* v. *Beesley* [1973] 1 W.L.R. 1295, the plaintiff alleged that any judge would be prejudiced against him because he was a layman suing a solicitor. In rejecting his claim, on that ground, to trial by jury Lord Diplock said,

> "If, as in the instant case, all rational considerations point to the conclusion that trial by judge alone would involve a shorter and less expensive hearing and would be more likely to achieve a just result than trial by jury, it would be the height of injustice to the defendant to deprive him of his right to have his case tried by the appropriate method merely because of the mistaken belief of the plaintiff that judges as a class are likely to be biased against him or in favour of his opponent. To allow the court's decision as to the mode of trial to be swayed by the existence of such a belief by one of the parties, however sincerely it might be held, would be to acknowledge that there was some substance in it and that our system of justice lacks the firm foundation of an impartial judiciary" (p. 1299).

The distinction between a possible, general "bias" which does not disqualify, as opposed to the individual prejudice or bias which does, has been illustrated in the case of domestic tribunals by *Roebuck* v. *N.U.M.* (*Yorkshire Area*) (*No. 2*) [1978] I.C.R. 676. The chairman of the committee which expelled the plaintiffs from the union was, as will be seen later in the chapter, disqualified from acting by bias arising from his personal interest in the case. It could have been argued that the other members of the committee also, as union members, had an interest where the charge was of acting in a manner detrimental to the interests of the union. Templeman J. however said, at p. 681,

> "True it is that all the members of the executive committee and the area council, in common with all members of a domestic tribunal where the interests of their own organisation are at stake, have a general inclination to defend the union and its officers against attack from any source; this fact, every trade unionist and every member of a domestic organisation knows and accepts."

Secondly, there can be little doubt that the courts would regard as falling outside the rule against bias, as they apply it, allegations of bias in a third sense, namely a prejudice, possibly partially or wholly unconscious, against particular sections of society arising from the age, social background and professional training of the judiciary. Such a thesis has, for example, been put forward recently by Professor J. A. G. Griffith in *The Politics of the Judiciary*. Judges, he argues, are part of a highly authoritarian society—although less authoritarian, Professor Griffith admits, than others—and use their power in the interests, as they see them, of the social order. They define the public interest from the viewpoint of their own class. If such a theory accurately represents the judicial attitude, "bias" in the sense of individual prejudice is, by comparison, unimportant. Our system of justice would indeed lack, in Lord Diplock's words "the firm foundation of an impartial judiciary." However, it is possible to dispute whether Professor Griffith's evidence proves his thesis. Should, for example, the case of *Attorney-General* v. *Jonathan Cape Ltd.* [1976] Q.B. 752, be regarded as an extension of the law to prevent publication of information relating to Cabinet business, as he seems to suggest, or, on the contrary, as a case limiting the extent to which the publication of such material can be controlled. It is possible too, to dispute the weight which he gives to particular decisions or dicta. At the very least cases such as *Ridge* v. *Baldwin* [1964] A.C. 40 and *Conway* v. *Rimmer* [1968] A.C. 910 can be described as more important and significant than, for example, Lord Denning M.R.'s animadversions in *Ward* v. *Bradford* (1972) 70 L.G.R. 27, on the qualities needed to be a successful schoolteacher to which the learned author takes such exception. In the words of a reviewer who, as a former Lord of Appeal, may be regarded by some as insufficiently impartial:

> "[Professor Griffith's] purpose is to show that there are certain types of cases that the judges as a body do not decide fairly. I am not sure that in the end he proves much more than that there are cases which he, often in accord with dissenting judges, would have decided differently from the final court."[9]

II. Interest and Favour

The common law distinguishes two types of bias, that arising from financial interests and that arising from such causes as relationship to a party or witness. The latter type of bias has often been described as a challenge to favour as opposed to the first type which is described as giving rise to an interest; *R.* v. *Rand* (1866) L.R. 1 Q.B. 230.

Any direct pecuniary interest, however small, is sufficient to disqualify a person from acting as a judge, a proposition strikingly illustrated by *Dimes* v. *Grand Junction Canal* (1852) 3 H.L.C. 759. Litigation between the canal company and the lord of the manor from one of whose copyholders it had bought land had occupied the courts for over 10 years before Lord Cottenham pronounced a decree in favour of the company. Dimes, the lord of the manor, discovered that the Lord Chancellor owned 90-odd shares in the canal company; he recommenced litigation and ultimately the House of Lords set aside Lord Cottenham's decree. Lord Campbell summed up the law in words which have been frequently repeated and applied:

> "No-one can suppose that Lord Cottenham could be, in the remotest degree, influenced by the interest that he had in this concern: but, my Lords, it is of the last importance that the maxim that no man is to be a judge in his own cause be held sacred. And that is not to be confined to a cause in which he is a party but applies to a cause in which he has an interest.... This will be a lesson to all inferior tribunals to take care not only that in their decrees they are not influenced by their personal interest but to avoid the appearance of labouring under such an influence."[10]

The decision in *Dimes'* case was followed in *London and North Western Ry. Co.* v. *Lindsay* (1858) 3 Macq. 99 where Lord Wensleydale refused, as a shareholder in the railway company, to participate in hearing the appeal.[11] In *Serjeant* v. *Dale* (1877) 2 Q.B.D. 558 the Bishop of London was held to be disqualified from determining whether a clergyman should be removed from his benefice because as one of two patrons who appointed alternately to the living he had an interest in the eyes of the law:

> "The law does not measure the amount of interest which a judge possesses. If he has any legal interest in the decision of the question one way he is disqualified, no matter how small the interest may be. The law, in laying down this strict rule, has regard not so much perhaps to the motives which might be supposed to bias the judge as to the susceptibilities of the litigant parties. One important object, at all events, is to clear away everything which might engender suspicion and distrust of the tribunal, and so to promote the feeling of confidence in the administration of justice which is so essential to social order and security" (*per* Lush J. at p. 567).

A common ground of disqualification of magistrates in the nineteenth century was their interest in the outcome of litigation as ratepayers who would ultimately bear the cost of unsuccessful proceedings, for example, *R.* v. *Recorder of Cambridge* (1857) 8 E. & B. 637. In *R.* v. *Hertfordshire JJ.* (1845) 6 Q.B. 753 the Court of Queen's Bench held that a magistrate who sat at quarter sessions on an appeal from a decision of his own was interested because of his contingent liability for costs if the applicant was successful. Licensing justices who had a financial interest in the granting or withholding of licences for the sale of alcohol would of course be disqualified at common law. Statute has reinforced this prohibition but also provided that no act done by any justice disqualified by the statutory prohibition shall be invalid by reason only of that disqualification; Licensing Act 1964 s. 193, as amended by the Courts Act 1971, Sched. 8. However, any financial interest falling outside the terms of the statutory provisions will still suffice to invalidate the justices' decision; *R.* v. *Barnsley Licensing Justices, ex p. Barnsley and District Licensed Victuallers Association* [1960] 2 Q.B. 167.

A financial interest, to be disabling, must be direct. In *R.* v. *Rand* (*supra*) Bradford Corporation sought, under statute, authority from the justices to take water from various streams to fill the reservoir of the municipally-owned waterworks. Two of the justices were trustees of bodies which had invested in bonds issued by the corporation. Mill owners affected by the granting of permission to the corporation objected that the two justices were disqualified because of the interest they must have had in the success of the activities of the corporation. The challenge on the ground of financial interest failed because the justices personally could neither lose nor profit as a result of the granting of permission and hence their interest was not direct. Any allegation of partiality on the ground of their trusteeships would be a challenge to favour.

In disqualifying judges and magistrates on the ground of the smallest financial interest the courts have applied to themselves a stricter rule than they apply to arbitrators. In the latter case, as will be seen in Chapter 7, the courts ask if there is a real likelihood of bias.[12] In *Ellis* v. *Hopper* (1858) 28 L.J.Ex. 1; 3 H. & N. 766, the Court of Exchequer refused to set aside a decision by stewards at a race meeting that a particular horse had won although one of the five stewards had an interest arising from his betting. It was held that the parties must have foreseen that species of interest. On the other hand, in *R.* v. *Farrant* (1887) 20 Q.B.D. 58 the court said that if, as alleged, a magistrate had bet on the outcome of a case in which he was involved he would have been disqualified by pecuniary interest.

A challenge to favour may arise in various circumstances involving such matters as personal friendship or relationship, participation by a judge in proceedings leading to the hearing so that he can be regarded as both accuser and judge, or the expression of views on earlier occasions which might be thought to affect his ability to give both parties a fair hearing.

The fear of bias arising from acquaintance or kinship with the disputants could hardly be more clearly shown than by the early statutes which forbade a judge from sitting on assize in the country of his birth, *e.g.* 8 Rich. 2, c. 2 and 33 Hen. 8, c. 24. These were not repealed until 1739, so far as criminal cases were concerned, and 1809, so far as civil litigation was concerned; 12 Geo. 2, c. 27 and 49 Geo. 3, c. 91. In modern times more than mere acquaintanceship or distant relationship would be needed before a judge were disqualified but there is no hard and fast rule. Lord Evershed M.R. declined to sit in a case involving the anaesthetist who attended him at his dentist.[13] The same judge felt that it was improper for him, as a church commissioner, to take part in an appeal to which the Church Commissioners were a party; *The Times*, October 30, 1956. Lord Denning M.R., in a similar case, took a different view. The

Commissioners included, he said, many dignitaries—among whom is the Master of the Rolls—but the dignitaries have nothing to do with the management of the Commissioners' affairs which are the concern of a board of governors; *Hanson* v. *Church Commissioners for England* [1978] Q.B. 823. Some degree of acquaintance may be unavoidable as, for example, if a High Court judge initiates proceedings in that court. Such a case would, if necessary, be covered by the doctrine of necessity which is discussed later in Chapter 6. Even so it might be possible—and preferable—to have such a case heard before a judge who had not been, for example, in the same chambers as the plaintiff judge or had practised on a different circuit.[14] In *Cottle* v. *Cottle* [1939] 2 All E.R. 535, 539, Sir Boyd Merriman said it would be "preposterous" to suggest

> "that because of the mere fact that some sort of acquaintance exists between a justice and parties, or even the fact that they have discussed business matters entirely unconnected with the case ... there was bias or a possibility of bias.... The whole essence of the local administration of justice and the great value of the functions of justices are that they do administer justice among people with whom they are acquainted, and of whose lives and family history they know something"

—a somewhat unreal picture of the work of magistrates in cities the size of Birmingham or Liverpool. Similarly, arbitrators will not be disqualified by acquaintance with one of the parties and indeed, as will be seen in Chapter 7, may even be in the employment of one of the parties. The question is one of degree. In *Cottle* v. *Cottle* (*supra*) the chairman of the bench hearing a summons brought by a wife against her husband was a friend of the wife's mother. There were various allegations that the wife had suggested that she could influence the chairman and that the women had been seen talking "in an animated manner" to him. Perhaps not surprisingly the summons was remitted to the justices to be dealt with by a different bench.

Questions of bias or favour can arise where the acquaintance or kinship is between the judge or tribunal and counsel or other person representing one of the parties. In the case of the courts there are accepted standards of professional behaviour. Thus, no barrister should habitually practise in any county court or Crown Court of which his father or near relative is the judge. There is no objection to a barrister practising in a court where his father is one of several judges. It has never been considered improper for a barrister to appear before his father in the High Court, Court of Appeal, or in the House of Lords.[15] To take advantage of such relationship would clearly be regarded nowadays as improper. Earlier centuries viewed matters differently; the position of "the Judge's Friend" or favoured barrister was well recognised. Boswell earned the greater part of his income at the Scottish Bar appearing before his father, Lord Auchinleck.[16] In the case of other tribunals and arbitrators the standard of behaviour will be tested by reference to the likelihood of a real likelihood of bias, as will be seen later in this chapter and in Chapter 7.

The decision of a judge or tribunal of any kind will be vitiated by bias if anyone involved in making the decision was so concerned in the preliminaries to the hearing that he can be described as both accuser and judge. A magistrate, for example, has been disqualified where he has heard charges arising out of facts which have been the subject of other proceedings brought by the local board of health of which he was a member (*R.* v. *Meyer* (1875) 1 Q.B.D. 173), or where she heard charges against a farmer of giving short weight when delivering vegetables to schools, brought at the instance of the local education committee, of which she was a member; *R.* v. *Altrincham Justices, ex p. Pennington* [1975] Q.B. 549. The court emphasised in the *Altrincham Justices* case that a justice must not be regarded as disqualified from sitting in a case brought by the police merely because he, or she, is a member of the relevant police authority. The police authority is concerned with the administration of the force; they are not concerned with the rights and wrongs of individual prosecutions. (Apart from any likelihood of bias arising from the specific facts of a particular case magistrates are, by section 3 of the Justices of the Peace Act 1949, prohibited from hearing actions brought by local authorities of which they may be members.)

The rule was applied to a professional disciplinary body in *Law* v. *Chartered Institute of Patent Agents* [1919] 2 Ch. 276. The council of the defendant institute approached the Board of Trade to seek the erasure of L's name from the register of patent agents on the ground that he had been guilty of "disgraceful professional conduct" under rule 31 of its charter. When this move failed the council met and purported to erase L's name itself under another rule, an attempt which failed because the council, which was now acting as judge, had earlier been accuser. In *Taylor* v. *National Union of Seamen* [1967] 1 W.L.R. 532 Ungoed-Thomas J. held that there had been a breach of natural justice where the body which heard T's appeal was chaired by the official of the union who had been responsible for initially preparing and presenting the charge against T. In *Roebuck* v. *N.U.M.* (*Yorkshire Area*) (*No. 2*) [1978] I.C.R. 676 Mr. Scargill had initiated proceedings for expulsion from the union of two miners who had given evidence in a successful libel action which he had brought against a newspaper. The evidence was not what had been hoped for; the behaviour of the witnesses was alleged to be detrimental to the interests of the union. Mr. Scargill presided at the meetings of the committee which decided to expel the two, and of the body which heard their unsuccessful appeal. Templeman J. set the decisions aside. In the learned judge's words, Mr. Scargill had played the roles of

> "the complainant, the pleader, the prosecutor, the advocate and the chairman ... his presence as chairman, and his conduct undoubtedly gave the impression that the dice were loaded against [the plaintiffs]. No amount of evidence can remove that impression, or establish affirmatively that the end result was unaffected by natural resentment and prejudice in the mind of Mr. Scargill.... Whether he recognised that fact or not, Mr. Scargill must inevitably have appeared biased against [the plaintiffs]. The appearance of bias was inevitable; the exercise of bias, conscious or unconscious, was probable."

The rule was applied to private clubs in *Howshall* v. *Evans* [1969] C.L.Y. 354; [1969] P.L. 169. The plaintiff had been reprimanded for his behaviour in 1964 by the committee of Shotton Conservative Club. In 1966 he wrote to the secretary of the club accusing members of the committee which had reprimanded him of lying and conspiracy. He was summoned before the new committee of the club, the chairman of which had been chairman of the 1964 committee.

Creighton J. held that the expulsion of Howshall was null and void, the chairman being both judge and prosecutor.

It is not necessary that the prosecutor should himself be one of the judges; his mere presence among the adjudicators is sufficient to invalidate a decision. This is illustrated by the case of *R.* v. *Barnsley Borough Council, ex p. Hook* [1976] 1 W.L.R. 1052, to which reference was made in Chapter 1 and which will be discussed again in Chapter 5. The manager of a street market at Barnsley received a complaint about the behaviour of Hook, one of the traders. He interviewed Hook and decided to ban him from trading at the market. Hook appealed to a committee of the local council and from that body to another committee. At both hearings the market manager was present. The Court of Appeal quashed the decision upholding the ban on Hook because "it is contrary to natural justice that one who is in the position of a prosecutor should be present at the deliberations of the adjudicating committee"; *per* Lord Denning M.R. at p. 1057.[17]

It is "a question of substance and of fact whether one of the judges has in truth also been an accuser," *per* Bowen L.J. in *Leeson* v. *General Medical Council* (1889) 43 Ch.D. 366, 384. (It might be added in view of the vigorous dissent of Fry L.J. that it is also a question of difficulty.) Leeson had been summoned to appear before a committee of the General Medical Council on a charge of infamous conduct in a professional respect. The proceedings had been initiated by the council of the Medical Defence Union. Two members of the committee of 29 were members of the Medical Defence Union but not of its council over whose activities they could exercise no control. The majority of the Court of Appeal held that the two members were not in substance accusers and judges. Bowen L.J.'s test was applied in *R.* (*Ellis*) v. *Co. Dublin JJ.* [1894] 2 I.R. 526. An application was made to quash a conviction on the ground that one of the justices who heard the case was a member of the finance committee of Dublin Corporation which had, on an earlier occasion, directed that the district surveyor should prosecute E for causing an obstruction. The justice had not attended the meeting at which the decision was taken, nor did he know of the directions given by the committee. The surveyor later prosecuted E, on his own initiative, when he refused to remove the obstruction. The Court of King's Bench refused to quash this conviction. The defendant might not like having a justice on the bench who, as a member of the finance committee, might be influenced by the fact that the prosecution, brought by the surveyor, would commonly be understood to be a prosecution by the finance committee. Nonetheless the court was not prepared to accept that "the feeling of the defendant [was] the true test of the question." Nor is "esprit de corps ... the same thing as the bias or interest that will disqualify a magistrate"; *per* O'Brien J. at p. 533.[18]

A judge or tribunal may be disqualified in a variety of circumstances where their behaviour or statements or other factors may suggest an inability to discharge their duties impartially; the question, as will be seen later, is whether the likelihood is sufficiently serious for the law to take account of it. The mere fact of being a teetotaller, or of believing alcohol should be more easily available, will not, for example, disqualify a justice from dealing with licensing applications.[19] Statutory provisions make it clear that mere membership of the licensing planning committee, which consists of selected justices and members of the local authority, does not disqualify a justice from hearing a licensing application; Licensing Act 1964, s. 130. On the other hand in *Frome United Dairies* v. *Bath Justices* [1926] A.C. 586 an applicant who was refused a licence by the compensation committee—to which appeal lay from the licensing justices—had that refusal set aside when he showed that three of the justices sitting on the compensation committee had, after participating in the meeting of the licensing justices, directed their clerk to instruct a solicitor to oppose the applicant's appeal. Similarly the Salmon and Freshwater Fisheries Act 1975, Sched. 4, Pt. II, para. 4, while providing that "a justice shall not be entitled to hear any case in respect of an offence committed on his own land or in relation to any fishery of which he is owner or occupier" also says that a "justice of the peace shall not be disqualified from hearing any case under this Act by reason only of being a subscriber to any society for the protection of fish." The Factories Act 1961, s. 164(7) prevents a justice hearing proceedings under s. 135 of that Act with respect to a factory of which he is the occupier or owner, or the husband, wife, parent, son, daughter, brother, or sister of the occupier or owner of the factory or a person engaged in, or an officer of any association of persons engaged in, the same trade or occupation as any person charged with the offence. Barristers are prohibited from constituting an election court for the trial of any petition relating to any local government area in which they reside or which is included in a circuit on which they practise; Representation of the People Act 1949, s. 115(3), as amended by the Courts Act 1971, Sched. 8.

An example of another type of possible bias is afforded by *R.* v. *Grimsby Borough Quarter Sessions, ex p. Fuller* [1956] 1 Q.B. 36 where the Recorder had in front of him a report on the prisoner which included, near the part he was consulting for a purpose to the prisoner's benefit, a list of previous convictions. The Divisional Court quashed the conviction on the ground that there was "a real likelihood of prejudice."[20] In another case an order binding D to be of good behaviour was quashed when it was shown that one of the justices had, before the hearing, been involved in altercations with D's family and had said, "As sure as I'm living I will not leave any member of the Feheens [the nickname of D's family] in Bohonagh"; *R.* (*Donoghue*) v. *Justices of Co. Cork* [1910] 2 I.R. 271. In *R.* (*Kingston*) v. *Justices of Co. Cork* [1920] 2 I.R. 658, the applicants for certiorari to quash a conviction for assault proved that two of the justices before whom they appeared were members of the United Irish League which had organised a boycott of the applicants' farm and had attended the meeting of the league at which the decision to boycott had been taken. The Court of King's Bench quashed the conviction; "motives of delicacy alone ought to have restrained [the] two magistrates from taking any part in the decision"; p. 665 *per* Gibson J.[21]

No doubt it was from motives of delicacy, rather than any real likelihood of bias, that no Law Lord with a known political background sat to hear the controversial case, arising under the Industrial Relations Act 1971, *Heaton's Transport Co.* v. *T.G.W.U.* [1973] A.C. 15. It is said, indeed, that a convention has developed that the Lord Chancellor and ex-Lord Chancellors do not participate in judicial matters affecting, even remotely, affairs of state.[22]

A judge whose words or actions show that he has preconceived opinions on the merits of the parties is disqualified by bias. In *Black* v. *Black* [1951] 1 N.Z.L.R. 723, for example, a magistrate, in the course of proceedings relating to access by the wife to the children who were in the husband's custody, commented that the husband's conduct was callous and he did not have a spark of manhood in him. The wife shortly afterwards commenced proceedings before the same magistrate for custody of the children. The order made in her favour was quashed by the Supreme Court. In *Healey* v. *Rauhina* [1958] N.Z.L.R. 945 the magistrate, in an action to which an insurance company was defendant, suggested throughout the action that such companies were no better than second-hand car dealers, and implied that they were of doubtful honesty. His judgment was quashed by certiorari. In *Ex p. Church of Scientology of California, The Times* February 21, 1978, the applicants, who had appeared before the Master of the Rolls on eight or nine earlier occasions, claimed that those hearings showed that the Master of the Rolls' judgment was affected by an unconscious prejudice against them. Lord Denning agreed to transfer the case to a court of which he was not a member.

Occasionally a judge may feel obliged to disqualify himself, because of a strongly held belief which he fears might affect his judgment. Counsel in the *Scientology* case drew the attention of the Court of Appeal to the statement by Mr. Justice Frankfurter in *Public Utilities Commission* v. *Pollak* 343 U.S. 451, 466 (1951). The question before the court was whether it was unconstitutional to allow the broadcasting of music and announcements on public buses.

> "There is a good deal of shallow talk that the judicial robe does not change the man within it. It does. The fact is that on the whole judges do lay aside private views in discharging their judicial functions. This is achieved through training, professional habits, self-discipline and that fortunate alchemy by which men are loyal to the obligation with which they are entrusted. But it is also true that reason cannot control the subconscious influence of feelings of which it is unaware. When there is ground for believing that such unconscious feelings may operate in the ultimate judgment, or may not unfairly lead others to believe they are operating, judges recuse themselves. They do not sit in judgment. They do this for a variety of reasons. The guiding consideration is that the administration of justice should reasonably appear to be disinterested as well

as be so in fact. This case for me presents such a situation. My feelings are so strongly engaged as a victim of the practice in controversy that I had better not participate in judicial judgment upon it. I am explicit as to the reason for my non-participation in this case because I have for some time been of the view that it is desirable to state why one takes oneself out of a case."

Perhaps the most striking example in the reports of a judge being held not to be biased despite a personal concern with the subject-matter of the litigation is to be found in *R.* (*Giant's Causeway, etc. Tramway Co.*) v. *Antrim JJ.* [1895] 2 I.R. 603. For many years Lord Macnaghten had engaged in correspondence with the directors of the railway company over a right of way which he alleged to exist over the railway line near his home. The learned Lord sat as one of the local justices when the company prosecuted a tramp for trespassing on its property. The tramp was acquitted and the company challenged the validity of the justices' decision, alleging bias on the part of Lord Macnaghten. Their claim failed on two grounds; an acquittal cannot be quashed by certiorari[23]; and the company had waived its right to object by agreeing at the first hearing that Lord Macnaghten should sit. Thus the Court of Queen's Bench was spared having to decide whether "one of the supreme arbiters of the law of the whole Empire" (*per* O'Brien J. at p. 641) could reasonably be suspected of bias. Two members of the court managed to convince themselves that, apart from any question of waiver, there was no possibility of bias. Holmes J., for example, thought the interest of Lord Macnaghten in the right of way was merely "the interest of a keen lawyer on a nice legal question" (p. 659).

Three cases which largely, but not exclusively, concern the courts in the strict sense, might be thought to present a special risk of bias: a judge sitting on appeal from an earlier judgment of his own; a judge hearing a case in which he had earlier been involved as counsel and a judge exercising his power to imprison for contempt committed in the face of his court.

So far as the first of these three cases is concerned, the common law has never seen any objection to judges of the superior courts sitting on appeal from their own previous decisions. The explanation is, probably, historical and practical. The common law courts usually sat *in banc* (*i.e.* as a full court) and considered as a court matters which came before them whether directly or as a result of rulings made by a single judge when hearing cases at *nisi prius*.[24] In Chancery matters there could often have been no effective appeal at all unless from the Lord Chancellor who pronounced the decree to the same judge, sitting in the House of Lords, whether as Lord Chancellor or ex-Lord Chancellor. Indeed to assemble a quorum of qualified peers at all was often difficult before the passing of the Appellate Jurisdiction Act 1876.[25]

Examples of judges sitting on appeal from their own decisions are not uncommon in the law reports. In the first half of the nineteenth century Lord Plunket, Lord Chancellor of Ireland from 1830 to 1841, (apart from a period of three months in 1835 when the office was held by Sir Edward Sugden) sat in the House of Lords on appeal from his own decrees on four occasions, behaviour described by a nineteenth-century biographer as not being in good taste.[26] In *Vandeleur* v. *Vandeleur* (1835) 3 Cl. & Fin. 82 he concurred in the reversal of his own previous decision. In *Anderson* v. *Wallace* (1835) 3 Cl. & Fin. 26 and *Miltown* v. *Trench* (1837) 4 Cl. & Fin. 276 the House of Lords agreed in upholding his decisions while in *Shaw* v. *Lawless* (1837) 5 Cl. & Fin. 129 Lord Plunket had the satisfaction of helping to restore a decision of his own which had been reversed on a rehearing by Sir Edward Sugden during the latter's brief tenure of office as Lord Chancellor of Ireland. In *Shore* v. *Wilson* (1842) 9 Cl. & Fin. 355 Lord Brougham and Lord Lyndhurst participated in hearing an appeal in a case which had been argued before Lord Brougham when he was Lord Chancellor, and, on his resignation before completion of argument, had been re-argued before his successor, Lord Lyndhurst. The parties, wisely as it turned out, agreed that the latter should give judgment even if he lost office before the end of the case. Such in fact happened. The ex-Lord Chancellor, advised by the judges, gave judgment sitting in Gray's Inn hall. Later in the century in *Grey* v. *Friar* (1853) 4 H.L.C. 565 Lord Cranworth L.C. heard an appeal from a judgment given by himself when Rolfe B. (The majority of the House upheld the reversal of the Baron's judgment by the Exchequer Chamber, the Lord Chancellor dissenting.) In *Knox* v. *Gye* (1872) L.R. 5

H.L. 656, Lord Hatherley L.C. dissented when his judicial colleagues upheld the reversal of the judgment which he had given as Page Wood V.-C. In this century Lord Reading sat in the House of Lords on appeals from his own decisions in the Court of Criminal Appeal in *R.* v. *Christie* [1914] A.C. 545 and *D.P.P.* v. *Beard* [1920] A.C. 479. In *R.* v. *Lovegrove* [1951] 1 All E.R. 804 Lynskey J. sat in the Court of Criminal Appeal on an appeal from one of his own decisions.

This practice has been defended judicially:

> "There is nothing in the nature of the thing which makes it improper for a judge to sit in review upon his own judgments. If he is what a judge ought to be—wise enough to know that he is fallible, and therefore ever ready to learn; great and honest enough to discard all mere pride of opinion, and follow truth wherever it may lead; and courageous enough to acknowledge his errors—he is then the very best man to sit in review upon his own judgments. He will have the benefit of a double discussion. If right at the first, he will be confirmed in his opinion; and if wrong, he will be quite as likely to find it out as anyone else" (*Piecre* v. *Delameter* 1 N.Y. 3, 18 (1847) *per* Bronson J.).[27]

However, as another judge has said, "Because laymen rarely appreciate the degree of mental detachment of which members of the judiciary are capable in relation to their own opinions . . . it seems highly desirable that the practice . . . should be acted upon as rarely as possible."[28] It is interesting that the legislature, when it created the Court of Appeal by statute, expressly forbade the Lords Justices of Appeal to hear appeals from their own previous decisions.[29] Similarly, whether or not there was a common law rule against justices sitting on appeal from their own decisions[30] such a practice has been forbidden from time to time by various statutory provisions.[31]

Cases such as *R.* v. *Barnsley Metropolitan Borough Council, ex p. Hook* (*supra*) show that the common law does not, as a general rule, believe that someone who has once adjudicated on a matter can, impartially, participate in the hearing of an appeal on the same question.[32] Nonetheless in certain circumstances it will be impossible to avoid a person being involved, in some sense at any rate, in an appeal against his or her previous decision. For example, in universities appeals from examiners' decisions may well be to those individuals sitting in another capacity or at least to a board containing some of the original examiners. Admittedly sometimes formally there may be no problem when, for instance, the "appeal" is not against the examiners' decision to fail a candidate but there is an application on non-academic grounds to be allowed to proceed or to repeat a year. This problem, in the context of universities, will be discussed later in Chapter 7. In other cases the solution may be provided by the doctrine of necessity which is discussed later in Chapter 8. What is clear is that the courts accept that such overlap of membership between the domestic tribunal which first hears a case and the body to which appeal lies is inevitable and, in the absence of any special factor giving rise to a likelihood of bias, unobjectionable; *Roebuck* v. *N.U.M.* (*Yorkshire Area*) (*No. 2*) [1978] I.C.R. 676, 682.

To be distinguished from the question of bias arising from a judge hearing an appeal from his own decision is the situation where a tribunal realises that its first hearing was defective and resolves to give the matter a second full and fair hearing. While such a procedure does not of itself violate natural justice the fairness of the subsequent proceedings will obviously be closely scrutinised by the courts. Where the tribunal is the only body with jurisdiction and its first decision has been quashed by the court the doctrine of necessity will be available to justify its second hearing.[32] Where possible courts will often direct that a rehearing is before a differently-constituted tribunal.[33]

Whether a judge should hear a case in which he has earlier been involved as counsel may be regarded as a specific instance of the rule forbidding a judge to be simultaneously accuser or party in litigation before him or, at any rate, a closely analogous situation. There seems to be no absolute rule. In *Shore* v. *Wilson* (*supra*) Lord Campbell declined to give judgment having argued the case at the Bar of the House and been elevated to the Bench before the litigation was completed. The matter was discussed more fully in *Thellusson* v. *Rendelsham* (1859) 7 H.L.Cas. 429, 430. Lord Chelmsford L.C. declined to take any part in the appeal (other than to preside as Lord Chancellor) since he had, while at the bar, been counsel in the very case then before the House. He did not, however, think himself disqualified and would have been prepared to hear the appeal had he been the only judge available to do so. Lord St. Leonards referred to his own connection as counsel in 1825 and 1831 with various matters indirectly concerned with the appeal before the House and stated that he felt bound to discharge his duty of advising the House. Lord Brougham emphasised the practical inconveniences, especially in Chancery, of a judge refusing to hear a case with which he had been concerned as counsel. For that reason he had himself, as Lord Chancellor, heard the case of *Tatham* v. *Wright* (1830) 2 Russ. & M. 1, which came before him shortly after he became Lord Chancellor. However, to "satisfy his own mind" he had obtained the assistance of Tindal C.J. and Alderson B.[34]

The third special case is the jurisdiction of judges to punish for contempt of court. In a general sense it might be argued that all judges have an interest in extending their powers and privileges by extending the law of contempt. That argument was raised in *Ex p. Fernandez* (1862) 10 C.B.(N.S.) 3 when the Court of Common Pleas was considering the power of a single assize judge to commit for contempt a witness who refused to answer questions put to him in court. Willes J. said:

> "We have been urged to be careful of being misled by our own way of thinking in this case because ... our privileges are involved ... I take leave to say that I am not conscious of the vulgar desire to elevate myself or the court of which I may be a member by grasping after a pre-eminence which does not belong to me; and that I will endeavour to be even [*sic*] valiant in preserving and handing down those powers to do justice and to maintain truth, which, for the common good, the law has intrusted to the judges" (p. 56).[35]

The question of bias is particularly acute, however, where a judge punishes a person for contempt in the face of the court, for example where a litigant abuses a judge personally or tells counsel to "shut your bloody gob" and hurls furniture into the well of the court.[36] There is no doubt that a judge has jurisdiction to deal with such cases although "it appears to be rough justice, it is contrary to natural justice and it can only be justified if nothing else will do"; *Balogh*

v. *Crown Court* [1975] Q.B. 73, 90 *per* Stephenson L.J.[37] The Administration of Justice Act 1960, s. 13 at least provides for an appeal from any order or decision of a court punishing for contempt.

III. The Test for Bias

The courts do not, normally, inquire whether a tribunal was, in fact, biased. In the case of a pecuniary interest disqualification is automatic; "the law does not allow any further inquiry as to whether or not the mind was actually biased by the pecuniary interest"; *per* Bowen L.J., *Lesson* v. *General Medical Council* (1889) 43 Ch.D. 366, 384.[38] Such an attitude can be represented as revealing of the materialistic view of human nature taken by the common law and contrasts with allegations of bias arising from non-financial factors where it is necessary to satisfy a test which has been variously described as involving "a real likelihood of bias" or "a reasonable suspicion of bias." The explanation of this approach is two-fold. First, the efficacy of the rule against bias would be greatly reduced if the complainant had to prove actual bias. Secondly, the law is concerned with public confidence in the administration of justice and the need to ensure that individuals *feel* that they have been given a fair hearing. It is, in the words of Lord Hewart, "of fundamental importance that justice should not only be done, but should manifestly and undoubtedly be seen to be done"; *R.* v. *Sussex JJ., ex p. McCarthy* [1924] 1 K.B. 256, 259.

What, however, do the phrases "real likelihood of bias" and "reasonable suspicion" mean? Does the use of different phrases by the courts involve a difference of opinion as to the test to be applied? It will be suggested that the "somewhat confusing welter of authority" (*per* Widgery L.J., *Hannam* v. *Bradford C.C.* [1970] 1 W.L.R. 937, 945) does not indicate a genuine difference of opinion on the correct test to apply but rather the existence of a confusing variety of ways of describing one test. The real difficulty is in applying the test to the facts of particular cases.

Whatever the test which must be satisfied before a decision can be set aside on the ground of bias it is clear that a decision will not be set aside on

> "the mere vague suspicions of whimsical, capricious and unreasonable people ... mere flimsy elusive morbid suspicions should not be permitted to form a ground of decision" (*R.* v. *Queen's County JJ* [1908] 2 I.R. 285, 294 *per* Lord O'Brien C.J.).[39]

Once, however, it is accepted in a particular case that the allegation is more than a morbid suspicion it becomes necessary to settle what further test or tests must be satisfied before the decision can be set aside. What does the "welter of authority" establish? Some judges clearly believe that there are different tests laid down in the case law and that it is necessary to choose the correct one. Thus, in *R.* v. *Barnsley Licensing JJ.* [1960] 2 Q.B. 167 the Court of Appeal upheld a finding of the Divisional Court that a decision of the justices was not void for bias. In the Divisional Court Salmon J. had dissented and on appeal Devlin L.J. said (at p. 187),

> "I am not quite sure what test Salmon J. applied. If he applied the test based on the principle that justice must not only be done but manifestly seen to be done, I think he came to the right conclusion on that test.... But in my judgment it is not the test.... We have to satisfy ourselves that there was a real likelihood of bias ... not merely satisfy ourselves that that was the sort of impression that might reasonably get abroad."

That dictum suggests the existence of two tests; the first, that of a reasonable suspicion of bias (equated by Devlin L.J. with Lord Hewart's requirement that justice should be seen to be done), the second, imposing a heavier burden of proof on the person making the allegation, that of a real likelihood of bias. Reading the judgment of Salmon J. one may wonder, however, if he intended to suggest the existence of two tests; thus he says:

> "In order successfully to impugn the decision of the justices a real likelihood of bias must be established.... How is this onus to be discharged? ... by establishing that there are real grounds on which ordinary right-thinking people might reasonably conclude that the decision may have been biased"; [1959] 2 Q.B. 276, 285.

Further support for the view that there are two distinct tests is to be found in *Metropolitan Properties* v. *Lannon* [1969] 1 Q.B. 577, where the Court of Appeal obviously regarded itself as applying a more liberal test than that which had found favour in the *Barnsley Licensing Justices* case. Metropolitan Properties applied for certiorari to quash a decision of a rent assessment committee reducing rents on flats owned by the company to a figure below that asked by the tenants and suggested by experts. The father of the chairman of the committee was a tenant of another company in the group to which Metropolitan Properties belonged. The son lived with his father and had as a solicitor acted in the latter's disputes with his landlords about a fair rent for the father's flat. Not surprisingly, perhaps, the Court of Appeal quashed the decision—a conclusion which, one might feel, would have followed inevitably, whatever the test of bias. Lord Denning M.R. said:

> "In considering whether there was a real likelihood of bias, the court does not look at the mind of the justice himself or at the mind of the chairman of the tribunal.... It does not look to see if there was a real likelihood that he would or did in fact favour one side at the expense of the other. The court looks at the impression which would be given to other people. Even if he was as impartial as could be, nevertheless if right-minded persons would think that in the circumstances there was a real likelihood of bias on his part, then he should not sit.... There must appear to be a real likelihood of bias. Surmise or conjecture is not enough.... There must be circumstances from which a reasonable man would think it likely or probable that the justice or chairman as the case may be would, or did, favour one side unfairly at the expense of the other. The court will not enquire whether he did, in fact, favour one side unfairly. Suffice it that reasonable people might think he did" (p. 599).

This dictum runs together the two tests of real likelihood and reasonable suspicion in a way which supports the suggestion made here that there is in fact only one test. What Lord Denning is clearly concerned with in his references to a real likelihood of bias is to emphasise the irrelevance of whether the court or tribunal was *in fact* biased. At the same time it must be admitted that, in a passage immediately preceding, the Master of the Rolls had, after quoting Lord Hewart's dictum, said that, in the *Barnsley Licensing Justices* case, "Devlin L.J. appears to have limited that principle considerably but I would stand by it." Danckwerts L.J. clearly believed that there were two distinct tests but felt on the facts able to find a likelihood of bias without deciding between them. Edmund Davies L.J. said:

> "With profound respect to those who have propounded the 'real likelihood' test I take the view that the requirement that justice must manifestly be done operates with undiminished force in cases where bias is alleged and that any development of law which appears to emasculate that requirement should be strongly resisted" (p. 606).

Hannam's case did nothing towards settling one way or the other whether there are two tests or not since all members of the court agreed that however the test for bias was formulated it would be satisfied on the facts before them. Widgery L.J. refused to add to what, as has been seen, he described as "a somewhat confusing welter of authority." His learned brothers refused, however, to follow his self-denying ordinance. Sachs L.J., at p. 942, gave some support to the view that there are two tests by saying that the *Metropolitan Properties* case involved "somewhat of a swing back towards the principle enunciated in the *Sussex Justice* case" and recognising the possibility of a difference between the real likelihood test and that propounded in the *Metropolitan Properties* case. If there was such a difference he preferred the test laid down in the latter case. Similarly, Cross L.J., by saying there was "little if any difference" between the two tests ensured that the view that there are two distinct tests would continue to flourish. He ran together real likelihood and reasonable suspicion in the following formula:

> "If a reasonable person who has no knowledge of the matter beyond knowledge of the relationship which subsists between some members of the tribunal and one of the parties would think that there might well be bias, then there is in his opinion a real likelihood of bias ... the question is not whether the

tribunal will in fact be biased, but whether a reasonable man with no inside knowledge might well think that it might be biased" (p. 949).

The position remains unclear after the latest cases. In *R.* v. *Altrincham JJ., ex p. Pennington* [1975] Q.B. 549, the court again did not have to inquire if there were two tests and, if so, which was the correct one because it had no doubt, on the facts, that the magistrate ought not to have sat; it was not necessary, according to Lord Widgery C.J., to embark on further detailed investigation of the law and the authorities.[40] The Chief Justice expressed the view that the two tests are often overlapping and one may be appropriate to one situation and another to another situation.

The antithesis between the two tests remains, it is suggested, somewhat unconvincing. It is hard to envisage a court holding that a reasonable man might properly suspect the existence of bias but refusing to interfere because it was not itself convinced of a real likelihood of bias. In the end all turns on the view the court takes of the facts. The judge who says there is no real likelihood of bias would just as likely say that any suspicion of bias was unreasonable; a judge who is prepared to find a reasonable suspicion of bias is hardly likely to deny that there was a real likelihood of bias. Perhaps it is unfortunate that the courts ever tried to improve on Lord Carson's simple test: Was there "such a likelihood of bias as entitled the court to interfere?" (*Frome United Dairies* v. *Bath JJ.* [1926] A.C. 586, 618).

Finally, what is the significance of Sachs L.J.'s suggestion in *Hannam* that an allegation that a man has been a judge in his own cause constitutes a ground of challenge separate from an allegation of bias. The distinction has no practical significance unless a man who is a judge in his own cause is automatically disqualified, quite apart from questions of real likelihood or reasonable suspicion of bias. However, there is no evidence in modern cases of any inclination in the courts to distinguish bias from judging one's own cause in this way; see *R.* v. *Altrincham JJ., ex p. Pennington* [1975] Q.B. 549, 552, *per* Lord Widgery C.J.

IV. Juries and Bias

The law relating to juries and discussions of the merits of that form of trial lie far outside the scope of this book.[41] However, developments in the last few years have emphasised that, although trial by jury has often been regarded as the foundation of the impartial administration of justice in England, juries, like magistrates or judges, may be biased. This section is intended to do no more than briefly outline the problems of bias in an area where they are not often discussed, at least in the context of natural justice.

Bias, in the case of juries, may be, or be thought to be, of three kinds. First a general prejudice on the part of a type of juror against certain types of defendants—or plaintiffs; for example white jurors may be alleged to be biased against black defendants.[42] Secondly there may be a particular bias on the part of a particular juror because, for example, of a relationship with one of the parties. Thirdly, a party may allege that bias on the part of the summoning officer has deprived him of his right to an impartially selected panel of jurors from which the jury is to be selected.[43]

To allow suggestions of bias, in the first sense in which that word was used in the previous paragraph, to be put forward would undermine the essence of the jury as a body of 12 individuals chosen at random. In a *Practice Note* (*Jurors: Excusal from Service*) [1973] 1 W.L.R. 134, Lord Widgery C.J. said:

> "A juror should be excused if he is personally concerned in the facts of the particular case, or closely connected with a party to the proceedings or with a prospective witness. He may also be excused at the discretion of the judge on grounds of personal hardship or conscientious objection to jury service.
>
> It is contrary to established practice for jurors to be excused on more general grounds such as race, religion, or political beliefs or occupation."

Lord Hailsham L.C., replying to questions in the House of Lords arising out of the Lord Chief Justice's statement, said:

> "One assumes in this country that a juror is not prevented from

trying a case impartially simply because he happens to belong to one religion rather than another or does not belong to any religion.

The same is true of political beliefs and general opinions. If you are not going to choose jurors at random you are undermining the whole jury system" (H.L. Deb., 5th Series. Vol. 338, col. 584).

In accordance with this approach potential jurors cannot be questioned, in the absence of evidence of bias, in the hope of discovering a disqualifying prejudice; *M.* v. *H.M. Advocate* [1975] Crim.L.R. 108.

Nonetheless the composition of a jury, apart from questions of individual bias raised by the parties, is not entirely random. First, by statute various categories of persons are ineligible for jury service —such as judges, lawyers and almost anyone connected with the law, down to shorthand writers employed in the courts. The mentally ill are similarly ineligible. Criminals who have been sentenced to imprisonment for life or for more than five years, are thereafter disqualified from acting as jurors for the rest of their lives. Anyone who has served a prison sentence of over three months who does not come within the preceding categories is disqualified for a period of 10 years. Members of Parliament, the armed forces and the medical professions are excused service as of right.[44] Secondly, under section 1 of the Sex Disqualification (Removal) Act 1919, a judge may direct that a jury may consist of men only or women only. The use of this provision was considered in *R.* v. *Sutton* (1969) 53 Cr.App.R. 128. The Court of Appeal refused to interfere with the exercise of his discretion by a judge who had ordered an all-female jury in a case of manslaughter by a woman of her young child. The judge would have preferred to have been able to order a jury of both sexes but with a majority of women. Lord Parker C.J. said that the court, although not prepared to set aside the judge's decision, disapproved of ordering exclusively female juries. Thirdly, in criminal cases a defendant may challenge peremptorily, that is without giving a reason for his challenge, up to three jurors.[45] Such a right may obviously be used in an attempt to secure what seems to be a more favourable, or less unfavourable, jury. Corresponding to the prisoner's right of peremptory challenge is the Crown's right to "stand by" a member of the panel when a jury is being chosen. A prisoner does not have this right although in exceptional cases the judge may allow the standing-by of a potential juror at the prisoner's request; *R.* v. *Chandler* (*No. 2*) [1964] 2 Q.B. 322. A recent statement of the Attorney-General has admitted that in certain types of trial the Crown investigates the background of members of the panel in order to be able to exercise the right to "stand-by" effectively to exclude "undesirable" individuals from juries. The Attorney-General said that the safeguards provided by Parliament in the Juries Act 1974 are not sufficient in all cases to ensure fair trials. In particular further steps have to be taken in the cases of (a) serious offences where strong political motives were involved such as IRA and other terrorist cases and cases under the Official Secrets Act: and (b) serious offences committed by a member or members of a gang of professional criminals. In these cases the circumstances may indicate that potential jurors may be susceptible to improper pressure or may, because of extreme political beliefs, be biased against either the prosecution or the defence. The Attorney-General has emphasised that a juror's political connections are wholly irrelevant unless they are of so extreme a character as to make it reasonably likely that they will prevent the juror from trying a case fairly or that he may exert improper pressure on his fellow jurors. In Official Secrets cases, there is the additional factor that it may be anticipated that some of the evidence will be heard *in camera*, when the possibility of a potential juror making improper use of that evidence, voluntarily or under pressure, may need to be borne in mind.

In order to ascertain whether in these exceptional cases any of these factors might seriously influence a potential juror's impartial performance of his duties, it may be right in the Minister's view to conduct a limited investigation of the panel. Such an investigation may comprise any one or more of the following sources available to the police: (a) a Criminal Record Office check: (b) a check on Special Branch records; and (c) a check with local CID officers to ascertain if a potential juror is known to be an associate of an accused or of those known to be sympathetic or antagonistic to his cause. No general inquiries beyond a check of police records are made save to the limited extent that they may be needed to confirm the identity of a juror about whom the initial check has raised serious doubts.[46]

The need for such steps in cases of the kind to which the Attorney-General has referred are hardly open to question—but neither is the undesirability of such an important matter being determined by officials, or ministers or both, without reference to Parliament.

In both civil and criminal cases either side may, if there is evidence of bias in the second sense in which that word was used in the preceding paragraph, challenge "for cause." Although this right enables a party to remove a juror with a particular interest in a case it is unlikely that parties will know, except in rare cases, of a juror's particular bias or even disqualification. A juror cannot be questioned in an attempt to establish bias unless a prima facie case has already been established; *R.* v. *Chandler* (*No. 2*) [1964] 2 Q.B. 322. Presumably the test of bias is, as in the case of judges and tribunals, a real likelihood or reasonable suspicion of bias. The case of *R.* v. *Marlowe*, *The Times*, March 23, 1973, does not provide the help which might have been hoped for on this question. M was a postman, charged in the Crown Court on seven counts of stealing postal packets. Two members of the jury were discovered to be postmen and the prosecution successfully applied for the discharge of the jury and the empanelling of a new one. M sought mandamus to quash the order of the jury and also purported to appeal. Both applications were heard by the same judges sitting first as a Divisional Court to deal with the application for mandamus and then as the Court of Appeal (Criminal Division) to hear the appeal. Both applications failed on jurisdictional grounds[47] so the question whether the judge had been right to discharge the jury did not arise—although the Lord Chief Justice did say that the judge's discretion might "possibly have been, he would not say, 'wrongly' but 'unwisely' exercised." The only remedy for M, if he were convicted by the second jury would be to try to bring his case within section 2(1)(*a*) of the Criminal Appeal Act 1968 and argue that the verdict "should be set aside on the ground that, under all the circumstances of the case ... it is unsatisfactory."

Notes

[1] D. E. C. Yale, "Iudex in Propria Causa: an *Historical Excursus*" [1974] C.L.J. 80.

[2] *Supra*, n. 1.

[3] See also *Veritas Shipping Corporation* v. *Anglo Canadian Cement* [1966] 1 Lloyd's Rep. 76.

[4] *Infra*, Chap. 8.

[5] W. A. Robson, *Justice and Administrative Law* (3rd ed., 1951), p. 410: *Gee* v. *Freeman* (1959) 16 D.L.R. 65, 74, "A judge who tries a theft charge may safely be assumed to be against theft."

[6] See Lord Cross, *The Lawyer and Justice* (Holdsworth Club, Birmingham, 1973), pp. 6–11.

[7] See, for example, the public interest following remarks of Judge McKinnon in a case brought under the Race Relations Act 1965; *The Times*, January 12, 1978; and the report in *The Daily Telegraph*, July 5, 1978 of action taken by the Lord Chancellor following a complaint by Mr. Leo Abse M.P. about comments made by Melford Stevenson J. concerning the Sexual Offences Act 1967.

[8] Similarly, Jerome Frank, *Law and the Modern Mind* (1930) esp. Part I, Chap. XII; *Courts on Trial* (1949) pp. 150 *et seq.* and 410 *et seq.*

[9] Lord Devlin, "Judges, Government and Politics" (1978) 41 M.L.R. 501, 508. See also Professor Claire Palley, *Times Higher Education Supplement*, January 6, 1978; K. Minogue, *Times Literary Supplement*, January 6, 1978 and acrimonious correspondence in the following weeks.

[10] "Long before judgment was given [Lord Cottenham] had not only quitted the woolsack but had left behind him the troubles of his transitory life: it was a common belief that Dimes had killed Lord Cottenham." Atlay, *Victorian Chancellors*, i, 415.

[11] See also *Smith* v. *Liverpool and London and Globe Insurance Co.* (1887) 14 R. 931, 938.

[12] In *Sellar* v. *Highland Ry.* 1919 S.C.(H.L.) 19 the House of Lords seems to have applied *Dimes* to disqualify an arbiter automatically because he owned shares in the railway. The House did not, however, consider the authorities discussed *infra* p. 150. It may be that the full facts do not appear from the report.

[13] *The Times*, March 13, 1958. See S. Shetreet, *Judges on Trial* (1976), p. 306.

[14] When Lawson J. sued his next-door neighbour, seeking damages for trespass and nuisance, Milmo J. secured the agreement of the defendant to his hearing the case; *The Daily Telegraph*, October 19, 1976.

[15] W. Boulton, *Conduct and Etiquette at the Bar* (6th ed., 1975), p. 40. *Cf. Shrager* v. *Dighton* [1924] 1 K.B. 274 where counsel applied for the appointment of a near relative as a referee. Atkin L.J. described such behaviour as "an error of judgment."

[16] F. D. M. (Mackinnon L.J.) "The Judge's Friend" (1946) 62 L.Q.R. 35.

[17] See also *R.* v. *London County Council, ex p. Akkersydyk* [1892] 1 Q.B. 190; *Allinson* v. *General Council of Medical Education* [1894] 1 Q.B. 750; *Cooper* v. *Wilson* [1937] 2 K.B. 309; for unsuccessful attempts to rely on this rule see *Kilduff* v. *Wilson* [1939] 1 All E.R. 429; *Day* v. *Williams* (1970) 46 T.C. 59, 67.

[18] See also *R.* v. *Pwllheli JJ., ex p. Soane* [1948] 2 All E.R. 815; *R.* v. *Camborne JJ., ex p. Pearce* [1955] 1 Q.B. 41.

[19] In *R.* v. *Taylor* (1898) 14 T.L.R. 185, one of two licensing justices had signed a petition in favour of granting a licence to the successful applicant. The decision was upheld because, in the view of the court, no reasonable person could suspect him of bias.

[20] Such a defect in procedure is, perhaps, better regarded as a breach of the *audi alteram partem* rule; see *Kanda* v. *Government of Malaya* [1962] A.C. 322, 366 *per* Lord Denning.

[21] Similarly *R.* (*Harrington*) v. *JJ. of Co. Clare* [1918] 2 I.R. 116. (Conviction of member of R.I.C., arising out of disturbances at Sinn Fein election procession; one of the justices in the procession.)

[22] Shetreet, *op. cit.* p. 313. *Marais* v. *G.O.C.* [1902] A.C. 109, where Lord Halsbury L.C. sat, shows that the convention did not exist before the turn of the century.

[23] "The law seeks not to lure the bird from the air that has once left the cage"; *per* O'Brien J. at p. 641.

[24] A practice cited by Lord Goddard C.J. to justify a trial judge sitting in the Court of Criminal Appeal on an appeal from one of his own judgments; *R.* v. *Lovegrove* [1951] 1 All E.R. 804. In the case of criminal appeals since 1966 see n. 29, *infra.*

[25] R. F. V. Heuston, "Who was the third lord in *Rylands* v. *Fletcher*" (1970) 86 L.Q.R. 160; D. E. C. Yale (1970) 86 L.Q.R. 311.

[26] J. Roderick O'Flanagan, *The Lives of the Lord Chancellors and Keepers of the Great Seal of Ireland* (1870), vol. ii, p. 586. The same writer admits that the Lord Chancellor had no "very great acquaintance with the old tomes in which the judges of England laid the foundation of their learning" (p. 483). Nor "so far as appears from his own judgments, did he take much trouble to acquaint himself with the decisions of contemporary judges" (p. 584).

[27] Quoted, R. E. Megarry, *Miscellany at Law* (1955), p. 314.

[28] R.E.M. (1951) 67 L.Q.R. 290.

[29] Supreme Court of Judicature Act 1873, s. 54; Supreme Court of Judicature (Consolidation) Act 1925, s. 68(4). The rule was extended to criminal appeals on the creation of the criminal division of the Court of Appeal; Criminal Appeal Act 1966, s. 2(3). See also the Northern Ireland (Emergency Provisions) Act 1973, Sched. 1, Pt. I, para. 8 which provides that a Commissioner, appointed under that Schedule to make detention orders against terrorists, could be appointed a member of the Detention Appeal Tribunal but could not hear appeals against his own decisions. (Sched. 1 was repealed by the Northern Ireland (Emergency Provisions) (Amendment) Act 1975, s. 9).

[30] Cases on disqualification almost always also involved questions of financial interest or statutory prohibitions; *e.g. R.* v. *Hertfordshire JJ.* (1845) 6 Q.B. 753; *Ex p. Clarke* (1890) 26 L.R.Ir.1.

[31] See now r. 5 of the Crown Court Rules 1971, S.I. 1971 No. 1292.

[32] *Infra*, Chap. 6.

[33] *Cf. Rotheray (E.) & Sons Ltd.* v. *Carlo Bedarida* [1961] 1 Lloyd's Rep. 220 where McNair J. set aside, rather than remitted, an arbitrator's award because it would, in the judge's view, be difficult with the best will in the world for the same arbitrator to approach the question a second time with an entirely open mind. In *McKenzie* v. *McKenzie* [1971] P. 33 the Court of Appeal directed a rehearing before a different judge because the original judge "in the circumstances would not wish to retry the case." In *R.* v. *Coroner for Durham, The Times*, June 29, 1978 the Divisional Court, on quashing a coroner's verdict, remitted the case to another coroner. In *Outlook Supplies* v. *Parry* [1978] 2 All E.R. 707 the Employment

Appeal Tribunal quashed a decision of an industrial tribunal because of a failure to give the applicant a proper hearing and remitted the case to a differently constituted tribunal: similarly *Humphreys* v. *Board of Managers of St. George's Church of England (Aided) Primary School* [1978] I.C.R. 546.

[34] In earlier centuries judges had no such scruples; see L. W. Abbott, *Law Reporting in England 1485–1585* (1973), pp. 81–82.

[35] Interestingly, Keating J., the only member of the court who had been on the assize in question and had been consulted by the judge who committed Fernandez, refrained from taking any part in the decision.

[36] *The Times*, May 5, 1978. Sir Robert Megarry V.-C. committed the disappointed litigant, an ex-student of Bradford University, to seven days' imprisonment. For the judgment which led to the outburst see *Patel* v. *University of Bradford Senate* [1978] 3 All E.R. 841; *infra* p. 158.

[37] See also *Maharaj* v. *Att.-Gen. for Trinidad and Tobago* [1977] 1 All E.R. 411 (P.C.). For a lengthy and interesting discussion see *Sacher* v. *United States* 343 U.S. 1 (1951). See additional note below.

[38] *R.* v. *Rand* (*supra*); *R.* v. *Sunderland JJ.* [1901] 2 K.B. 357. This automatic qualification does not apply to arbitrators; *infra*, Chap. 7.

[39] See also *R.* (*Taverner*) v. *Co. Tyrone JJ.* [1909] I.R. 762, 768 and *R.* (*Donoghue*) v. *Co. Cork JJ.* [1910] 2 I.R. 271, 276.

[40] See also *R.* v. *Eastern Traffic Area Licensing Authority, ex p. Wyatt* [1974] R.T.R. 480; *Re Watson, ex p. Armstrong* (1976) 9 A.L.R. 551, 561–563.

[41] See generally, W. R. Cornish, *The Jury* (1968) Allen Lane.

[42] See Alan Dashwood, "Juries in a Multi Racial Society" [1972] Crim. L.R. 85.

[43] The right to "challenge the array," preserved by the Juries Act 1974, s. 12(6).

[44] Juries Act 1974, Sched. 1.

[45] Juries Act 1974, s. 12(1)(*a*), as amended by the Criminal Law Act 1977, s. 43.

[46] *The Times*, October 11, 1978. For the view of the National Council for Civil Liberties see H. Harman and J. Griffith, *Justice Deserted* (1979).

[47] (i) Prerogative orders do not lie to the Crown Court in relation to trials on indictment; *Ex p. Meredith* [1973] 1 W.L.R. 435; *R.* v. *Smith* (*Martin*) [1975] Q.B. 531; *infra*, p. 197 (ii) an appeal under the Criminal Appeal Act is possible only by a "person convicted."

Further Developments: Contempt of Court

Rooney v. *Snaresbrook Crown Court*, *The Times*, June 17, 1978. The appellant had been fined for contempt of court, having allegedly sacked an employee who was absent from work on jury service. The Court of Appeal quashed the conviction since the judge to whom the juror had complained had taken upon himself the role of prosecutor and had "almost cross-examined" the employer. The case should have been dealt with by another judge.

CHAPTER 3

THE RIGHT TO BE HEARD

ALTHOUGH it has been said that "in the quest for justice under the Rule of Law there has been no more spontaneously acceptable idea than the principle embodied in the maxim *audi alteram partem*"[1] it is no more settled what this right entails than where it applies. Does it, for example, require that notice be given of proceedings? Is there a right to an oral hearing? To cross-examine witnesses? To be legally represented? Can the hearing be conducted by one body and the decision made by another? Usually, in a case where there is a right to a hearing, an allegation of a breach of natural justice relates to one of these, or a similar, matter; corollaries, as it were, of the basic right to be heard.

However, the breach may sometimes arise from the complete absence of a hearing. In *Fleet Mortgage* v. *Lower Maisonette* [1972] 1 W.L.R. 765, for example, a party was completely unaware of proceedings involving him. A landlord had brought an action seeking forfeiture of a lease; by agreement between the parties an order was made but suspended on condition that the tenant complied with certain stipulations. The original landlord later assigned his reversion. Without giving any notice to the tenant the assignee landlord applied to a master for leave to issue a writ of possession on the grounds that the tenants were in breach of the stipulations contained in the consent order. Pennycuick V.-C., in setting aside the writ, said "apart from any provisions in the Rules of the Supreme Court it appears to me too clear for words that natural justice required that notice of this application should be given to the tenants."

The exercise by justices of their power to bind over to be of good behaviour has also given rise to some striking examples of breach of natural justice. In *Sheldon* v. *Bromfield JJ.* [1964] 2 Q.B. 573, justices dismissed a charge of assault against M but bound over M and two prosecution witnesses to keep the peace. The witnesses had been unaware of the possibility of being bound over. The Divisional Court held that the justices had acted contrary to natural justice. Lord Parker said:

> "It has been argued here on behalf of the justices that provided, as in this case, the persons whom it is proposed to bind over have had, in effect, their say by being examined, cross-examined and re-examined, there is no need at all that they should know what is passing through the court's mind, and indeed that the justices can bind them over without giving them any advance notice or any opportunity of dealing with it. I must say that I shudder at any idea that that can be done although it is said that it is done quite generally. It seems to me to be elementary justice that, in particular, a mere witness before justices should, at any rate, be told what is passing through the justices' minds, and should have an opportunity of dealing with it" (p. 578).

In *R.* v. *Hendon Justices, ex p. Gorchein* [1973] 1 W.L.R. 1502 G had brought a private prosecution against P. Before the proceedings began the magistrates asked G and P if they were prepared to be bound over; they both refused. P was convicted and both parties were bound over. G successfully claimed that the binding over was in breach of natural justice. A complainant, like a witness, does not expect to be bound over and should not be, without an opportunity to speak in his own defence. A similar claim by a defendant, who had been acquitted of a criminal charge by magistrates but bound over, without any prior warning, was unsuccessful in *R.* v. *Woking Justices, ex p. Gossage* [1973] Q.B. 448. Lord Widgery distinguished the position of a defendant from that of witnesses:

> "[He] comes before the court knowing that allegations are to be made against him, knowing that he can be represented if appropriate, and knowing that he can call evidence if he wishes.... That is not to say that it would not be wise and indeed courteous in these cases for justices to give such a warning" (p. 451).

Another unsuccessful resort to natural justice was made in *R.* v. *North London Metropolitan Magistrate, ex p. Haywood* [1973] 1 W.L.R. 965. H and B brought summonses against each other alleging assault. Their behaviour in the court was such that the magistrates bound both parties over. The Divisional Court held that in such a case where the behaviour justifying the binding over was committed in the face of the court neither party required any opportunity of justifying themselves before an order was made.

Other examples of courts failing to hear a party at all before reaching a decision are provided by cases where judges have ordered solicitors to pay, personally, the costs of actions without first giving them an opportunity of explaining their behaviour; *Abraham* v. *Jutson* [1963] 1 W.L.R. 658; *R.* v. *Smith* (*Martin*) [1975] Q.B. 531.[2] In other cases, without adverting to natural justice, the courts have emphasised that a trial judge must not take into consideration, when sentencing a prisoner, offences which the prisoner has not expressly admitted and asked to be taken into consideration; *D.P.P.* v. *Anderson* [1978] 2 All E.R. 512. In *R.* v. *Huchison* [1972] 1 W.L.R. 398 the prisoner was convicted on one charge of incest. After conviction the judge heard evidence from the prisoner and his daughter, accepted the latter's account that the father had frequently had intercourse with her, and sentenced him on that basis. The Court of Appeal reduced the sentence because "the course followed by the trial judge was wrong, and did in effect deprive the appellant of his right to trial by jury in respect of those other offences."

An unusual example of a decision vitiated by a complete failure to grant a hearing is provided by *Hiles* v. *Amalgamated Society of Woodworkers* [1968] Ch. 440. H had been acquitted by a disciplinary committee of his union of a charge of being in breach of a union rule. A member of the committee who disagreed with the decision "appealed" to the executive committee; the first H knew of the appeal was when he was informed that it had been successful and the original decision had been reversed. Stamp J. held that even if the rules, on their true construction, permitted appeals by aggrieved judges, the failure to warn H of the appeal vitiated the decision of the executive committee.

Where there is a right to be heard it is no defence to a plea of no warning or hearing that the tribunal was merely reaching a provisional decision which it is prepared to depart from after hearing the person aggrieved; *R.* v. *Newmarket Assessment Committee, ex p. Allen Newport Ltd.* [1945] 2 All E.R. 371.

In some cases a party has appeared before a tribunal but has been so hampered in the presentation of his case that he has been held not to have had a hearing. Sometimes this has been because of improper intervention by the tribunal—constant interruptions, for example, from a clearly exasperated judge. Cases of that kind are discussed later in Chapter 4. Other examples arise when, for example, magistrates refuse to allow counsel to address them on the facts; *Disher* v. *Disher* [1965] P. 31; or if magistrates dismiss a complaint without allowing the complainant's solicitor to argue that the defendant has a case to answer; *Mayes* v. *Mayes* [1971] 1 W.L.R. 679. In *R.* v. *Billericay JJ., ex p. Rumsey* [1978] Crim.L.R. 305, a Divisional Court held that a refusal by justices to hear a plea in mitigation by counsel required the quashing of their sentence. (The court itself, acting under section 6(1) of the Administration of Justice Act 1960 then imposed a new sentence of the same length as the original one.) In *R.* v. *Middlesex Crown Court ex p. Riddle*, *The Times*, October 8, 1975 the Crown Court was guilty of a denial of natural justice by refusing to allow R, who was appealing from a conviction in a magistrates' court to make a speech after he had given evidence.

A right to be heard and defend oneself is illusory without time to prepare a defence and knowledge of the cast to be met. What is sufficient notice will vary with the facts as will the detail which must be given of the case to be met.

> "A case may be of so uncomplex a character and the issues may be so well known to all parties concerned that no more particular notice of any charge may be required, an opportunity for the party of whom complaint is made to state his case being sufficient" (*Stevenson* v. *United Road Transport Union* [1977] 2 All E.R. 941, 951, *per* Buckley L.J.).

In *Willis* v. *Childe* (1851) 13 Beav. 117 a schoolmaster learned, shortly before it was to take place, of a meeting of trustees to confirm a decision, which they had already reached, to dismiss him. He wrote to the trustees two days before the second meeting. A few hours before the meeting he was informed that the trustees would hear him. That was held inadequate notice. In *R.* v. *North, ex p. Oakey* [1927] 1 K.B. 491 the Court of Appeal granted prohibition to prevent an ecclesiastical court enforcing an order against a vicar. The court held that a citation attached to the porch of his church announcing an application for a faculty to restore a painting which had been damaged did not constitute adequate notice to the vicar of his liability to have to pay the costs of the restoration.

The details of the notice which a party is entitled to in the case of the courts or administrative tribunals are to be found in statutory rules and orders.[3] Provision must also be made for the party whose whereabouts are, for one reason or another, unknown. The Rules of the Supreme Court, for example, provide that in the case of actions relating to land, a writ may be served by being affixed to some conspicuous part of the land if no-one appears to be in possession and service cannot otherwise be effected; R.S.C., Ord. 10, r. 4. In the case of squatters whose identity cannot be established proceedings may begin by originating summons which is served by being affixed to the main door or other conspicuous part of the land; R.S.C., Ord. 113, r. 4. The Matrimonial Causes Rules 1977 make provision for dispensing with the requirement of serving notice of a petition where such service is, in the opinion of the registrar, impracticable or it is otherwise necessary or expedient to dispense with personal service.[4] Presumably a domestic tribunal could validly hear a charge where it had unsuccessfully taken all reasonable steps to discover the person concerned, at any rate where its rules so provided.

The courts attach such weight to the giving of adequate notice that, even where tribunals have correctly followed statutory provisions, they will be astute to help a party who did not, in fact, receive notice. For example in *R.* v. *Kensington and Chelsea Rent Tribunal, ex p. MacFarlane* [1974] 1 W.L.R. 1486, Lord Widgery C.J. while admitting that an order made in such circumstances would not be open to challenge by certiorari, suggested that a tribunal might rehear a case if it were satisfied that the party had a reasonable excuse for not receiving his notice.[5]

Where a person has been given notice of the charge against him he may invoke natural justice if the notice is so vague or ambiguous as to prevent him from preparing a satisfactory defence. An extreme example of this difficulty is presented by *Sloan* v. *General Medical Council* [1970] 1 W.L.R. 1130 where a doctor, S, appealed against a decision of the General Medical Council to strike him off the medical register. The Privy Council recognised the principle but rejected the appeal, holding that the doctor had not been hampered in his defence although the charge against him was on a literal reading capable of two contradictory meanings. S had been accused of infamous conduct in connection with an illegal operation: he argued that, as the charge was worded, if he proved he had not performed the operation he would have been struck off for having pretended to the patient that he had in fact operated: if he proved that he had operated he would be struck off for performing an illegal operation. The Privy Council, however, was satisfied that the doctor knew that the General Medical Council intended the charge to be one of not performing an operation which he had purported to perform.

The right to know the precise charge one has to meet is recognised by the Rules of the Supreme Court, Ord. 18, r. 19 and the general jurisdiction of the court to strike out writs which may prejudice or embarrass a party or are otherwise an abuse of the process of the court; *Re Willcocks* (*W.R.*) *& Co.* [1974] Ch. 163. In cases of contempt of court it has been said that no-one should be punished "unless the specific offence charged against him be distinctly stated, and an opportunity of answering it given to him"; *Re Pollard* (1868) L.R. 2 P.C. 106, 120; quoted in *Maharaj* v. *Att.-Gen. of Trinidad and Tobago* (*No. 2*) [1978] 2 W.L.R. 902, 910 *per* Lord Diplock.

Notice, to be effective, must be notice of the charge or subject matter of dispute to be decided by the court or tribunal. In *Andrews* v. *Mitchell* [1905] A.C. 78, a member of a friendly society was summoned before the committee, charged with an offence punishable by fine. After hearing his defence the committee expelled him on a different charge, acting under another rule. The House of Lords held that the expulsion was void. Similarly, in *Maradana Mosque* v. *Badi-Ud-Din Mahmud* [1967] 1 A.C. 13 the Privy Council held that there had been a breach of natural justice when the minister told the managers of a school of one allegation against them to which they prepared a defence but, in his decision, made it plain that he was taking over the school in reliance on a breach of a statutory provision of which the managers had had no notice at all. In *R.* v. *Paddington Rent Tribunal, ex p. Bell Properties Ltd.* [1949] 1 K.B. 666 a tribunal's decision was quashed because, in reducing the rent, it was influenced by a matter which had suggested itself at a view of the premises after the hearing, on which the landlord had had no chance to comment. The problem has arisen in a number of planning cases as exemplified by *Fairmount Investments Ltd.* v. *Secretary of State for the Environment* [1976] 1 W.L.R. 1255 where the House of Lords quashed a compulsory purchase order on the ground that the inspector had based his report on his view that the foundations of certain houses were inadequate although that question had not been raised at the hearing.[6]

The opportunity to present an effective answer or defence may necessitate seeking an adjournment of proceedings; "Sometimes, if justice is to be done, adjournments are essential"; *Hanson* v. *Church Commissioners for England* [1978] Q.B. 823, 838, *per* Roskill L.J. In *R.* v. *Thames Magistrates' Court, ex p. Polemis* [1974] 1 W.L.R. 1371 the conviction of a ship's captain was quashed because he had been served with a summons at 10.30 a.m., returnable at 7.00 p.m. on the same day. The justices refused to grant an adjournment beyond 4.00 p.m. because the ship was sailing that evening. Lord Widgery C.J. said, "If the court cannot conduct a trial in accordance with the rules of natural justice before the ship sails, then the justices must adjourn the matter because the rules of natural justice are paramount" (at p. 1378).[7] Where it is not sufficiently clear what case a person accused has to meet an adjournment may be ordered to enable the necessary particulars to be provided and give an opportunity to prepare a defence; *R.* v. *Pharmaceutical Services Committee, ex p. Gordon D. Conway Ltd., The Times*, November 7, 1970. Sometimes the court or tribunal should itself invite a party to ask for an adjournment, for example if magistrates realise that the defendant is directing his case to a particular charge but they are contemplating exercising their powers to convict, in the light of the facts, on a different charge under another statutory provision; *Morriss* v. *Lawrence* [1977] R.T.R. 205.

A party who has had lengthy notice of proceedings cannot expect to obtain an adjournment as of right by producing at the very last moment an excuse such as an objection, based on religious grounds, to attending a hearing on a particular day; *Ostreicher* v. *Secretary of State for the Environment* [1978] 1 W.L.R. 810. Nor can a party claim an adjournment, as of right, if he would not have required the delay had he taken the trouble to observe the appropriate rules of procedure of the tribunal or other body in question; *Rigby* v. *British Steel Corporation* [1973] I.C.R. 160. Where, even on the admission of the person seeking an adjournment, a further delay cannot be expected to affect the outcome, a court may properly refuse the request; *Teo Hook Seng* v. *Public Prosecutor* [1978] Crim.L.R. 378. The defendant in that case had sought an adjournment on the ground that his experts had not finished their analysis of substances which had been found in his possession and which the Crown alleged contained, to an extent forbidden by law, a prohibited drug. It had not been suggested that the Crown's experts had been incorrect in identifying the particular drug. The only question was as to its concentration in the substance in which it had been found. On the Crown's evidence the drug was present in such large quantities that there could be no real likelihood of the defendant's experts being able to produce evidence that the concentration was below the level forbidden by statute; any difference in figures could only be a matter of academic interest. The Privy Council held that, in the circumstances, the court had been entitled to refuse to grant an adjournment.

A party to an action is, according to Jenkins L.J. prima facie entitled to have it heard in his presence; *Grimshaw* v. *Dunbar* [1953] 1 Q.B. 408, 416. This is true, in the case of the ordinary courts, whether proceedings are civil or criminal.

> "Thieves are not judged but they are by to hear,
> Although apparent guilt be seen in them" (Shakespeare, *Richard II*, 4.1.122).

Only in special circumstances will a party be removed from the court during a trial; for example, if the accused shouts threats at a witness; *R.* v. *Ince*, *The Times*, May 5, 1973. However, natural justice does not require that the hearing should in all cases be oral. That has been settled since *Local Government Board* v. *Arlidge* [1915] A.C. 120 when the House of Lords held that a householder whose property had been condemned as unfit for human habitation had no right to insist on an oral hearing at the appeal to the local government board against the local authority's decision.[8] At times the question of a right to an oral hearing will resolve itself into a question of statutory interpretation[9]; a statute itself may clearly give a tribunal a discretion whether to hold an oral hearing or not.[10] In so far as any general principle can be laid down it is suggested that there is no right to an oral hearing unless the refusal of an oral hearing would prejudice the applicant—and even in such a case statute may take away the right. Normally, for example, written submissions in a case where the truthfulness of the applicant is not in issue are sufficient. But there are situations where the applicant does not wish to bring new facts to the tribunal's attention but to convince them that his version of a disputed story is true. In *Rose* v. *Humbles* [1970] 1 W.L.R. 1061 a taxpayer successfully appealed on this ground against the refusal of the Inland Revenue Commissioners to postpone the hearing of his appeal against assessment until he was sufficiently well to appear in person; the refusal, said Buckley J., caused substantial injustice when:

> "on one footing, the whole outcome of the case depended on whether he was to be believed in regard to his claim to have made winnings from bettings accounting for the whole of the unexplained increase in his wealth ..." (p. 1071).[11]

The rights of parties to oral hearings before arbitrators has been the subject of considerable litigation and will be discussed in Chapter 7.

The right to a hearing and to adequate notice may still be of little value if the individual does not know the evidence against him.

> "For a court to take into consideration evidence which a party to the proceedings has had no opportunity during trial to see or hear ... [strikes] at the very root of the judicial process" *Brinkley* v. *Brinkley* [1965] P. 75, 78 *per* Scarman J.

From another angle this rule can be expressed in the form that the tribunal must afford "a real and effective opportunity to the litigant to deal with or meet" the case against him; *R.* v. *Architects Registration Tribunal, ex p. Jagger* [1945] 2 All E.R. 131. In that case the Divisional Court quashed the decision of the tribunal which had had before it three letters relating to the applicant which he had not been allowed to see. In *Kanda* v. *Government of Malaya* [1962] A.C. 322 the Privy Council held that a right to be afforded "a reasonable opportunity of being heard" contained in the Malayan Constitution had not been observed when K had been dismissed from the police force as a result of a decision taken by an officer who, unknown to K, had before him a critical report from an earlier board of inquiry.[12]

A particular instance of relying on evidence not available to the parties is found in cases where judges, inspectors or members of tribunals, in the absence of the parties—or one of them—view the scene of an alleged offence or the site of a proposed building development. In *Goold* v. *Evans* [1951] 2 T.L.R. 1189, the Court of Appeal ordered a new trial where the county court judge had viewed premises in the absence of the parties. In *Salsbury* v. *Woodland* [1970] 1 Q.B. 324, however, the Court of Appeal recognised that a judge may "view" the site of the action on his own where he is merely looking at the site as opposed to a demonstration of what happened although Harman L.J. thought even this type of viewing "undesirable" (p. 346).[13]

Judges, and, indeed, anyone who must decide any dispute, cannot approach the matter with a mind empty of all information except that produced by the parties. How much use may be made by judges and tribunal members of their own knowledge and experience has frequently been the subject of litigation. First, the law recognises that notorious facts—that it rains in Manchester, or that rain is wet—do not need to be proved. The range of such facts may vary from time to time. Recently the fact that the Commissioners of Customs and Excise make careless errors in assessing liability for value added tax has been added to their number; *Customs and Excise Commissioners* v. *Holvey* [1978] Q.B. 310, 313, *per* Peter Pain J. Judges, and no doubt anyone deciding a dispute, may take judicial notice of facts of this kind, that is they may rely on their own knowledge, even if they need to be assisted by experts[14] as for example in *McQuaker* v. *Goddard* [1940] 1 K.B. 687 where the doctrine was held to extend to the details of the sexual life of the camel.

Beyond the limits set by judicial notice members of tribunals can, to some extent, rely on their own special knowledge, whether of a locality, derived from living there, or of professional or industrial matters, as a result of past experience. To hold otherwise would be to reduce, if not deny, the value of lay magistrates and administrative tribunals. Justices may properly take into account their own knowledge of the locality, for example, to decide whether waters are tidal; *Ingram* v. *Percival* [1969] 1 Q.B. 548. A magistrate who is a doctor may use his special knowledge in interpreting the evidence which he has heard, for example, where the question is whether a party had suffered a genuine fit; *Wetherall* v. *Harrison* [1976] Q.B. 773.[15] Members of administrative tribunals have been held to be entitled to rely on "their cumulative knowledge and experience of the matter in hand" in addition to the evidence before them; *Metropolitan Properties* v. *Lannon* [1969] 1 Q.B. 577, 603, *per* Edmund Davies L.J.[16] Thus members of a rent assessment committee may take the scarcity of accommodation into account, where that is relevant, although no evidence has been given on the point; *Crofton Investment Trust Ltd.* v. *Greater London Rent Assessment Committee* [1967] 2 Q.B. 955. In *Dugdale* v. *Kraft Foods Ltd.* [1977] I.C.R. 48, the Employment Appeal Tribunal applied a similar test to members of industrial tribunals. They may draw on their knowledge and experience to fill gaps in the evidence given to them but where their experience differs from the evidence given before them, they ought not to rely on their own knowledge and experience without putting the matter to the witness concerned.[17] Nor should members of tribunals attempt to supplement their professional knowledge and expertise by carrying out private experiments. Thus, where it is alleged that it is unsafe to drive at a certain speed round a bend in a road, a member of the tribunal should not put that claim to the test by driving along that part of the road himself at various speeds; *Hickmott* v. *Dorset C.C.* (1977) 243 E.G. 671.

A problem of particular importance in relation to statutory inquiries in planning matters and also, to a lesser degree in arbitrations, is the extent to which, after the hearing in the presence of the parties is concluded, the inspector, minister, arbitrator or umpire, can conduct further discussions and consult third parties such as lawyers or other experts. These problems will be discussed in

Chapter 7.

In some cases the courts have recognised limits to the right of a party to know the evidence before a tribunal. Thus the public interest in suppressing crime may be invoked to justify withholding the source of information from a party as in *R.* v. *Gaming Board for Great Britain, ex p. Benaim and Khaida* [1970] 2 Q.B. 417 where the Court of Appeal held that applicants for gaming licences must be given sufficient details of objections raised against them to afford them a proper opportunity to answer, but that they had no right to insist on knowing the source of the evidence in the hands of the Board. This decision can be contrasted with *Ex p. Brown*; *Re Tunstall* (1966) 67 S.R. (N.S.W.) 1 where the attempt by the Crown to cross-examine a witness in reliance on a document which was withheld on the ground of Crown privilege was held to be a breach of natural justice. The line is difficult to draw; few would deny that in some cases, apart from national security, public interest justifies protecting the source of information from disclosure, as for instance, the House of Lords held with regard to the identity of complainants to the National Society for the Prevention of Cruelty to Children; *D.* v. *N.S.P.C.C.* [1978] A.C. 171.

A compromise, to which the courts have had resort in some cases where communication of evidence to the person seeking a hearing may be thought to be undesirable, for example, cases involving mental illness, is illustrated by *R.* v. *Kent Police Authority, ex p. Godden* [1971] 2 Q.B. 662 where the Court of Appeal held that natural justice required the communication to the medical advisers of a police officer of the reports and information communicated by the local police authority to a doctor who was to examine the officer with a view to declaring him permanently unfit for work. If the individual is not prepared to accept this compromise the court may solve the problem by deciding the tribunal is under no obligation to reveal the evidence before it to anyone. In *R.* v. *Archbishop of Canterbury, ex p. Morant* [1944] 1 K.B. 282 the patron of a living wished to challenge the refusal of a bishop to approve his nomination to that living and accordingly exercised his right under the Benefices (Exercise of Rights Presentation) Measure 1931 to take the "decision before the Archbishop for review." The archbishop, in upholding the bishop's refusal, took into account a confidential letter containing material derogatory of the patron. He communicated the contents of the letter in confidence to the patron's legal adviser, who was appearing before the archbishop as the patron's friend, not as counsel. The Court of Appeal refused to quash the decision, holding that the archbishop was not exercising quasi-judicial functions; "I cannot imagine any function more personal, more intimate and more delicate than the bishop's approval of a clerk"; *per* Lord Greene M.R. at page 294. Resort to the modern terminology of "fairness" would, it is suggested, produce just the same result. Wardship proceedings provide further examples of a similar problem and in *Official Solicitor* v. *K.* [1965] A.C. 201 the House of Lords held that the court was entitled to withhold from parties confidential reports submitted by the Official Solicitor as guardian *ad litem*. At the same time the House expressed the undesirability of looking on the submission of such reports as a matter of course.[18] The House of Lords recognised the desirability in some cases of withholding medical reports from a party in *McIvor* v. *Southern Hospital Board* [1978] 1 W.L.R. 757. Nonetheless, it went on to hold that the new provisions of the Administration of Justice Act 1970, ss. 31 and 32, which permit an order for the production of documents to be made against a person who is not a party to proceedings, were so worded that they had no right to limit the order for disclosure to the applicant's legal adviser. Even so, Lord Diplock thought that there might be exceptional cases where the court, in its discretion, would refuse to make an order upon an undertaking by the other person to make the documents available to someone other than the applicant.

The exceptional nature of such cases as those discussed in the preceding paragraphs was emphasised in *Midland Cold Storage* v. *Turner* [1972] I.C.R. 230 where Sir John Donaldson refused to allow a party to adduce evidence on the condition that it was not disclosed to the other parties. Cases where evidence had been so received were explicable, in the view of the learned judge, as examples of the courts acting in a "quasi-paternal capacity." Even in those instances the evidence does not come from one of the parties but from disinterested, outside bodies such as doctors or social workers.

The next aspect of the right to a hearing to be considered is the procedure and the rules of evidence to be followed. As was seen in

Chapter 1, the technical common law rules of evidence must not be confused with natural justice. The distinction is between what nineteenth-century judges called "the technical rules of special pleading" on the one hand, which are here irrelevant and, on the other hand, "the substantial rules of justice"; *Ex p. Ramshay* (1852) 18 Q.B. 173, 195; *Smith* v. *R.* (1878) 3 App.Cas. 614, 623. It is not contrary to natural justice, for example, for a tribunal to receive hearsay evidence; *Miller (T. A.)* v. *Minister of Housing and Local Government* [1968] 1 W.L.R. 992.

Whether there is a right to cross-examination will depend on the nature of the body, the gravity of the matter at issue and the source of the body's jurisdiction. In *Osgood* v. *Nelson* (1872) L.R. 5 H.L. 636, Martin B., speaking on behalf of the judges called to the House of Lords, advised that the Corporation of the City of London, in removing O from his office, had observed the rules of natural justice since their procedure reached the standard followed in the ordinary courts. Among the elements of that procedure which the learned Baron picked out was the opportunity of cross-examining witnesses. Since the Corporation *had* reached the standard of the ordinary courts the case does not, however, determine how far short of that standard the Corporation could have fallen without violating the rules of natural justice. The right to cross-examination has been most firmly stated in modern times in cases involving proceedings in magistrates' courts or county courts; *Grimshaw* v. *Dunbar* [1953] 1 Q.B. 408, 416, *per* Jenkins L.J.; *Blaise* v. *Blaise* [1969] P. 54. In *Bassett* v. *Bassett* [1975] Fam. 76, a case in which a wife was seeking an order to exclude her husband from the matrimonial home pending further proceedings, the Court of Appeal held that in such circumstances the magistrates could refuse a right to cross-examine and proceed simply on affidavit evidence where there is sufficient undisputed material to enable the court to reach a proper decision. Views on the right to cross-examine witnesses before tribunals other than the courts conflict. Such a right is supported by Mackinnon L.J. in *R.* v. *Newmarket Assessment Committee, ex p. Allen Newport Ltd.* [1945] 2 All E.R. 371, 373, and by Diplock L.J. in *R.* v. *Deputy Industrial Injuries Commissioner, ex p. Moore* [1965] 1 Q.B. 456, 490. The dictum in that case was followed and applied in *Nicholson* v. *Secretary of State for Energy* (1977) 76 L.G.R. 693. Further support is found in *University of Ceylon* v. *Fernando* [1960] 1 W.L.R. 223 where the hearing given to F, a student, was held to satisfy the rules of natural justice although he had not cross-examined witnesses. He had not asked to exercise such a right and Lord Hodson indictated that the decision of the Board might well have been different had he made such a request and it had been refused. In *R.* v. *Secretary of State for Home Affairs, ex p. Hosenball* [1977] 1 W.L.R. 766, the Court of Appeal held that the Home Secretary was not, in deciding whether to deport an alien, bound by the rules of natural justice. But, said Lord Denning M.R., if he had been bound, the party aggrieved would have had the right to test evidence by cross-examination. On the other hand the existence of such a right in the case of administrative tribunals was denied by Lord Denning M.R. in *Kavanagh* v. *Chief Constable of Devon and Cornwall* [1974] Q.B. 624. Here again the answer may be that everything turns on the particular case, the formality of the tribunal in question, for example, and the gravity of the issue at stake.[19] A dictum of Maugham J. in *Maclean* v. *The Workers Union* [1929] 1 Ch. 602, suggests that there is no right to cross-examine in the case of domestic tribunals. However, it cannot be safely assumed that other judges would follow Maugham J. in his obvious reluctance to interfere in the affairs of domestic tribunals.

A person appearing before a tribunal may feel that the value of a right to a hearing is largely dependent on the right to legal representation. If a tribunal refuses permission to a person appearing before it to be legally represented, if he so desires, is it violating natural justice? A right to counsel, although now recognised in all actions before the ordinary courts, was for many centuries, denied in the cases where, because of their gravity, it might have been thought most necessary by modern standards.[20] Legal representation is still not allowed before certain administrative tribunals but it may be argued that the controversy over this prohibition shows the fundamental importance attached to the right in the second half of the twentieth century.[21] The courts, in a number of recent cases, have emphasised the importance of a right to legal representation in hearings before tribunals, although in every case the applicant concerned failed to establish his right.

In *Pett* v. *Greyhound Racing Association* (*No. 1*) [1969] 1 Q.B.

125 the Court of Appeal issued an interlocutory injunction to restrain the defendant from holding an inquiry into the running of P's greyhounds unless he was allowed to appear and to be legally represented. Attention was drawn in the judgments to the gravity of the charge and its consequences. Lord Denning expressly admitted what the other judges implied, that there may not be such a right in minor matters, although even in such cases it seems that the Court of Appeal might have been assuming a right to representation subject to the power of the party, if he wished, to waive that right by contract. However, at the trial Lyell J., undeterred by the views of the Court of Appeal, held that a right to legal representation was not a part of natural justice. The learned judge relied on *University of Ceylon* v. *Fernando* [1960] 1 W.L.R. 223 which had not been cited in the Court of Appeal. That decision of the Privy Council Lyell J. regarded as conflicting with the views of the Court of Appeal. He quoted the Board's reference to "elementary and essential principles of 'fairness'" and continued:

> "I find it difficult to say that legal representation before a tribunal is an elementary feature of the fair dispensation of justice. It seems to me that it arises only in a society which has reached some degree of sophistication in its affairs" ([1970] 1 Q.B. 46, 65).

But if the Court of Appeal went too far in *Pett* in suggesting a general right to legal representation, Lyell J. with respect, erred in suggesting such a right could never be required by natural justice. It is arguable that when the Privy Council in *Fernando's* case referred to elementary principles it was not contrasting primitive and sophisticated societies as the learned judge suggests but basic principles common to all courts and tribunals as opposed to the highly technical rules of evidence peculiar to common law courts. In *Enderby Town F.C.* v. *The Football Association* [1971] Ch. 591, the Court of Appeal emphasised that everything depends on the facts of the particular case. A rule of the FA prohibited clubs which appealed to it against decisions of county football associations from being legally represented. Enderby Town F.C., having appealed to the FA, sought an injunction to prevent the appeal being heard unless the club was allowed legal representation. The Court of Appeal held that since the club could, if it had wished, have sought a declaration of its legal rights from the courts it could not complain of the offending rule if it chose to submit to the appellate jurisdiction of the FA. All the members of the court discussed the right to legal representation. Both Fenton Atkinson L.J. and Cairns L.J. were prepared to recognise that clubs might exclude legal representation by an absolute rule. Fenton Atkinson L.J. gave examples of statutory exclusions of the right and referred to the paucity of case law on the subject. He concluded:

> "If such a rule is indeed contrary to natural justice, a very large number of persons, including our legislators, must have been very insensitive over a long period of years to what natural justice requires" (at p. 609).

Lord Denning, resiling slightly from what seemed to be the absolute rule he had propounded in *Pett*, admitted that

> "It may be a good thing for the proceedings of a domestic tribunal to be conducted informally without legal representation. Justice can often be done in them better by a good layman than by a bad lawyer" (at p. 605).

The right to representation, he said, depends on the discretion of the tribunal which must be genuinely exercised: in *Pett* the court had intervened because the Greyhound Racing Association had an inflexible practice of refusing representation. A rule which purported expressly to exclude a right to representation would probably be void unless it could be construed as directory and not imperative so that a tribunal could permit legal representation in an exceptional case when justice demanded it (p. 606).

A further retreat from any idea of a general right to legal representation is to be found in *R.* v. *Race Relations Board, ex p. Selvarajan* [1975] 1 W.L.R. 1686 and *Maynard* v. *Osmond* [1977] Q.B. 240. In *Selvarajan's* case the question of legal representation was not directly before the Court of Appeal. The applicant's complaint related to the delegation by the Board of its powers to a committee of its members. However, Lord Denning M.R. at p. 1693, discussed generally the duty of the Board when hearing complaints.

The Master of the Rolls said it belonged to a category of organisations which must conduct investigations and form an opinion. (Other such bodies include the Gaming Board and inspectors under the Companies Acts.) Their duty is to act fairly. Each body is "master of its own procedure. It need not hold a hearing. It can do everything in writing. It need not allow lawyers. It need not put every detail of the case against a man." The Master of the Rolls also emphasised that what fairness requires "depends on the nature of the investigation and the consequences it may have on persons affected by it," so keeping open the possibility of the courts in a particular case saying that a right to legal representation exists.

In *Maynard* v. *Osmond* (*supra*), a claim to a right by a police constable to be legally represented when appearing before his chief constable failed because the Court of Appeal held that the Police (Discipline) Regulations 1965, made under the Police Act 1964, which expressly provided for representation only by another policeman, were *intra vires*. Lord Denning M.R. expressed the view that the Regulations were, in any event, entirely fair since the prosecution was presented by a police officer, not a lawyer, and the police officer defending the accused would do so with courage and independence.[22] Because of his knowledge of the inner workings of the police force he would probably be able to conduct the defence more effectively than a lawyer. Assuming that the Regulations were clearly within the four corners of the Act any attempt to justify them is of little importance. If, however, considerations such as those enunciated by the Master of the Rolls influenced the court in holding *intra vires* the Regulations which they might otherwise have held *ultra vires* then, with respect, it must be said that these considerations are largely irrelevant. The applicant clearly did not accept them or he would not have appealed.[23] The faith of a third party in the ability of a representative is unimportant. What matters is the faith of the person represented. On the general question of a right to representation, in the absence of statutory provisions, Lord Denning reaffirmed his belief in a right to legal representation where a person is charged with a serious offence. A tribunal should have a discretion to allow representation unless clearly forbidden. The Master of the Rolls, however, accepted, as did Orr L.J., that a domestic tribunal may operate under a contractual rule which absolutely prohibits legal representation. Waller L.J. relied heavily on the fact that

> "These regulations deal with disciplinary matters and . . . , although the powers of the Chief Constable are wide, he is dealing with the discipline of his own force, he is facing one of his men for whom he is responsible and . . . it is not surprising if the regulations provide for a man-to-man procedure" (p. 259).

The use by the courts of the concept of "disciplinary proceedings" to minimise the requirements of natural justice or even to exclude them entirely will be discussed later in Chapter 6. Here it is only necessary to point out that, before *Maynard* v. *Osmond*, it had been used by the Court of Appeal to deny a right to legal representation to a prisoner when appearing before a board of visitors on a charge of misbehaviour in prison; *Fraser* v. *Mudge* [1975] 1 W.L.R. 1132.

A party may wish to be represented not by a lawyer but by a friend or an adviser such as a trades union official. In the case of statutory tribunals this problem will often be dealt with by statutory regulation. In the case of domestic tribunals the right so far as it is based on natural justice[24] will depend on such factors as the seriousness of the charge and the gravity of the consequences.

Apart from a claim to representation a party may simply seek to have a friend or other person to assist and advise him even if that person does not seek a right to speak. In *McKenzie* v. *McKenzie* [1971] P. 33 the Court of Appeal held that a litigant was entitled to be accompanied by an adviser who could assist by giving advice and taking notes.[25] It might be thought that such a right applies—or should apply—to other tribunals where there is a right to legal representation, but even more in many cases where there is no such right as, for example, where a prisoner is facing a charge before a board of visitors as in *Fraser* v. *Mudge* (*supra*).

Next it is necessary to consider whether the right to a hearing involves the right that the decision is taken by the person who heard the evidence. Must he who decides also hear? This may present practical problems in large organisations such as government departments, administrative bodies with regulatory functions, or universities. Some of the particular problems which may arise in this context will be discussed in Chapter 4. The general principle, however, is clear. The collecting of evidence may be delegated, subject of course to the rules, statutory or contractual, governing a particular tribunal. There is, however, a strong presumption against any power to delegate the right to make the decision. It is not an absolute rule, as shown by *Re S. (A Barrister)* [1970] 1 Q.B. 160 where it was said (at p. 172):

> "Assuming that [counsel] is correct in his contention that a judicial or quasi-judicial duty cannot as a matter of general principle be delegated the question to be determined would be whether, in the interest of justice, delegation in this particular case can and should be allowed."

Re S. (A Barrister) provides a striking example of the courts holding that the making of a decision had not been delegated. S argued that the judges had delegated to the Inns of Court their disciplinary powers over barristers and therefore the Inns could not themselves further delegate those powers to the Senate of the Four Inns. Five judges, sitting as Visitors to Gray's Inn, held that the judges had never "in the narrow sense" delegated their powers to the Inns but merely concurred in the Inns selecting who are fit to be called to the Bar while the exercise of all the Inns' powers remained subject to the judges' jurisdiction. By setting up a senate the machinery was changed but the judges' duty and power to control the profession remained unaltered.

Many cases turn on the construction of statutory provisions or contractual terms. For example, in *Barnard* v. *National Dock Labour Board* [1953] 2 Q.B. 18 and *Vine* v. *National Dock Labour Board* [1957] A.C. 488 dockers who had been suspended successfully obtained declarations that the suspensions were nullities because statute had conferred disciplinary powers on the Dock Labour Board and purported delegations of those powers by the Board were *ultra vires*. In other cases the solution may be a finding of fact that, whether or not delegation is possible, it has not, on the facts before the court, occurred. A large body which sets up a committee to conduct a hearing and receive evidence is not, for example, delegating its powers provided the evidence is laid before the body making the final decision.[26] Only if, as in *Jeffs* v. *New Zealand Dairy Production and Marketing Board* [1967] 1 A.C. 551, the committee does not transmit to the parent body the evidence it has received, does the question of the validity of delegating powers of decision arise. That decision was distinguished by the Court of Appeal in *R.* v. *Race Relations Board, ex p. Selvarajan* [1975] 1 W.L.R. 1686, on two grounds. First, that the legislation under which the Board operated did not prevent delegation to some members only. Secondly, the Board anyway had before it sufficient information to make its own assessment of the case. After a complaint had been investigated by a conciliation committee, as provided for by the Race Relations Act 1968, the Board decided to refer the matter to a committee of seven of its own members. An employee of the Board collected evidence and prepared a report, headed "clearly predictable case." Four members of the committee received only the report; the chairman and two others had copies of all the papers. The committee, differing from the conciliation committee, decided that there had not been discrimination. The Court of Appeal refused certiorari to quash the decision. Lord Denning M.R. thought that the Board had acted fairly, as he defined that duty in words quoted earlier. Lawton L.J. said, at p. 1698,

> "How the board does what Parliament has entrusted it to do is not a matter for the courts to decide as long as it acts fairly and in good faith. It is for the board, not the courts to decide how much information each of its members should have when considering a particular case. As long as the board, or one of its constituent committees, has enough information to enable it to make a fair assessment of the case the courts will not interfere. How it gets the information is for the chairman and his advisers to decide."[27]

The procedure to be followed with regard to the collecting of evidence is to be determined by practical considerations in each case subject to any applicable statute or contract. This is clearly shown by *Local Government Board* v. *Arlidge* (*supra*) where the House of Lords rejected the arguments that the applicant was entitled to know which member of the Board had decided his appeal and that he who hears must decide. Viscount Haldane said at p. 132:

"When Parliament entrusts it [the Local Government Board] with judicial duties, Parliament must be taken in the absence of any declaration to the contrary to have intended it to follow the procedure which is its own and is necessary if it is to be capable of doing its work effectively."

Two final points should be made about the limits to the right to be heard. First, although tribunals or courts must be careful to allow a party to put his case fully they are not required to sit, in Lord Widgery C.J.'s phrase, "pinioned in their seats" while a party talks endlessly. A point is reached at which a tribunal is entitled to conclude its proceedings; *R.* v. *Middlesex Crown Court, ex p. Riddle*, *The Times*, October 8, 1975.[28] Secondly, once that point has been reached the tribunal is entitled to reach its conclusions and announce them. There is no right to be heard a second time.[29]

"The rules of natural justice do not require the decision-maker to disclose what he is minded to decide so that the parties may have a further opportunity of criticising his mental processes before he reaches a final decision. If this were a rule of natural justice only the most talkative of judges would satisfy it and trial by jury would have to be abolished" (*Hoffman La Roche & Co.* v. *Secretary of State for Trade and Industry* [1975] A.C. 295, 368, *per* Lord Diplock).

Notes

[1] *Demara Turf Club* v. *Phang* (1961) Sup.Ct. of British Guiana (1963) 26 M.L.R. 412, 416.

[2] See *infra*, Chap. 8. *Cf. Swordheath Properties* v. *Floydd* [1978] 1 W.L.R. 550, where the Court of Appeal deferred giving reasons for its decision until the county court judge had been given an opportunity to comment on the suggestion that he had deliberately given judgment against the applicants, knowing that he had no jurisdiction but in the hope that they would not appeal.

[3] *e.g. Wilson* v. *Secretary of State for the Environment* [1973] 1 W.L.R. 1083; *R.* v. *Kensington and Chelsea Rent Tribunal, ex p. MacFarlane* [1974] 1 W.L.R. 1486.

[4] See also *R.* v. *Immigration Appeal Tribunal, ex p. Ekrem Mehmet* [1977] 1 W.L.R. 795 (regulation made under Immigration Act 1971 dispensing with the need of notice in the case of persons whose addresses are unknown held *intra vires*).

[5] See also *R.* v. *Cornwall Rent Tribunal, ex p. West* (1974) 118 S.J. 699.

[6] See also *H. Sabey & Co. Ltd.* v. *Secretary of State for the Environment* [1978] 1 All E.R. 586; *General Accident Fire and Life Assurance Co.* v. *Secretary of State for the Environment* (1977) 241 E.G. 842; *infra* Chap. 7.

[7] Similarly, *R.* (*Harrington*) v. *Co. Clare JJ.* [1918] 2 I.R. 116; *R.* v. *Medical Appeal Tribunal* (*Midland Region*), *ex p. Carrarini* [1966] 1 W.L.R. 883; *Kiely* v. *Minister for Social Welfare* [1971] I.R. 21; *Ottley* v. *Morris*, *The Times*, June 24, 1978. For an unsuccessful attempt to claim insufficient time to prepare a defence see *Government of Australia* v. *Harrod* [1975] 1 W.L.R. 745 (H.L.).

[8] *R.* (*Cairns*) v. *L.G.B.* [1911] 2 I.R. 331, 345, *per* Maddon J.; "The claimant should be given an opportunity of presenting his case to the Board in some way suitable to the character of the inquiry, and it would probably be in writing."

[9] See, *e.g.* *Wiseman* v. *Borneman* [1971] A.C. 297, affirming [1968] Ch. 429.

[10] *R.* v. *Deputy Industrial Injuries Commissioner, ex p. Moore* [1965] 1 Q.B. 456.

[11] Affirmed on this point, without discussion, by the Court of Appeal; [1972] 1 W.L.R. 33. See also *R.* v. *Immigration Appeal Tribunal, ex p. Ekrem Mehmet* [1977] 1 W.L.R. 795.

[12] See also *Re Estate of Roscrea Meat Products Ltd.* [1958] I.R. 47; *R.* v. *Deputy Industrial Injuries Commissioner, ex p. Jones* [1962] 2 Q.B. 677; *Shareef* v. *Commissioner for Registration of Indian and Pakistani Residents* [1966] A.C. 46.

[13] On the different point of the effect of the judge *not* visiting the scene of the crime when the parties, witnesses and jury do, see *Tameshwar* v. *The Queen* [1957] A.C. 476.

[14] J. B. Thayer, *A Preliminary Treatise on Evidence at the Common Law* (1898) Little Brown & Co., Chap. VII (which reveals, *inter alia*, that American courts do not require proof that human beings are not 9 feet tall or that gin is intoxicating); G. D. Nokes, "The Limits of Judicial Notice" (1959) 75 L.Q.R. 59; Sir Rupert Cross, *Evidence* (4th ed., 1974), Chap. VII. Sir Richard Eggleston, *Evidence, Proof and Probability* (1978), Chap. 10.

[15] Similarly, *R.* v. *Medical Appeal Tribunal, ex p. Hubble* [1958] 2 Q.B. 228, 240 *per* Diplock J., affirmed [1959] 2 Q.B. 408.

[16] See further *Keane* v. *Mount Vernon Colliery Co. Ltd.* [1933] A.C. 309 (sheriff substitute acting as arbitrator under Workmen's Compensation Act 1925 entitled to take into account, in determining the cost of the "ordinary necessaries of life," his judicial knowledge of local conditions); *Reynolds* v. *Llanelly Associated Tinplate Co.* [1948] 1 All E.R. 140 (county court judge not entitled to rely on some particular, highly specialised knowledge as to what a certain type of workman might earn).

[17] See further G. Ganz, *Administrative Procedures* (1974) Sweet & Maxwell, pp. 32 *et seq.*; J. A. Smillie, "The Problem of Official Notice: Reliance by Administrative Tribunals on the Personal Knowledge of their members" [1975] P.L. 64; C. Manchester, "Judicial Notice and Personal Knowledge" (1979) 42 M.L.R. 22.

[18] See also *Re D.* (*Infants*) [1970] 1 W.L.R. 599; *Re P.A.* (*An Infant*) [1971] 1 W.L.R. 1530; *Re M.* (*An Infant*) [1973] 1 Q.B. 108 (discussed later in Chap. 9) and *Collymore* v. *Att.-Gen. of Trinidad and Tobago* [1970] A.C. 538; [1970] P.L. 105, 107. A judge cannot receive evidence in private which he promises not to reveal to anyone else; *H.* v. *H.* (*Child: Judicial Interview*) [1974] 1 W.L.R. 595 (C.A.).

[19] *Cf.* two recent decisions of the Employment Appeal Tribunal; *Khanum* v. *Mid-Glamorgan Health Authority* [1979] I.C.R. 40; *Bentley Engineering Co. Ltd.* v. *Mistry* [1978] I.R.L.R. 436.

[20] The right to counsel in case of felony was granted by statute in 1836; 6 & 7 Will. 4, c. 114.

[21] See the Reports of the Council on Tribunals for 1960, paras. 40 *et seq.*; 1967, paras. 58 *et seq.*; 1969–70, paras. 31 *et seq.*; 1976–77, p. 6; J. E. Alder, "Representation before Tribunals" [1972] P.L. 278.

[22] It emerges from the judgment of Waller L.J. that the applicant had approached eight courageous and independent officers, each of whom had refused to undertake his defence.

[23] The Court of Appeal devoted a considerable part of its judgment to explaining why it was, on the other hand, fair that senior officers had a right to legal representation.

[24] See Alder, *supra*, n. 21, arguing for a right to representation based on the law of agency.

[25] "An exceptional case"; *Mercy* v. *Persons unknown*, *The Times*, June 4, 1974; C. T. Latham, "The McKenzie Friend" (1974) 138 J.P. 428.

[26] *Cf. The State* (*Keller*) v. *Galway C.C.* [1958] I.R. 142 (chief medical officer not able to delegate decision whether person "substantially handicapped" but not required to examine every applicant personally. He could proceed on the basis of reports from doctors to whom he delegated the task of examining).

[27] For Parliamentary comment see H.C. Deb. (5th Ser.), vol. 940, cols. 1839 *et seq.* The Race Relations Act 1976, Sched. 1, para. 13 provides expressly for the possibility of delegation by the Commission for Racial Equality of any of its functions to a committee or to two or more commissioners. Arrangements for the discharge of its duties are to be made by the Commission and approved by the Secretary of State. See also the Price Commission Act 1977, s. 1(4) and Sched. 1.

[28] Similarly *Winchester County Council* v. *Secretary of State for the Environment* [1978] J.P.L. 467.

[29] *Ex p. Ramshay* (1852) 18 Q.B. 173.

Further Developments: The Right to know what Evidence is before the Court (pp. 68 *et seq.*)

R. v. *Leyland JJ., ex p. Hawthorn* [1979] 2 W.L.R. 28 (D.C.) marks an extension of this part of the rule relating to the right to a fair hearing. A conviction was quashed where the prosecution had failed to inform the prisoner of the existence of witnesses known to the police, whose evidence the prosecution had decided not to use. Although it was not the conduct of the tribunal which was in question, *certiorari* was an appropriate remedy as it was in cases of fraud and collusion.

CHAPTER 4

JUSTICE MUST BE SEEN TO BE DONE

THE distinction between justice being done and being seen to be done has been emphasised in many cases. Perhaps the most frequently quoted dictum is that of Lord Hewart C.J. in *R.* v. *Sussex JJ., ex p. McCarthy* [1924] 1 K.B. 256, 259; "It is of fundamental importance that justice should not only be done but should manifestly and undoubtedly be seen to be done."[1] The distinction has been invoked in many, widely differing circumstances, to such an extent that it has been thought necessary to warn against "the erroneous impression that it is more important that justice should appear to be done than that it should in fact be done"; *R.* v. *Camborne Justices, ex p. Pearce* [1955] 1 Q.B. 41, 52, *per* Slade J.

The requirement that justice should be seen to be done may be regarded as a general principle which in some cases can be satisfied only by the observance of the rules of natural justice or as itself forming one of those rules. Both explanations of the significance of the maxim are found in Lord Widgery C.J.'s judgment in *R.* v. *Home Secretary, ex p. Hosenball* [1977] 1 W.L.R. 766, 772, where after saying that "the principles of natural justice are those fundamental rules, the breach of which will prevent justice from being seen to be done" he went on to describe the maxim as "One of the rules generally accepted in the bundle of the rules making up natural justice." Although in most cases it will be of no importance how the maxim is classified the question may arise whether failure to ensure that justice is seen to be done nullifies a decision, an inevitable consequence of a breach of natural justice.[2] In cases where the maxim is invoked in connection with allegations of bias or a failure to give a proper hearing there is, of course, no doubt of the invalidity of the decisions challenged. In *R.* v. *Essex Justices, ex p. Perkins* [1927]

2 K.B. 475, for example, justice, it was said, was not seen to be done, where there was a likelihood of bias arising from the fact that the clerk to the magistrates was a member of the firm of solicitors which acted for the applicant's wife. The maxim has similarly been relied on where decisions have been invalidated because the tribunal has received, or appeared to receive, evidence in the absence of one of the parties, for example *R.* v. *Bodmin JJ., ex p. McEwen* [1947] 1 K.B. 321 where a witness was summoned by the justices to their room after they have retired to consider their verdict and *R.* v. *Stratford-upon-Avon JJ., ex p. Edmonds* [1973] R.T.R. 356, where the prosecutor spoke to justices after the conclusion of the hearing to inquire if they had copies of the relevant statutory provisions. On the other hand in *R.* v. *Arrowsmith* [1975] Q.B. 678 A had been convicted of offences under the Incitement to Disaffection Act 1934 arising out of the distribution by her of leaflets to members of the armed forces. On an earlier occasion she had distributed copies of the same leaflet but the Director of Public Prosecutions had refused leave for a prosecution under the 1934 Act. The Court of Appeal declined to quash her conviction although it quashed her original sentence because, in the words of Lawton L.J.,

> "It is, however, one of the principles of the administration of justice in this country that not only should justice be done (and justice would have been done to this woman by a long sentence), but it must appear to be done. The appellant may have drawn the inference from the Director of Public Prosecution's inaction and decision that nothing would happen to her if she went on distributing these leaflets.... She has got some grounds for thinking that she has not been treated fairly.... In the interests, not of justice but of the appearance of justice, the appropriate order for this court to make is that the sentence be quashed and a sentence be substituted which will allow for this appellant's immediate release" (p. 691).

This decision, if correct, suggests that the maxim is not part of natural justice or, at any rate, that it may be used in a loose, non-technical way where a defect in procedure does not go to the essential validity of a decision. But there is no doubt that the maxim may be used to nullify a decision in circumstances not involving any suggestion of bias or failure to give a full hearing, as illustrated by *R.* v. *Southwark Juvenile Court, ex p. J.* [1973] 1 W.L.R. 1300, where certiorari issued to quash the conviction of a 13-year-old boy because the justices had refused to allow a social worker, employed by the local authority in whose care the convicted boy was, to be present in court during the hearing. The Divisional Court held that section 47(2) of the Children and Young Persons Act 1933, which authorised the presence of the social worker at the hearing as "a person directly concerned," was directory not mandatory so that the refusal to admit her did not go to the jurisdiction of the court. Nonetheless it granted the order sought on the ground that any fair-minded person present at the juvenile court might well have come to the conclusion that justice was not seen to be done.

It is the recognition of the importance of the requirement that justice is seen to be done that justifies the giving of a remedy to a litigant even when it may be claimed that a decision alleged to be vitiated by a breach of natural justice would still have been reached had a fair hearing been given by an impartial tribunal. The maxim is applicable precisely when the court is concerned not with a case of actual injustice but with the appearance of injustice, or possible injustice. In *Altco Ltd.* v. *Sutherland* [1971] 2 Lloyd's Rep. 515 Donaldson J. said that the court, in deciding whether to interfere where an arbitrator had not given a party a full hearing, was not concerned with whether a further hearing would produce a different or the same result. It was important that the parties should not only be given justice, but, as reasonable men, know that they had had justice or "to use the time hallowed phrase" that justice should not only be done but be seen to be done. In *R.* v. *Thames Magistrates' Court, ex p. Polemis* [1974] 1 W.L.R. 1371, the applicant obtained an order of certiorari to quash his conviction by a stipendiary magistrate on the ground that he had not had sufficient time to prepare his defence. The Divisional Court rejected the argument that, in its discretion, it ought to refuse relief because the applicant had no defence to the charge.

> "It is again absolutely basic to our system that justice must not only be done but must manifestly be seen to be done. If justice was so clearly not seen to be done, as on the afternoon in

question here, it seems to me that it is no answer to the applicant to say: 'Well, even if the case had been properly conducted, the result would have been the same.' That is mixing up doing justice with seeing that justice is done" (*per* Lord Widgery C.J. at p. 1375).[3]

In *Maxwell* v. *Department of Trade* [1974] 1 Q.B. 523, 540 Lawton L.J. expressed a similar idea when he said, "Doing what is right may still result in unfairness if it is done in the wrong way."[4] It is because the assurance that justice has been seen to be done is, in itself, an important element in the public confidence in the settlement of disputes, whether in the courts or by other bodies, that, for example, the rules of natural justice may apply even to what might be regarded as "open and shut cases." Megarry J. explained why, when warning of the danger of regarding any case as "open and shut";

> "'When something is obvious' (it may be said), 'why force everybody to go through the tiresome waste of time involved in framing charges and giving an opportunity to be heard? The result is obvious from the start.' Those who take this view do not, I think, do themselves justice. As everybody who has anything to do with the law well knows, the path of the law is strewn with examples of open and shut cases which, somehow, were not; of unanswerable charges which, in the event, were completely answered; of inexplicable conduct which was fully explained; of fixed and unalterable determinations that, by discussion, suffered a change. Nor are those with any knowledge of human nature who pause to think for a moment likely to underestimate the feelings of resentment of those who find that a decision against them has been made without their being afforded any opportunity to influence the course of events" (*John* v. *Rees* [1970] Ch. 345, 402).[5]

The necessity that justice should be seen to be done not only explains the applicability in certain cases of the two central rules of natural justice but also itself provides the justification for setting aside decisions on a variety of grounds, some of which could only be explained with difficulty as instances of failure to grant a hearing or of the likelihood of bias. In *R.* v. *Smith* (*Winston*), *The Times*,

April 30, 1975 a pupil barrister who had had long discussions with the prisoner about his case appeared in court at the trial sitting behind prosecuting counsel to whose chambers he belonged. On appeal Smith's conviction was quashed because, while it was not suggested that the pupil passed on to prosecuting counsel any information he had obtained from the prisoner, justice could not be said to be seen to be done.

The maxim is also of use in explaining a wide range of cases where decisions have been invalidated because of defects in the composition of tribunals or serious irregularities in their procedure. Often, the maxim is not directly referred to in such cases, the courts using instead such a phrase as "grave irregularity." Nonetheless, it is submitted it is the need for justice to be seen to be done which explains and justifies such decisions. Defects in the composition of tribunals which are relevant here are of two kinds, the participation by non-members and, on the other hand, the non-participation by members, in a tribunal's deliberations. There is no doubt that "the actual participation of a non-member of a judicial body in the taking of a decision involves want of jurisdiction"[6] while, conversely, the mere presence of a non-member does not invalidate the decision if he did not participate in the decision; *Leary* v. *National Union of Vehicle Builders* [1971] Ch. 34, 54 *per* Megarry J. But the question is often whether the non-member *seemed* to participate. Lord Denning M.R. in *Ward* v. *Bradford Corporation* (1972) 70 L.G.R. 27, 33 disapproved of a person who is not a member of a tribunal retiring with the members on this very ground, that it might "give the impression that he is taking part in their deliberations when he is not entitled to do so, for then justice would not be seen to be done." Thus in *R.* v. *East Kerrier JJ., ex p. Mundy* [1952] 2 Q.B. 719 the clerk to the justices went to their room carrying a piece of paper with details of the prisoner's previous convictions. On returning to court the justices announced that they were convicting the prisoner and called for proof of further convictions, if any. Their decision was quashed. Devlin J. said (at p. 724), "We are not concerned with a case of actual injustice.... We are concerned with an infringement of the rule that justice must not only be done but must also manifestly appear to be done."[7] In *Re B.* (*Adoption by Parents*) [1975] Fam. 127 where a social worker involved in adoption proceedings retired with the justices, their determination was quashed because justice had not been seen to be done.[8] (In the case of justices' clerks there are a number of situations in which it is recognised as entirely proper that they retire with the magistrates: when magistrates request their clerk to join them for the purpose of advising them on the law: see *R.* v. *Welshpool Borough Justices, ex p. Holley* [1953] 2 Q.B. 403, or on the sentences imposed by other courts: see *Practice Note* (*Justices' Clerks*) [1953] 1 W.L.R. 1416, or on a mixed question of law and fact, see *R.* v. *Consett Justices, ex p. Postal Bingo Ltd.* [1967] 2 Q.B. 10.)

It is not necessary to establish that evidence has been given in the absence of the parties or the non-member has participated in deciding the case, or both. However, where the alleged participation by a non-member takes place in a tribunal's public deliberations it may be possible to uphold the challenged decision because it can be proved that the decision was that of the tribunal alone and justice can be seen to have been done; *R.* v. *Recorder of Burnley, ex p. New Empire* (*Burnley*) *Ltd.* [1940] 2 All E.R. 412.

Whether a tribunal's decision is invalid because of non-participation of some of the members is a question which can arise in various ways. There may have been improper delegation to some members of the power of deciding as opposed to the duty of collecting evidence on which the tribunal will make up its own mind; *Jeffs* v. *New Zealand Dairy Production and Market Board* [1967] 1 A.C. 551.[9] In other cases the question may be how many members constitute a tribunal. For example section 28 of the Finance Act 1960 created a tribunal and subsection 7 of that section provided that "For the purposes of this section the tribunal shall consist of (*a*) a chairman ... (*b*) two or more persons appointed by the Lord Chancellor." Four such appointments had been made and Pennycuick V.-C. held that the tribunal consisted of five persons and a decision taken by four alone of those five was void. The Court of Appeal and House of Lords both, however, held that there was nothing in the Act to compel the conclusion that a validly constituted tribunal must consist of a chairman plus all persons appointed under paragraph (*b*); *Howard* v. *Borneman* (*No. 2*) [1976] A.C. 301; affirming [1975] Ch. 201; reversing [1974] 1 W.L.R. 15. The case turned, according to Lord Kilbrandon, with whose speech the other members of the House concurred, "upon a narrow point of statutory construction" (p. 311); the proper meaning of section 28(7) was that the tribunal was validly constituted by the chairman plus any two of the appointees under paragraph (*b*). An example of a clearer statutory provision is to be found in section 68(1) and (3) of the Supreme Court of Judicature Act 1925 which expressly recognises that appeals need not be heard by all the members of the Court of Appeal.

Once it is established who constitutes a tribunal, it is clear that all the members must participate in its decision. In *R.* v. *Kensington and Chelsea Rent Tribunal, ex p. MacFarlane* [1974] 1 W.L.R. 1486, 1490 Lord Widgery C.J. recognised this principle when he said "[Counsel] has given us a timely reminder that under the Act the tribunal consists of a chairman and two other members; he submits quite rightly that no decision can be taken except by a tribunal so constituted." An interesting example of this principle is supplied by *Morris* v. *Gestetner Ltd.* [1973] 1 W.L.R. 1378. By a majority an industrial tribunal found that Morris had been unfairly dismissed. The members of the tribunal who had found in the workman's favour then went on to consider whether to recommend his re-engagement, the dissenting member taking no part in this further deliberation. While Sir John Donaldson agreed with the dissentient member on the issue of unfair dismissal he went on to say:

> "We can quite understand that as, on his view, there had been no unfair dismissal he thought that he had neither the power nor the duty to consider re-engagement. The tribunal having decided, albeit by a majority, that the appellant had been unfairly dismissed, it was for the tribunal and every member of it to consider whether there should be a recommendation. This second issue could also have been decided by a majority and the members composing it might not have been the same as decided the first issue" (p. 1383).

Where there is a quorum it will not, of course, be necessary for every member of a tribunal to be present at a meeting. However, every member must be summoned to a meeting, subject to possible exceptions in the cases of severe illness or distance. It is not for the chairman to decide who should have notice of a meeting;

Lane v. *Norman* (1891) 66 L.T. 83; *Young* v. *Ladies Imperial Club* [1902] 2 K.B. 523.

Has justice been seen to be done if the members of a tribunal have not engaged in consultation between themselves before reaching their decision? In *Parr* v. *Winteringham* (1859) 28 L.J.Q.B. 123, 125 Lord Campbell C.J. described the duty of arbitrators as being to "meet together . . . deliberate together and . . . give a joint judgment." The Chief Justice upheld a decision of race stewards, reached after two of them sent a letter to the third informing him of their view and asking him to sign it, which he refused to do, precisely because they were not judges or arbitrators.[10] In one instance, at least, a failure to consult has been held to be an example of justice not being seen to be done. The complainant in *Ex p. Ladbroke Group*, *The Times*, February 28, 1969 had unsuccessfully applied for the renewal of a betting licence. The chairman of the committee sat some distance from his colleagues and appeared to reach his conclusion without consulting them. Justice, it was held, had not been seen to be done and certiorari issued to quash the decision. In *Olympia Press Ltd.* v. *Hollis* [1973] 1 W.L.R. 1520, a large number of allegedly obscene books had been seized and summonses issued under the Obscene Publications Act 1959, s. 3. The justices divided the books among themselves for reading, no justice reading all the books but every book being read by more than one justice. Olympia Press claimed that "each one should have read all, because natural justice demands that the decision is reached by each justice on every piece of material." The Divisional Court rejected this argument because it was satisfied that after reading the books the justices had discussed them together so as to arrive at a collective opinion, so distinguishing the case from the earlier decision of *Burke* v. *Copper* [1962] 1 W.L.R. 700, where the facts suggested that individual justices had reached their own conclusion on the obscenity of particular items. In that case one copy of a particular photograph appeared in a bundle—presumably examined by one justice—which was held not to be obscene, while another copy of the same photograph appeared in a bundle—presumably looked at by a different and more censorious justice—which was held to be obscene. Had all the books in the *Olympia Press* case been read by all the justices would that have obviated the need for a "proper and full discussion ... such as would be necessary to arrive at a collective opinion?" Surely not, if there had been differing views as to the obscenity of particular books. But should not the principle go further and require discussion before a collective decision is reached even where there seems to be a unanimous or near unanimous view?

In *Howard* v. *Borneman* (*No. 2*) (*supra*) Lord Kilbrandon remarked briefly that such a suggestion was "without substance. No serious explanation of the purpose of such consultations, in the case of unanimity, was or could have been given" (p. 313). To arrange for consultation where there was disagreement would, however, be "wise." With respect, the necessity for consultation between members of a tribunal merits further consideration, at any rate in cases where a tribunal has a discretion as to the action it may take after reaching a conclusion. *Howard's* case should perhaps be considered as a further example of the court's reluctance to impose too high a standard of procedure on bodies which are merely conducting the preliminary stages of an inquiry. In some circumstances no doubt consultation can be effected by an exchange of writing but in others something more may well be necessary.

The necessity of justice being seen to be done has been referred to in cases where there have been changes in the personnel of a court or tribunal in the course of hearing a dispute. In *Munday* v. *Munday* [1954] 1 W.L.R. 1078 maintenance proceedings had begun before three justices; on the second day of the hearing the bench was augmented by two further justices; those two and a sixth justice sat to hear the third and final day of the proceedings. Lord Merriman P., having held that the hearings were in breach of the Magistrates' Court Act 1952, s. 98, went on to say "There are wider considerations still, for it seems to me that this is pre-eminently a case in which the principle that justice must not merely be done but must manifestly be seen to be done has been infringed."[11] Where the parties agree to a case continuing before a new judge, or a change in the composition of a bench of magistrates, the maxim will probably not apply,[12] although in *Bolton* v. *Bolton* [1949] 2 All E.R. 908 Lord Merriman P. was clearly unhappy about upholding a decision of magistrates, despite the agreement of the parties to one magistrate hearing the wife's evidence and a second magistrate reading a note of that evidence and hearing the rest of the case.

Surprisingly, perhaps, the maxim does not seem to be invoked to justify or explain the rule that the courts must sit in public although Lord Atkinson in *Scott* v. *Scott* [1913] A.C. 417, 463 did justify public hearings as not merely giving "the best security for the pure, impartial and efficient administration of justice" but also as "the best means for winning for it public confidence and respect"—which is the objective of requiring, in various ways, that justice be seen to be done.[13] Lord Widgery C.J., in *R.* v. *Denbigh Justices, ex p. Williams* [1974] Q.B. 759, 764, referring to an argument that the hearing of the case by justices in the absence of members of the public had resulted in justice not being seen to be done and was contrary to natural justice, said

> "I say no more about it other than to observe that it is conceded by counsel that there is no case in the books in which it has been said to be a breach of the rules of natural justice to exclude members of the public from the court room. The point is not important in the present case . . . it being perfectly clear that the statute requires these proceedings to be in open court."

Nonetheless where there is not a convenient statute the question still arises, why should it be a basic principle that the courts administer justice publicly. Perhaps the reluctance to speak of justice being seen to be done in this context arises from the fact that the requirement of publicity is peculiar to courts and, in some cases, tribunals established by statute. No one has suggested that an obligation to sit in public binds all decision-making bodies and, indeed, legislation such as the Domestic and Appellate Proceedings (Restriction of Publicity) Act 1968 might be thought to show a lessening of belief in the overriding importance of sitting in public in the case of the courts themselves.

Other irregularities which may appropriately give rise to complaints that justice has not been seen to be done include such matters as judges falling, or appearing to fall, asleep during the course of a trial. In *R.* v. *Edworthy*, *The Times*, February 18, 1961 a conviction by court-martial was quashed when it was established that the judge advocate had fallen asleep in the course of the trial. In *R.* v. *Langham*, *The Times*, April 25, 1972 the judge was alleged to have slept for 15 minutes during a trial in which the defendants were convicted of murder. The Court of Appeal, however, concluded from an examination of the judge's summing-up that he had not been asleep at the time alleged; a mere appearance of being asleep was not sufficient to invalidate the trial. Again litigants may feel that justice has not been seen to be done when the judge has intervened excessively in the course of the trial, for example, by questioning witnesses to an improper extent, so that he might be thought to have descended into the arena and become "liable to have his vision clouded by the dust of the conflict"; *Yuill* v. *Yuill* [1945] P. 15, 20 *per* Lord Greene M.R. In *R.* v. *Hircock* [1970] 1 Q.B. 67, the judge sighed and groaned during the address of defence counsel to the jury, putting his head in his hands and saying audibly several times "Oh God." In *R.* v. *Southampton JJ., ex p. Atherton* [1974] Crim.L.R. 108 the magistrates pronounced sentence before hearing a plea in mitigation. They then heard counsel on the prisoner's behalf and reduced the size of the fine which they had originally imposed. The verdict was quashed because "It might have been thought by intelligent and well instructed members of the public sitting in court that justice was not being seen to be done." In that case Lord Widgery C.J. distinguished between

> "conduct on the part of the presiding judge which may be regarded as discourteous and may show signs of impatience—and, indeed, conduct which cannot be commended in any way—but which does not in itself invite the jury to disbelieve the defence witnesses, and conduct which positively and actively obstructs counsel in the doing of his work."

Hircock fell into the former category; the conviction was upheld but the sentence reduced. On the other hand in *R.* v. *Clewer* (1953) 37 Cr.App.R. 37, a conviction was quashed when the transcript of the trial showed that defence counsel had not been able to put his case fairly to the court. Lord Goddard C.J. said,

> "The first and most important thing for the administration of the criminal law is that it should appear that the prisoner is having a fair trial, and that he should not be left with any sense of injustice on the ground that his case has not been fairly put before the jury" (p. 40).[14]

Any appearance of a bargain by a judge with the defence in a criminal trial about sentence in return for a plea of guilty may also result in the quashing of a conviction as in *R.* v. *Turner* [1970] 2 Q.B. 321, or sentence as in *R.* v. *Atkinson* [1978] 1 W.L.R. 425, 428, where Lord Scarman said plea bargaining "was a sensitive area in which the appearance of justice was part of the substance of justice."[15] Indeed any behaviour on the part of the judge which might leave a prisoner with a "real sense of grievance" will result in the setting aside or reduction of the sentence. In *R.* v. *Beard* [1967] Crim.L.R. 376, for example, the sentence was reduced where a judge had expressed his displeasure at finding a guardsman in the dock before him and indicated that, as a Brigade of Guards officer, he could not be expected to show any mercy. In *R.* v. *Deary*, *The Times*, June 8, 1976 a Recorder had assured counsel for the prisoner that there was no question of a custodial sentence in any circumstance. D pleaded guilty and a custodial sentence was imposed, the Recorder having been outvoted by the lay justices sitting with him. On appeal, the sentence was set aside because, even if in some sense correct, "there was here a rather unpleasant circumstance . . . some real sense of grievance might be felt by the appellant."

The importance of the need for justice to be seen to be done might also be thought to be relevant in any discussion of whether natural justice requires that reasons be given for decisions. In *Fountaine* v. *Chesterton* (1968) 112 S.J. 690, Megarry J. said that a right to know the reasons for a decision did not form part of natural justice. More recently the same learned judge has said, "It is clear that there is no general obligation to give reasons for a decision"; *McInnes* v. *Onslow Fane* [1978] 3 All E.R. 211, 219. The correctness of the learned judge's statement of the law is unarguable. Thus magistrates are not, normally, under a duty to give reasons for their decisions; administrative bodies, similarly, have been held not to be under any such duty.[16] But equally there is no doubt that in many circumstances there is a duty to give reasons and that the courts and the legislature increasingly recognise the desirability of such a duty. In *Rothermere* v. *Times Newspapers* [1973] 1 W.L.R. 448, 455, for example, Cairns L.J. said that in deciding whether to order a trial by jury or by judge alone, "The fact that a judge has to give reasons for his decision is to my mind a point in favour of trial by judge alone." In *Alexander Machinery Ltd.* v. *Crabtree* [1974] I.C.R. 120, 122 Sir John Donaldson said that in the case of industrial tribunals, "In the absence of reasons it is impossible to determine whether or not there has been an error of law. Failure to give reasons therefore amounts to a denial of justice and is itself an error of law." Buckley L.J. said in *Capital Properties* v. *Swycher* [1976] 1 Ch. 319, 326, "Litigants are entitled to know on what grounds their cases are decided." The judge at first instance should not, the lord justice observed scathingly "have spared himself the trouble of expressing his reasons for deciding as he did." In *Breen* v. *A.E.U.* [1971] 2 Q.B. 175, 191 Lord Denning M.R., as seen in Chapter 1, argued that fairness might require the giving of reasons as a fundamental of good administration. As the Master of the Rolls pointed out, the courts, in the absence of a reason for a decision by a Minister, may be prepared to assume that there was no good reason and quash the decision; *Padfield* v. *Minister of Agriculture, Fisheries and Food* [1968] A.C. 997.[17] Writers have described the giving of reasons as "of the essence of a judicial decision"[18] or "a particular virtue" of law.[19] Both the Committee on Ministers' Powers[20] and the Committee on Administrative Tribunals and Enquiries[21] emphasised the need to give reasons for decisions, the former body indeed invoking natural justice. In many instances such a requirement is now imposed by Act of Parliament[22] or statutory instrument.[23] The duty under these provisions "is a responsible one and cannot be discharged by the use of vague general words"; *Elliott* v. *London Borough of Southwark* [1976] 1 W.L.R. 499, 510, *per* James L.J.[24] The European Convention of Human Rights requires the court itself to give reasons for its decisions (Art. 51). The right to a fair trial, which is contained in Article 6, does not expressly extend to a reasoned decision but that, it has been said, is implicit in the requirement of a fair hearing.[25] Organs of the EEC are required to give reasons for their decisions.[26]

With the desirability of giving reasons for decisions so widely recognised it surely can be argued that a failure to do so amounts to a failure to be manifestly seen to be doing justice, whether the body concerned is a court, a statutory tribunal or a domestic tribunal. The burden of establishing a right not to give reasons should be firmly on the person giving the decision and should only be capable of being discharged in special circumstances. There may be cases where giving reasons will be embarrassing or hurtful to parties, but against that must be weighed the resentment of the party who does not know why he has lost and the lack of confidence on the part of third parties in the decisions of a tribunal which, unexplained, seem inexplicable. (The practical difficulties faced by the Parole Board in giving reasons for its decisions are discussed later in Chapter 6.) Perhaps the best known argument against the giving of reasons is that of Lord Mansfield advising a general who, as governor of a West India island, had also to sit as a judge:

> "Lord Mansfield said to him, 'Be of good cheer—take my advice, and you will be reckoned a great judge as well as a great commander-in-chief. Nothing is more easy; only hear both sides patiently— then consider what you think justice requires, and decide accordingly. But never give your reasons;—for your judgment will probably be right, but your reasons will certainly be wrong.'"[27]

Lord Mansfield's words, while amusing, are a denial of any system of adjudication based on rules—whether rules of law or the terms of membership of a club or union. Except in a system of palm tree justice a party is entitled to know why a decision was reached, or how else can he challenge its correctness? Nor, contrary to what Lord Mansfield's advice might suggest, is anything more likely to ensure that a person reaches the right decision than an obligation to justify it by reasons. This argument was clearly put by Lord Bramwell in *Allcroft* v. *Bishop of London* [1891] A.C. 666, 678, a case in which the House of Lords held that it had no jurisdiction to order the Bishop to take proceedings under the Public Worship Regulation Act 1874:

> "Then it is said why if his decisions cannot be reviewed is he to state his reasons? Lindley L.J. has given an excellent answer to this. It is that he may be under the necessity of forming a careful opinion, and one that will bear public examination. It is like the constitutional duty of judges who give their reasons for their judgment though there is no appeal; as in the case of your Lordships' House, and as formerly the judges of the

superior court gave on motions for new trials, for example, and other cases, and as they do now though there is no appeal."

Notes

[1] Similarly *R.* v. *Byles* (1912) 77 J.P. 40, Avory J.; *Shrager* v. *Basil Dighton Ltd.* [1924] 1 K.B. 274, 284 *per* Atkin L.J.; *R.* v. *East Kerrier JJ., ex p. Mundy* [1952] 2 Q.B. 719, 724, *per* Devlin J.; *R.* v. *Kent Police Authority, ex p. Godden* [1971] 2 Q.B. 662, 670 *per* Lord Denning M.R.

[2] *Infra*, Chap. 8.

[3] Similarly *Stringer* v. *Minister of Housing* [1970] 1 W.L.R. 1281, 1297 where Cooke J. said that the question was whether the Minister had "precluded himself from acting with fairness and impartiality both in appearance and in fact."

[4] "It is not a question of whether the tribunal has arrived at a fair result . . . the question is whether the tribunal has dealt fairly and equally with the parties before it in arriving at that result"; *Barrs* v. *British Wool Marketing Board*, 1957 S.C. 72, 82 *per* Lord President (Clyde).

[5] See further, *infra*, Chaps. 5 and 6.

[6] De Smith, *op. cit.* p. 236, n. 51.

[7] See also *R.* v. *Stafford JJ., ex p. Ross* [1962] 1 W.L.R. 456.

[8] See also *R.* v. *Aberdare JJ., ex p. Jones* [1973] Crim.L.R. 45; *R.* v. *Bodmin JJ., ex p. McEwen* [1947] 1 K.B. 321, 325 *per* Lord Goddard C.J.

[9] Noted, K.J. Keith, (1968) 31 M.L.R. 87.

[10] *Infra*, p. 148.

[11] See also *Re D.* (*Minors*) (*Wardship: Jurisdiction*) [1973] Fam. 179. In *Fulker* v. *Fulker* [1936] 3 All E.R. 636 where a final order was made by four justices, only two of whom had participated in earlier proceedings and heard the evidence, the case was remitted to the magistrates because "it is impossible to uphold an order based, as this was, on evidence which had never been heard at all *viva voce* by two of the justices."

[12] *The Forest Lake* [1968] P. 270; *Re Application of British Reinforced Concrete Engineering Co. Ltd.* (1929) 45 T.L.R. 186—both cases explaining the rather guarded words of Scrutton L.J. in *Coleshill* v. *Manchester Corporation* [1928] 1 K.B. 776; *The Hopemount* (1943) 75 Ll.L.Rep. 94; *H.M.S. Vanity* (1946) 79 Ll.L.Rep. 594; *Ferguson* v. *Ferguson*, 1936 S.C. 808.

[13] See also *Daubney* v. *Cooper* (1829) 10 B. & C. 237, 240 *per* Bayley J.; *McPherson* v. *McPherson* [1936] A.C. 177 and *Re Agricultural Industries Ltd.* [1952] 1 All E.R. 1188. For an interesting example of a limit to the principle see *R.* v. *Waterfield* [1975] 1 W.L.R. 711 (public has no right to be present in the courtroom during the showing of obscene films to jury as exhibits in the course of a trial).

[14] Similarly *R.* v. *Hulusi*; *R.* v. *Purvis* (1974) 58 Cr.App.R. 378 (assault arising out of alleged attempt to charge two Scotsmen in a Soho club £68 for a bottle of whisky). The interests of justice may entitle a judge in some circumstances to intervene in the course of a trial; *R.* v. *Fotheringham* (1975) 119 S.J. 613. See generally on judicial misbehaviour S. Shetreet, *Judges on Trial* (1976) North Holland Publishing Company, especially pp. 209–224 and 294–303.

[15] See also *R.* v. *Wilkins* (1977) 66 Cr.App.R. 49; *R.* v. *Grice* (1977) 66 Cr.App.R. 167; *R.* v. *Ryan* [1978] Crim.L.R. 306; *R.* v. *Llewellyn, The Times*, March 3, 1978.

[16] *R.* v. *Northumberland Compensation Appeal Tribunal, ex p. Shaw* [1952] 1 K.B. 338, 352 *per* Denning L.J.; *R.* v. *Gaming Board for Great Britain, ex p. Benaim and Khaida* [1970] 2 Q.B. 417, 431 *per* Lord Denning M.R.

[17] But *cf. Gouriet* v. *Union of Post Office Workers* [1978] A.C. 435.

[18] Lloyd, *Introduction to Jurisprudence* (3rd ed., 1972), Stevens, p. 47.

[19] Alan Watson, *The Nature of Law* (1977) Edinburgh, p. 67. See also C. Parker, "A Right to Know the Reasons for a Decision of a Magistrates' Court" in *Fundamental Rights*, ed. Bridge, Lasok, Perrott, Plender (1973), p. 189. M. Akehurst, "Statements of Reasons for Judicial and Administrative Decisions" (1970) 33 M.L.R. 154. J. L. Montrose, "Reasoned Judgments" (1958) 21 M.L.R. 80.

[20] (1932) Cmd. 4060, p. 80.

[21] (1957) Cmnd. 218, para. 98.

[22] Tribunal and Inquiries Act 1971, s. 12; Dumping at Sea Act 1974, s. 2; Housing Act 1974, s. 114(2); Consumer Credit Act 1974, s. 32; Bail Act 1976, s. 5(3).

[23] *Infra*, Chap. 7, n. 53 (Planning Inquiries Rules). For a general survey see Geoffrey A. Flick, "Administrative Adjudications and the Duty to Give Reasons—A Search for Criteria" [1978] P.L. 16.

[24] See also *Iveagh (Earl)* v. *Minister of Housing and Local Government* [1964] 1 Q.B. 395; *Re Poyser and Mills' Arbitration* [1964] 2 Q.B. 467; *Givaudan & Co.* v. *Minister of Housing and Local Government* [1967] 1 W.L.R. 250; *French Kier Developments* v. *Secretary of State for the Environment* [1977] 1 All E.R. 296; Bailey, Cross, Garner, *Cases and Materials on Administrative Law* (1977) Sweet & Maxwell, pp. 482–486.

[25] F. G. Jacobs, *The European Convention on Human Rights* (1975) Oxford, p. 102.

[26] R. M. Lauwaars, *Lawfulness and Legal Force of Community Decisions* (1973) Sijthoff, Leiden, pp. 151 *et seq.*

[27] J. Campbell, *Lives of the Chief Justices*, vol. 2, p. 572. Lord Mansfield's words are sufficiently well known to be included in the *Oxford Dictionary of Quotations.*

Further Developments: Plea Bargaining (p. 95, n. 15)

To the many recent decisions on plea-bargaining and, generally, on the undesirability of private discussions between judge and counsel, add *R.* v. *Eccles* [1978] Crim. L.R. 757 and *R.* v. *Winterflood, The Times*, November 21, 1978 (C.A.).

The Importance of giving Reasons (p. 95)

The importance of giving reasons for decisions has been emphasised in two recent cases. In *Re a debtor* [1979] 1 All E.R. 434, 439 Buckley L.J. referred to the view of Stamp J. in *Re a debtor* [1971] 1 W.L.R. 261, 266, that an appellate court would be justified in inferring that a judge who did not give reasons for a decision had gone wrong in exercising a discretion vested in him. However, in the case before the Court of Appeal it was clear from a note of the submissions made to the Register whose order was being appealed against that, although he had given no reasons for the way he had exercised his discretion, he must have had the relevant arguments before him when he made his decision.

In *Bowman* v. *McKeown, The Times*, November 23, 1978 the Court of Appeal said that a judge who had a litigant appearing in person before him should give clear reasons for his decision; the more awkward or difficult a litigant might be, the more important it was that the judge should do his duty with regard to giving reasons.

Chapter 5

WHEN DO THE RULES OF NATURAL JUSTICE APPLY?

I. Introduction: Fairness

Previous chapters have shown the uncertainty which pervades the law about the content of the rules of natural justice. In this chapter, in which it is intended to discuss in what circumstances the rules apply, the law will be seen to be at least as uncertain as in those earlier chapters. In many cases no distinction will be drawn between the right to a hearing and the rule against bias because, normally, if one principle applies both apply. Nonetheless it must be borne in mind that, in certain situations, there may be a right to an unbiased tribunal but no right to a hearing—which justifies, and explains, the description of the maxim *nemo iudex in re sua* as "the first and most fundamental principle of natural justice."[1] Thus in *R.* v. *Aston University Senate, ex p. Roffey* [1969] 2 Q.B. 538, which is discussed later, in Chapter 7, Donaldson J. said, "It [the principle of *audi alteram partem*] will certainly not apply in every case in which there is a right to natural justice" (p. 552). More usually, however, the courts describe such cases, where the right to an impartial tribunal exists but no right to a hearing, as involving not natural justice but the duty to act fairly. A lay client for instance, has no right to a hearing before his architect exercises his power to make decisions under a standard form of RIBA contract about the quality of work executed by the builder, but he is entitled to expect the architect to be free from bias—as is the builder. In such a case,

> "It is the position of independence and skill that affords the parties the proper safeguards and not the imposition of rules requiring something in the nature of a hearing" (*Hounslow L.B.C.* v. *Twickenham Garden Developments* [1971] Ch. 233, 259, *per* Megarry J.)

Re HK: fairly
Bushell – not in all cases

Similarly, to say that a student has no right to be heard by the examiners who assess his work "is not, of course, to say that the university is free to trample on the student's rights: for he is entitled to have his application duly considered by whatever bodies have the power of decision"; *Leary* v. *National Union of Vehicle Builders* [1971] Ch. 34, 52 *per* Megarry J.[2]

It has already been seen in Chapter 1 that the tendency of the courts at present is to apply the rules of natural justice to a very wide range of decision-making processes. In *Gaiman* v. *National Association for Mental Health* [1971] Ch. 317, 333, Megarry J. suggested that the rules apply

> "To all powers of decision unless the circumstances suffice to exclude them. These circumstances may be found in the person or body making the decision, the nature of the decision to be made, the gravity of the matter in issue, the terms of any contract or other provision governing the power to decide and so on."

Without wishing to deny that there is, at present, almost a presumption that natural justice applies to all decision-making, for the purposes of this chapter Megarry J.'s dictum will be turned on its head and the circumstances he enumerates discussed as factors supporting a contention that natural justice is applicable in a certain situation. In the next chapter attention will be paid to factors which lead to an exclusion of natural justice—such as the unimportance of a decision.

Before discussing these factors it is necessary to consider the view, formerly frequently expressed in judgments, that the clue to the applicability of the rules of natural justice is to be found in the duty of a body or tribunal to act judicially, a concept which might fairly be said to have proved to be even more vague than most legal concepts.[3] No satisfactory definition of "acting judicially" ever evolved and indeed the reasoning of the courts seemed at times to be that a body ought to observe the rules of natural justice; therefore it was acting judicially. While it might be felt that nothing would be lost by abandoning all reference to the existence of a duty to act judicially, the courts continue to refer to this concept (for example in *R.* v. *Kent Police Authority, ex p. Godden* [1971] 2 Q.B. 662) and even to talk of "quasi-judicial" functions, for example Salmon L.J.

in *Ex p. Godden* and Pennycuick V.-C. in *Glynn* v. *Keele University* [1971] 1 W.L.R. 487. However, the concept has clearly lost much of its importance, the courts tending increasingly to look to the substance rather than the form.[4] Some judges are happy to say that the duty to observe the rules of natural justice applies to bodies whether or not they are exercising a judicial function. Others retain the shell of the rule and give a wide meaning to "acting judicially." In *R.* v. *Barnsley Metropolitan Borough Council, ex p. Hook* [1976] 1 W.L.R. 1052, for example, Lord Denning M.R. held that the rules of natural justice applied to the revocation of a licence to trade at a market because of the importance of the right to the stall-holder; it was irrelevant whether the council was exercising an administrative or judicial function. Scarman L.J. and Sir John Pennycuick reached the same conclusion because, in their view, the council was under a duty to act judicially.

Another approach is exemplified in the dictum, quoted in Chapter 1, of Lord Parker C.J.: "[It] is not, as I see it, a question of acting or being required to act judicially, but of being required to act fairly"; *Re H.K. (An Infant)* [1967] 2 Q.B. 617, 630.

A single test of fairness which settles both the question, do the rules apply, and, what are the contents of the rules; for example, on the facts of this case does the applicant's right to a hearing involve the right to legal representation, has been adopted with enthusiasm in subsequent cases. In *Re Pergamon Press Ltd.* [1971] Ch. 388 the Court of Appeal held that inspectors conducting an inquiry under the Companies Act 1948, s. 165(*b*) must act fairly but that although that meant that directors must be given a hearing it did not entitle them to insist on cross-examining witnesses. Lord Denning said that the duty to act fairly "rests on them as on many other bodies although they are not judicial nor quasi-judicial but only administrative" (p. 399). Sachs L.J. said

> "It is ... not necessary to label the proceedings 'judicial,' 'quasi-judicial,' 'administrative,' 'investigatory'; it is the characteristics of the proceedings that matter, not the precise compartment or compartments into which they fall" (p. 402).

However, as will be seen later, there can be differences of opinion as to what fairness demands in a particular situation. The courts, in other words, may seem to extend the scope of judicial review by using an all-embracing test of fairness but nullify, at least to a large extent, the effect of that extension by the content that they give to the requirement of fairness in particular cases. One writer has claimed, for example, that decisions on the admission of Commonwealth immigrants subsequent to *Re H.K..(An Infant)* "have shown how easy it is for the courts to narrow the meaning of 'acting with fairness' to the point of extinction."[5]

Whether the courts talk of judicial functions or fairness, the decision to apply minimum rules of procedure to a particular situation is ultimately a question of policy, as was clearly recognised by Lord Wilberforce in *Malloch* v. *Aberdeen Corporation* [1971] 1 W.L.R. 1578, 1594. For this reason alone the fairness test is preferable since that approach emphasises the necessity of balancing various factors whereas the judicial function approach can well lend itself to "sterile conceptualism."

It must be remembered that, as was pointed out in Chapter 1, there is an ambiguity in the use by the courts of the notion of fairness. Sometimes it is used as a test to determine whether the rules of natural justice apply and, if so, what those rules require. Natural justice is equated with "fair play in action"; *Wiseman* v. *Borneman* [1971] A.C. 297, 309 *per* Lord Morris; or with the duty to act fairly; *Hoffman-La Roche (F) & Co.* v. *Secretary of State for Trade and Industry* [1975] A.C. 295, 368 *per* Lord Diplock. In *Hanson* v. *Church Commissioners for England* [1978] Q.B. 823, 837, Roskill L.J. said the question whether a tribunal had acted in accordance with the rules of natural justice, "put in simpler language simply means: did the committee act fairly. . . ."[6] In other cases, however, judges have clearly used the concept as distinct from natural justice and, in effect, asked two questions: is natural justice applicable to this situation? If the answer is no, then what, anyway, does fairness require? Such a distinction may perhaps be discerned in *R.* v. *Liverpool Corporation, ex p. Liverpool Taxi Owners Association* [1972] 2 Q.B. 299, which is discussed later in Chapter 6, and in *Pearlberg* v. *Varty* [1972] 1 W.L.R. 534 where Lord Pearson, in words quoted earlier in Chapter 1, contrasted tribunals exercising judicial or quasi-judicial functions, which are required to apply the rules of natural justice, with other bodies, exercising administrative or executive functions, where the courts may imply an obligation to act fairly. "Fairness," in this sense of a standard lower than that required by natural justice, is often used in cases such as those referred to at the beginning of this chapter where, for one reason or another, the courts are not prepared to imply that there is a right to a hearing, or only in an attenuated form. Sachs L.J. succinctly illustrated the use of fairness in this second sense when he referred to "that measure of natural justice [which] a reasonable man would regard as fair procedure in particular circumstances"; *Re Pergamon Press* [1971] Ch. 388, 402. In *R.* v. *Secretary of State for the Home Department, ex p. Hosenball* [1977] 1 W.L.R. 766, 781 Lord Denning M.R. emphasised that the duty to act fairly would often apply to a body which was not obliged, for one reason or another, to observe the normal rules of natural justice.[7] The idea of fairness may, on the other hand, provide, in the future, the justification for requiring a higher standard than that traditionally associated with natural justice, for example, the giving of reasons for a decision or the right to legal representation.[8] In the following paragraphs and chapters, as in the earlier chapters, the duty to act fairly will be considered where appropriate in discussing various aspects of the rules of natural justice.

II. The Applicability of the Rules

The person or body making the decision

Of the particular factors to which the courts advert in discussing the applicability of the rules of natural justice, the first is the person or body making the decision. That the rules of natural justice apply to proceedings in a court of law, for example, is hardly open to question. Litigation involving natural justice in court proceedings usually arises from differences over the content of the rules, not their applicability. Nonetheless, as was seen earlier, even the courts may, inadvertently, condemn unheard,[9] or reach decisions which appear to be infected with the possibility of bias.[10] It must not be thought that the courts can never act without first granting a hearing:

> "Many an ex parte injunction is granted against a person who has no notice of the charge and no opportunity of being heard;

and when in the Court of Appeal counsel assails the learning and competence of a trial judge, asserting his law to be unsound and his findings of fact unwarranted I am sure that he will not be deterred by the thought that the judge will not be heard in his own defence" (*Hounslow L.B.C.* v. *Twickenham Garden Developments* [1971] Ch. 233, 259 *per* Megarry J.).

Nineteenth-century authorities, quoted in Chapter 1, established that the rules of natural justice apply to domestic tribunals, professional disciplinary committees established by statute and similar bodies which resemble, to a greater or lesser extent, the courts in the way they deal with disputes. In this century it has been equally clearly established that the rules apply to decisions of trades unions' committees when disciplining members or dismissing officials; *Lawlor* v. *Union of Post Office Workers* [1965] Ch. 712.[11]

At the other end of the spectrum are ministerial decisions, to which the application of the rules requiring a hearing and an impartial tribunal involves difficulties. Whatever the uncertainty inherent in the concepts of "judicial," "legislative" and "executive" functions, Ministers exercise, in some circumstances, powers and duties not exercisable by other citizens. Whether, for example, a ministerial decision to authorise a particular instance of compulsory purchase is regarded as a "judicial," "quasi-judicial" or "executive" act, it has similarities to decisions regularly made in courts and tribunals. On the other hand, a Cabinet decision to extend the range of powers of compulsory purchase by introducing new legislation is an executive or political act of a kind very different in scope and importance. Similarly the decision to authorise in time of war the destruction of property worth millions of pounds cannot, realistically, be equated with the private citizen's right at common law to destroy property if that is necessary to protect lives or even other property.[12] For decisions of such a kind there is a special remedy available—in theory—in the form of ministerial responsibility and accountability to the Houses of Parliament.[13] In the case of Cabinet decisions, and those of elected assemblies such as the House of Commons and local authorities the ultimate remedy is "in the pressure of public opinion at the polling booth"; *Randall* v. *City of Northcote* (1910) 11 C.L.R. 100, 120, *per* Higgins J. The special difficulties presented by ministerial decisions will be discussed in Chapter 7.

In between the extremes of courts and Ministers, lie a number of other individuals and bodies, some already discussed, who or which may, to varying degrees, be subject to natural justice or a duty to act fairly—university vice-chancellors and examiners, the committees of clubs, disciplinary committees of trade unions, engineers, surveyors, architects, bishops. However, the cases dealing with these bodies can best be discussed in connection with other matters such as the gravity of the consequences of a tribunal's decision or the question of interference with property rights.

The gravity of the consequences

The gravity of the consequences of a decision is a further factor to which the courts have repeatedly referred. In holding that natural justice applied to a body of examiners which considered academic and non-academic matters the Divisional Court in *R.* v. *Aston University Senate, ex p. Roffey* [1969] 2 Q.B. 538 took account of the fact that "so much [was] at stake" (at p. 554). Again, in *Re Pergamon Press* [1971] Ch. 388, the Court of Appeal emphasised the gravity of the consequences of the publication of the inspectors' report. The courts are particularly likely to regard any decision as having grave consequences if it affects proprietary rights. Thus a committee which would otherwise be entitled to dismiss an employee without a hearing must observe the rules of natural justice if its decision involves the forfeiture of the employee's pension rights; *Fullbrook* v. *Berkshire Magistrates' Courts Committee* (1970) 69 L.G.R. 75; *R.* v. *Kent Police Authority, ex p. Gooden* [1971] 2 Q.B. 622; *infra*, p. 127. Similarly, expulsion from a club must follow the rules of natural justice, if such expulsion interferes with the property rights of the complainant.[14] Conversely,

> "The mere membership of [an] association, involving no real interest in property and no question of livelihood or reputation, does not seem . . . to be prima facie a matter in respect of which there is any strong claim to have the principles of natural justice, at any rate on motion" (*Gaiman* v. *National Association for Mental Health* [1971] Ch. 317, 336 *per* Megarry J.).

G, a member of a company limited by guarantee, was expelled by a resolution of the council of management; he failed in his claim that such expulsion should only have taken place after he had had a hearing. Megarry J. distinguished companies limited by shares where expulsion involves deprivation of valuable property rights.

The emphasis on proprietary rights must not be converted into the proposition that "the right to natural justice depends on the right to a few pieces of silver"; *John* v. *Rees* [1970] Ch. 345, 398 *per* Megarry J. In *Gaiman's* case, for example, the judge took into account, among other things, the existence of a set of statutory rules governing companies and their members and the duty of the council to the company as a whole which might require great speed whereas natural justice would involve delay.

The protection given by the courts to "rights" is not, of course, confined to property rights. The meaning the courts attach to "right" is obviously of great importance once interference with a right is made a serious element in assessing the applicability of natural justice. A good example of a very wide interpretation of "right" in this context is provided by the cases in which the courts talk of the "right to work" and protect that "right" by resort to natural justice, for example, where the complaint is against a union for expulsion from membership, or in some cases, where a person is refused membership of an association. These cases will be discussed in Chapter 6. In *R.* v. *Barnsley Metropolitan Borough, ex p. Hook* [1976] 1 W.L.R. 1052, which has been referred to earlier in this chapter, all three members of the Court of Appeal referred to the importance of the right to trade in the market because, without it, Hook could not "earn his living" or follow "his livelihood." However, as will also be seen in the following chapter, the right to work does not give an employee a right to be heard by his employer before dismissal. At common law the master-servant relationship has always been regarded as the classic case where natural justice does not apply. No doubt was thrown on the traditional rule in *Malloch* v. *Aberdeen Corporation* [1971] 1 W.L.R. 1578 although Lord Wilberforce warned, at p. 1595, that it must be used carefully and confined to pure master and servant cases where there is no element of public employment or service, no support by statute, nothing in the nature of an office or status which is capable of protection.[15]

In *Schmidt* v. *Secretary of State for Home Affairs* [1969] 2 Ch. 149, 170 Lord Denning M.R. suggested that the ambit of natural justice extended not merely to protect rights but any "legitimate expectation of which it would not be fair to deprive [a person] without hearing what he has to say."[16] Lord Denning illustrated what he meant by giving the example of an alien whose permission to stay in the United Kingdom had been revoked before the expiration of the time originally granted. In such circumstances he might well have had a right to a hearing because he had a legitimate expectation that he would be allowed to stay for the period originally granted. Schmidt, however, had no right to a hearing because he had been allowed to stay for the period originally granted. He had no legitimate expectation that permission would be granted to stay beyond that period. Schmidt might, justifiably, have felt that the consequences of the Secretary of State's decision were, for him, at least as serious as those for other litigants, such as the Aston students, where the gravity of the consequences involved an obligation to observe the rules of natural justice. But the courts, as we have already seen, are unwilling to interfere with the Home Secretary's exercise of his powers over aliens—or non-patrials. Whether the applicant is being refused permission to extend his stay or is being deported as an illegal entrant the attitude of the courts is best expressed in Lord Denning's words in *R.* v. *Governor of Pentonville Prison, ex p. Azam* [1974] A.C. 18, 31; the matter is one entirely "for the discretion of the Secretary of State. The statute [Immigration Act 1971] places no limit on his discretion. If he exercises it honestly, I do not think that the court can interfere with his discretion." The courts may impose in such circumstances a duty to act fairly—*R.* v. *Secretary of State for the Home Department, ex p. Hosenball* [1977] 1 W.L.R. 766, 781 *per* Lord Denning M.R.—but such a safeguard is of doubtful value.[17]

What degree of personal interest in the outcome of a decision can be regarded as giving rise to the type of "legitimate expectation" referred to by Lord Denning M.R. in *Schmidt* v. *Secretary of State for Home Affairs* [1969] 2 Ch. 149, is difficult to define. The question, who has a right to be heard before a decision is reached, is sometimes considered as one of *locus standi*; who has the right to challenge, by the particular remedy being sought, the decision which is being attacked. A landowner may be very happy with the grant of planning permission; can his neighbours or members of the public object? As will be seen in Chapter 8 the answer may vary with the remedy being sought.

An example of the distinction between a legal right or legitimate expectation, on the one hand, and personal disappointment at an unwelcome decision on the other, is provided by *Brown* v. *A.U.E.W.* [1976] I.C.R. 147. A and B had been candidates in a union election. A won but the executive council set the result aside and ordered a second election. A appealed to the union appeal body which upheld his contention that the executive council had no right to set aside the first result. In the meantime, however, the second ballot had been held, in which B obtained the greater number of votes. B claimed that he had a right to be heard by the appeal body before it reached its conclusion on the validity of the executive council's decision. Walton J. found, on the true construction of the rules, that the council had no power to set aside the first ballot, and hence the appeal body had no option but to reach the conclusion it did. However, the learned judge went on to say that in any case B's claim to a hearing would have failed because the dispute or *"lis"* was between A and the executive council. Although B, in one sense, had an interest in the outcome of the proceedings no legal right of his was at stake. He had entered the second election knowing that it might turn out to be a nullity.

In some cases a right to a hearing has been denied on the ground that the claim or interest or legitimate expectation is a mere "privilege" or "licence." This distinction is discussed later in Chapter 6.

The terms of any contract or other provision governing the power to decide

The final factor in Megarry J.'s catalogue was "the terms of any contract or other provision governing the power to decide." Whether the rules of natural justice, which would otherwise normally be applicable, can be excluded by contract, will be discussed later[18]; clearly they can by statute. Here contracts and statutes are being discussed in so far as their terms strengthen the argument that natural justice applies. In the simplest case where a contract or statute provides expressly that expulsion from a society or profession may only take place after an inquiry the courts will require the inquiry to comply with the rules of natural justice.[19] Will the courts imply a right to a hearing or to an impartial tribunal where the contract or statute is silent? Much turns on the factors already discussed and it may be, subject to the considerations of public policy discussed in Chapter 6, that the silence of a contract is sufficient to tip the balance against the applicability of natural justice although, if natural justice prima facie applies "in the process of construction the court will be slow to conclude that natural justice has been excluded"; *John* v. *Rees* [1970] Ch. 345, 400. In the case of statutes, as has already been seen in Chapter 1, silence does not imply the inapplicability of natural justice. On the contrary, "the justice of the common law will supply the omission of the legislature"; *Cooper* v. *Wandsworth Board of Works* (1863) 14 C.B.(N.S.) 180, 194 *per* Byles J.[20] In the next chapter some exceptional cases will be discussed where the common law will not imply natural justice into a statute, for example, because Parliament has itself defined the procedure to be followed in reaching a decision or because the decision is merely the preliminary to further proceedings to which natural justice is applicable.

Notes

[1] Report of the Committee on Ministers' Powers, Cmd. 4060 (1932), p. 76.

[2] See also *McInnes* v. *Onslow-Fane* [1978] 3 All E.R. 211; *Central Council for Education and Training in Social Work* v. *Edwards*, *The Times*, May 5, 1978. For a further discussion of architects, and other professional experts and students, see Chap. 7.

[3] *Supra*, p. 19.

[4] *Cf.* the similar approach in the case of the availability of certiorari, *e.g. R.* v. *Criminal Injuries Compensation Board, ex p. Lain* [1967] 2 Q.B. 864; *R.* v. *Hillingdon London Borough Council, ex p. Royco Homes* [1974] Q.B. 720.

[5] W. Birtles, "Natural Justice Yet Again" (1970) 33 M.L.R. 559, 561.

[6] "Common fairness, you can call it natural justice if you wish"; *R.* v. *Secretary of State for the Home Department, ex p. Hosenball* [1977] 1 W.L.R. 766, 784, *per* Geoffrey Lane L.J. Similarly, *Maxwell* v. *Department of Trade and Industry* [1974] Q.B. 523, 539 *per* Lawton L.J.

[7] See also *R.* v. *Birmingham City Justices, ex p. Chris Foreign Foods* (*Wholesalers*) [1970] 1 W.L.R. 1428; *R.* v. *Secretary of State for the Home Department, ex p. Mughal* [1974] Q.B. 313; *Kavanagh* v. *Chief Constable of Devon and Cornwall* [1974] Q.B. 624.

[8] *Supra*, p. 12.

[9] *Supra*, p. 60.

[10] *Supra*, pp. 33 *et seq.*

[11] See further, p. 129.

[12] *Burmah Oil Co. Ltd.* v. *Lord Advocate* [1965] A.C. 75, 99 *per* Lord Reid; 136 *per* Lord Hodson; 143 *per* Lord Pearce; 164 *per* Lord Upjohn.

[13] See *Liversidge* v. *Anderson* [1942] A.C. 206; *Gouriet* v. *Union of Post Office Workers* [1978] A.C. 435; *R.* v. *Secretary of State for Home Affairs, ex p. Hosenball* [1977] 1 W.L.R. 766, 783 *per* Lord Denning M.R. O Hood Phillips and Paul Jackson, *Constitutional and Administrative Law* (6th ed., 1978) Sweet & Maxwell, pp. 313 *et seq.*

[14] *Cassel* v. *Inglis* [1916] 2 Ch. 211. The absence of a proprietary right does not entail the absence of a right to an impartial hearing although it may affect the remedies available to protect such right; *Lee* v. *Showmen's Guild of Great Britain* [1952] 2 Q.B. 329 (C.A.).

[15] *Supra*, pp. 15 *et seq.*

[16] See also *McInnes* v. *Onslow Fane* [1978] 3 All E.R. 211, 218 *per* Megarry V.-C.

[17] *Supra*, n. 5.

[18] *Infra*, p. 125.

[19] *Labouchere* v. *Earl of Wharncliffe* (1879) 13 Ch.D. 346 (expulsion from club); *Lapointe* v. *L'Association de Bienfaisance et de Retraite de la Police de Montreal* [1906] A.C. 535 (P.C.) (loss of pension rights); *General Medical Council* v. *Spackman* [1943] A.C. 627 (striking doctor's name off register after "due inquiry." S. 33(2) of the Medical Act 1956 reversed *Spackman* but has itself been repealed by the Medical Act 1978 which establishes an elaborate new procedure for dealing with complaints of unprofessional conduct against medical practitioners); *Stevenson* v. *United Road Transport Union* [1977] 2 All E.R. 941 (C.A.).

[20] Recent examples of a similar attitude on the part of the House of Lords are provided by *Ridge* v. *Baldwin* [1964] A.C. 40; *Malloch* v. *Aberdeen Corporation* [1971] 1 W.L.R. 1578; *Atkinson* v. *United States Government* [1971] A.C. 197, 232 *per* Lord Reid. See also *Cmr. of Police* v. *Tanos* (1957) 98 C.L.R. 383, 396 *per* Dixon J.

Chapter 6

EXCLUSION AND NON-APPLICABILITY OF THE RULES OF NATURAL JUSTICE

By implication and, sometimes, expressly, the previous chapter indicated situations where the rules of natural justice do not apply: such as where the consequences of a decision are not serious in the eyes of the law; or where there are no property rights or other interests involved which the courts are prepared or able to protect. However, a number of situations require particular mention because they raise problems quite unconnected with the previous chapters. For example, in a situation where natural justice would normally be applicable, can a person waive his right to the protection afforded by the right to a hearing? Other cases referred to directly or impliedly earlier also merit particular attention here because of their topical importance. Thus, the exclusion of the rules of natural justice by contract from a situation where they would normally be applicable, for example, expulsion from a trades union, is a problem which links the subject-matters of this and the previous chapter.

I. The Nature of the Decision

In this section, it is proposed to discuss whether there are any general tests by which it can be ascertained that natural justice does not apply to a decision-making process before considering what special factors, such as waiver by a party of his rights, may exclude the operation of the rules from a situation to which, prima facie, they would apply.

Preliminary proceedings

In the previous chapter it was seen that any body making a decision affecting a party's rights or legitimate expectations must observe the rules of natural justice. Conversely a decision which does not affect rights, because, for example, it is a prelude to taking further proceedings in the course of which the party concerned will have an opportunity to be heard, will, very likely, not itself be subject to the requirements of natural justice, or only in a modified form. A fortiori, the decision by, for example, the responsible Minister or official to initiate the procedure necessary to reach a preliminary conclusion or to examine the existence of a prima facie case can be taken without first giving the person affected a hearing; *Wiseman* v. *Borneman* [1971] A.C. 297, 308 *per* Lord Reid; *Norwest Holst Ltd.* v. *Department of Trade* [1978] Ch. 201. *Balen* v. *I.R.C.* [1978] 2 All E.R. 1033.

The duties of persons charged with the responsibility of holding preliminary inquiries which may lead to further proceedings have been considered in a number of recent cases arising under legislation dealing with the collection of taxes and under the Companies Act 1948. In *Wiseman* v. *Borneman* [1971] A.C. 297 a taxpayer claimed the right to appear before a tribunal which, under section 28 of the Finance Act 1960, had to determine whether there was a prima facie case "for proceeding in the matter." The statute provided for the giving of notice to the taxpayer who could submit a written declaration which would be laid before the tribunal together with any counter-submission from the Commissioners of the Inland Revenue. The Court of Appeal and the House of Lords upheld the judgment of Pennycuick J. that the taxpayer had no right to appear before the tribunal. In the Court of Appeal great weight was attached to the distinction between a final determination of the rights of the parties and a decision that there is or is not a prima facie case. While the court decided as a matter of statutory interpretation that there was no right to an oral hearing it also indicated that had the tribunal been empowered to make a final determination it would have been more ready to imply into the statute a right to a hearing. Three members of the House of Lords deprecated the distinction drawn by the Court of Appeal since even a provisional finding of a prima facie case could have such serious consequences that justice required a hearing. In *Pearlberg* v. *Varty* [1972] 1 W.L.R. 534, the courts again held a taxpayer had no rights to a hearing—in this case under section 6(1) of the Income Tax Management Act 1964 which requires that before certain assessments are made a commissioner has to be "satisfied by an inspector or other officer ... that there are reasonable grounds for believing that tax has or may have been lost to the Crown owing to the ... wilful default or neglect of any person." While the Court of Appeal and the House of Lords both reached this decision as a matter of statutory interpretation, section 6 failing to make any reference to a right to a hearing while other sections expressly conferred such a right, Lord Denning expressed the view that there remains a difference between what he called a prima facie decision and a final decision: "In reaching a prima facie decision, there is a duty on any tribunal to act fairly; but fairness depends on the task in hand"; [1971] 1 W.L.R. 228, 737. Lord Hailsham, in the House of Lords, described the provisional nature of a decision as a "significant factor" in deciding whether there was a right to a hearing although, not, as stressed in *Wiseman* v. *Borneman*, the conclusive factor. In *Re Pergamon Press* [1971] Ch. 388, the Court of Appeal had to consider the case of inspectors holding an inquiry under the Companies Act 1948 which would result in the publication of a report which could be the prelude to the winding-up of the company or judicial proceedings. The directors of the company unsuccessfully claimed the right to see the transcripts of the evidence of witnesses adverse to them and a right to cross-examine witnesses. The court held, however, that the inspectors must act fairly:

> "Before they condemn or criticise a man they must give him a fair opportunity for correcting or contradicting what is said against him. They need not quote chapter and verse. An outline of the charge will usually suffice" (*per* Lord Denning M.R. at p. 400).[1]

Subsequent proceedings established that fairness did not require that the inspectors, after hearing the parties, should put their tentative conclusions to them for further comment before issuing their report; *Maxwell* v. *Department of Trade and Industry* [1974] Q.B. 523.[2]

In some instances preliminary decisions may—or must—be taken before the party concerned can be given any form of hearing, or warning, at all. The power of the courts to grant *ex parte* injunctions has been mentioned earlier.[3] Search warrants, for example under the Forgery Act 1913, s. 16, may issue without the party affected being heard; *R.* v. *Peterborough Justice, ex p. Hicks* [1977] 1 W.L.R. 1371. To give warning of proceedings under the Bankruptcy Acts 1914 may be undesirable as enabling a debtor to take steps to dispose of, or conceal his assets; *Burston Finance* v. *Godfrey* [1976] 1 W.L.R. 719, 725. In all these cases *ex parte* proceedings are a prelude to later proceedings in which both parties will have the opportunity to be heard. It is, therefore, all the more significant that the courts hedge about the exercise of this jurisdiction so carefully. In *Ansah* v. *Ansah* [1977] Fam. 138 the Court of Appeal discharged an *ex parte* injunction, issued by a county court judge, which was not subject to a precise time limit on its operation; Ormrod L.J. commented that "Orders made *ex parte* are anomalies in our system of justice" (p. 142). The President of the Family Division has expressed his concern at the growing number of applications for *ex parte* injunctions in his Division and emphasised that such injunctions should only be sought where there is real immediate danger of serious injury or irreparable damage; *Practice Direction* [1978] 1 W.L.R. 925.[4] Similarly the courts are reluctant to interpret a statute as giving them a power to act *ex parte*; *R.* v. *Havering Justices, ex p. Smith* [1974] 3 All E.R. 484.

Administrative officials, too, may require to be entitled to act without warning, for example to seize goods, whether contaminated food or pornographic magazines. The justification again is a practical one together with the existence of a right in subsequent proceedings to challenge the legality of the seizure. The Customs, for instance, may forfeit indecent or obscene books or articles which anyone attempts to import into the United Kingdom.[5] There is a right to challenge such seizure within a month, a right which, apparently, the Customs officials do not draw to the attention of the owner of the books or articles. Nor are they prepared to reveal the titles on a black list which has been compiled by the Commissioners of Customs and Excise.[6] The Post Office, likewise, may seize obscene material sent through the post.[7]

Does the fact that the individual or body conducting the preliminary hearing has the right to suspend the person charged from his post, or membership of an organisation, pending the final hearing, necessarily entail the application of the rules of natural justice? The Privy Council adverted to this question, among others, in *Furnell*

v. *Whangerei High Schools Board*, [1973] A.C. 660. Furnell, a teacher employed at a high school in New Zealand, claimed to be entitled to a hearing before a sub-committee which had been set up by the schools board to advise the board whether to proceed further with investigations into complaints relating to Furnell's conduct as a teacher. The method of dealing with such complaints was laid down by statute in what Lord Morris, delivering the opinion of the majority of the Judicial Committee described as a "multi-tiered and elaborate code." Only after a sub-committee had recommended that further action be taken on a complaint was it open to a schools board to proceed further. On receipt of an adverse report the board could suspend the teacher while the complaint was further investigated. At that stage the code required that the teacher concerned be given full details of the charge. The board might, after considering any explanation or statement from the teacher, decide to take no further action, deal with the charge itself, or refer the matter to the director general who might, as in Furnell's case, decide on a hearing before the teachers' disciplinary board. The majority of the Privy Council thought that natural justice did not involve a right to be heard before the sub-committee because that stage of the process operated in the teachers' interests, protecting them, for example, from complaints based on idle tittle-tattle. In comparison with the inspectors in *Re Pergamon Press Ltd.* (*supra*), the sub-committee "do not either condemn or criticise." Viscount Dilhorne, with whom Lord Reid concurred, thought that natural justice did require a right to be heard since, under the regulations as he interpreted them, the board might in reliance on the sub-committee's report deal with the charge itself, under a regulation (reg. 6) containing no provision for a hearing or investigation. While the teacher in such a case would have had an opportunity to comment on the findings of the sub-committee "the opportunity to make a statement and to give an explanation after condemnation by a sub-committee is, where the board deals with the case under regulation 6 analogous to a prisoner being asked whether he has anything to say before he is sentenced." The risk of temporary suspensions following an adverse report did not, in the view of the majority, import a duty to grant a hearing because although "suspension may involve hardship" it was not intended as a penalty (p. 682). Viscount Dilhorne, on the other hand, thought that this was a sufficiently serious consequence to require the sub-committee to grant a hearing. In *Lewis* v. *Heffer* [1978] 1 W.L.R. 1061 the Court of Appeal expressly held that the right to a hearing depends on the distinction between suspension as a penalty and, on the other hand, as a temporary measure; what the court called "good administration," while a complaint is investigated. As *Furnell's* case shows, judges may differ on where to draw the line between the two categories.

There is no right to a hearing where there is not even a provisional decision or preliminary proceedings but merely the preparation of evidence to be used later in the making of a decision. That distinction was made, and illustrated, in *R.* v. *St. Lawrence's Hospital Statutory Visitors* [1953] 1 W.L.R. 1158. Under the Mental Deficiency Act 1913 the decision to continue the detention of persons sent to mental hospitals under court orders was made by a board of control which, in reaching its conclusions, had to take into account reports from visitors who were required to interview patients and give an opinion on the appropriateness of their detention. The mother of one patient sought certiorari to quash the report of visitors who had refused to allow her, accompanied by counsel, to be present when they interviewed her daughter. The Divisional Court rejected her application on the ground that the visitors' report was merely a report of their opinion, no more nor less than a piece of evidence. The board was also required to take into account reports from doctors submitted at the request of patients' relatives. The principle in the *St. Lawrence Hospital* case is unassailable. Witnesses cannot be expected to grant a hearing before giving evidence to which a party objects. Evidence is, in a sense, necessarily *ex parte*. The duty of the tribunal is to reach a decision after hearing the evidence and comments on it and other material adduced by the applicant or defendant or aggrieved party, as the case may be. Whether, however, a report of the kind in this case should be regarded merely as evidence is open to doubt. It may be assumed that the board attached special weight to it. Precisely because it was a report of the visitors' opinion it should, arguably, only have been made in circumstances which ensured that they were in full possession of all relevant facts—and in circumstances in which they appeared to be so to the parties concerned.

Right or privilege?

There is authority for the proposition that a body need not observe the rules of natural justice where its decision, although final, relates not to a right but to a privilege or licence. This distinction is popular with the courts when they wish to narrow the scope of natural justice.[8] It is, however, an unattractive distinction.[9] First, "privilege" or "liberty" or "licence" suggest unimportant matters. They are appropriate terms perhaps, in Hohfeldian analysis, to distinguish the right *stricto sensu* of a farmer to walk across his own land as opposed to the licence which he may grant to a hiker to sit and picnic on that land. To use such terms when considering whether an applicant is entitled to a hearing before being admitted to a body or granted a certificate without which he cannot follow his trade or profession, is to conceal the gravity of what the court is doing. Secondly, even if the granting of permission to enter a country or practise a profession is a discretionary matter so that the official or tribunal is under no duty to grant permission to any particular applicant—and therefore, in Hohfeldian terms, no particular applicant has a right to the permission he seeks—that does not conclude the separate question, has an applicant for such permission a right to have his claim considered according to certain minimum standards of procedure? Thirdly, the distinction is not one that can be drawn in advance of a judicial decision that a particular claim falls on one side of the line or the other. This is not to say that in individual cases the judicial reluctance to apply the rules of natural justice cannot be explained or justified by considerations of the kind discussed elsewhere in this chapter, without recourse to the unsatisfactorily vague test of "privilege or right."

In a number of recent cases the courts have revived the distinction between "privilege" and "right" and, while denying the protection of natural justice in the former category of claims, have emphasised that in such cases applications must be considered fairly. Fairness, it seems, is a standard which varies with the importance of the issue at stake, and the court's view of the social value of the privilege which is being claimed. In *Breen* v. *A.E.U.* [1971] 2 Q.B. 175, 191, for example, Lord Denning said "If a man seeks a privilege to which he has no particular claim—such as an appointment to some post or other—then he can be turned away without a word." He went on to say that nonetheless statutory and in some cases domestic bodies must act fairly and this may involve a hearing—although it is not entirely clear from the judgment of the Master of the Rolls whether this duty applies where an initial application is being considered or only where an existing privilege is being terminated. In the earlier case of *R.* v. *Gaming Board for Great Britain, ex p. Benaim and Khaida* [1970] 2 Q.B. 417[10] it was not a right to a hearing that was at issue, but what that right entailed. The applicants, who had been refused a gaming licence by the Board, sought, unsuccessfully, an order of certiorari claiming that natural justice gave them the right to know the sources of the evidence on which the Board acted. Lord Denning, at p. 430, expressed distrust of distinctions between judicial and administrative proceedings but only after himself drawing a distinction of no greater value or clarity when he said (at p. 429):

> "It is an error to regard [the applicants] as having any right of which they are being deprived.... What they are really seeking is a privilege—almost, I might say, a franchise—to carry on gaming for profit, a thing never hitherto allowed in this country."

What fairness or natural justice demands may vary from case to case; the law is not, however, likely to be helped by reliance on such imprecise distinctions as that between right and privilege. A licence to run a casino is as closely connected with the right to work as membership of a trade union. It is difficult to avoid the suspicion that the Court of Appeal felt that gambling, if no longer illegal, was an activity to be viewed with disfavour by the law. On the other hand, however unattractive the dichotomy between right and privilege, the actual decision may be regarded as a reasonable attempt at justice where there is an acute conflict of private interest and public policy.[11]

Some support for the view advanced above, that the court in *Ex p. Benaim and Khaida* was, in effect, refusing to lend its assistance to a gambler because his livelihood was, although no longer illegal, not one of which the law approved, may be found in *R.* v. *Liverpool Corporation, ex p. Liverpool Taxi Fleet Operators' Association* [1972] 2 Q.B. 299. Under the relevant legislation Liverpool Corporation could "licence to ply for hire ... such a number of hackney coaches ... as they [thought] fit." After discussions with the taxi owners the corporation undertook not to increase the number of licences until legislation had been introduced to regulate minicabs. The corporation was advised its undertaking was legally ineffective and, without further consultation with the taxi owners, resolved to increase the number of hackney licences. Since a licence, once issued, could be freely sold, an increase in the number of licences would reduce the resale value of existing licences. The taxi owners successfully sought prohibition to prevent the corporation acting on its resolution. The Court of Appeal, instead of rejecting the application by reference to privileges and licences, upheld the owners' contention because fairness demanded a hearing when the applicants would be so greatly affected by the decision. This decision did not, however, raise the question whether the taxi owners—unlike the gamblers—had a right to know what evidence, if any, was before the corporation.

The effect of contract: membership of organisations

Just as the applicant to a statutory body for a licence has, in the past, often been held not to be entitled to have his claim considered in accordance with natural justice, so other decisions have denied the right to a fair hearing by a domestic tribunal and professional bodies in the absence of a contractual link between the applicant and the body making the decision. A typical example is afforded by the facts of *Byrne* v. *Kinematograph Renters Society* [1958] 1 W.L.R. 762. The defendant organisation decided to stop hiring out films to B, a cinema owner. B claimed that such a decision could only be reached by a process which satisfied the requirements of natural justice. B had no knowledge either of the existence of the committee of the KRS which decided to refuse to do further business with him, or of the existence of inspectors upon whose reports the committee acted. Although, according to the *All England Law Reports*, Harman J. found that the process by which the KRS decided whether or not to continue doing business with cinema owners was as "about as far from what a lawyer would consider a judicial one as can be imagined" ([1958] 2 All E.R. 579, 584), he held that there was no obligation to observe natural justice in the absence of a contractual link and since B was unaware of the disciplinary committee's existence it was impossible to imply a contract involving submission to the jurisdiction by B in consideration of the KRS promising to observe natural justice when deciding whether to cease trading with him.

Although making the right to a fair hearing dependent on the existence of a contract provides one explanation why, for example, workers applying for jobs or students seeking university places have no right to be heard before their applications are refused it also gives an undesirable power to domestic bodies exercising monopolistic control over, for example, entry into professions. In *Nagle* v. *Feilden* [1966] 2 Q.B. 633 the Court of Appeal went a long way to providing a solution by invoking public policy. N, a woman racehorse trainer, had been refused a licence by the stewards of the Jockey Club in pursuance of a general policy of refusing licences to women trainers—the absurdity of the rule in practice being shown by the fact that the stewards would grant licences to women trainers' head lads. The stewards unsuccessfully sought to strike out, as showing no cause of action, N's claim for a declaration that the stewards' policy was contrary to public policy. Lord Denning, while recognising that "if a man applies to join a social club and is blackballed he has no cause of action," continued: "but we are not considering a social club. We are considering an association which exercises a virtual monopoly in an important field of human activity."[12] Cases which had been decided on a contractual basis were, the Master of the Rolls said, decided on a legal fiction:

> "The true ground of jurisdiction in all these cases is a man's right to work ... a man's right to work at his trade or profession is just as important to him as, perhaps more important than, his rights of property. Just as the courts will intervene to protect his rights of property so they will also intervene to protect his right to work."[13]

Once it is conceded that the courts will control the grounds on which bodies such as the Jockey Club may refuse to grant licences, it surely follows that the procedure for the consideration of applications is subject to judicial control.

The position of applicants for licences has been recently considered by Megarry V.-C. in *McInnes* v. *Onslow-Fane* [1978] 3 All E.R. 211. The learned Vice-Chancellor suggested that natural justice or fairness apply to initial applications as to forfeiture of existing licences or membership rights.[14] But, whereas in the latter case there is a right to a hearing, in the former case the body considering the application need not grant a hearing although it must "reach an honest conclusion, without bias, and not in pursuance of any capricious policy" (p. 219). This duty does not entail an obligation to give reasons. The learned judge also expressed the view that

> "The courts must be slow to allow any implied obligation to be fair to be used as a means of bringing before the courts for review honest decisions of bodies exercising jurisdiction over sporting and other activities which those bodies were far better fitted to judge than the courts. This is so even where those bodies are concerned with the means of livelihood of those taking part in those activities" (p. 223).

In *Stinato* v. *Auckland Boxing Association* [1978] N.Z.L.R. 1, the New Zealand Court of Appeal held that an applicant for a licence to box professionally had a right to a hearing. The facts of that case were somewhat unusual and might, in any case, come into a third category described by Megarry V.-C., "the expectation cases" where the applicant has no existing right but an expectation, in the light of previous events, that his application will be successful. Stinato held a licence as a professional boxer. He was summoned before the governing body of the sport on a charge of misconduct. The governing body then realised that his licence would shortly expire by lapse of time and it decided to abandon the complaint of misconduct and simply refuse to grant a new licence. The Court of Appeal held that proof of such allegations would give the court jurisdiction to intervene on the ground that the boxer was entitled to an opportunity of answering the charge but not necessarily to an oral hearing. However, in the exercise of its discretion the court refused to grant relief.

The main obstacle to suggesting that applications for membership or the grant of a licence are subject to natural justice is presented by the decision of the House of Lords in *Faramus* v. *Film Artistes Association* [1964] A.C. 925, which does not appear to have been cited in *McInnes*' case. One of the rules of the association provided that no person who had been convicted of a criminal offence would be eligible for membership of the association. F, although a convicted person, was admitted to membership. When his convictions came to light, the union maintained he was not and never had been a member of the union, a contention upheld by the House of Lords; although the form of election had been gone through, F had never been validly elected because he lacked an essential qualification for membership. Lord Evershed denied that F had in the circumstances any right to a hearing:

> "The case is in no sense analagous to the case of rules applicable to someone whose contract of membership is being terminated, where it may well be that for their validity the rules must make provision to enable such a person at any rate to have a proper opportunity to put his case . . ." (p. 941),

or, as Lord Pearce succinctly stated the law: "Cases of expulsion without a fair hearing come in a different category from cases of refusal of an applicant for membership" (p. 947).

This decision does not establish that there can never be a right to be heard, or an opportunity to answer a charge, before being refused a licence or membership of a body. Nor does it establish that bodies considering applications need not act fairly. Indeed the House of Lords indicated that, but for the statutory immunity of trades unions they would have been prepared to intervene on the ground of unreasonable restraint of trade. Dicta suggesting that natural justice does not apply to "application cases" are also to be found in *Weinberger* v. *Inglis* [1919] A.C. 606. A member of the Stock Exchange who was not re-elected by the committee unsuccessfully sought relief in the courts. The majority of the House of Lords held that W had had a fair hearing before the committee reached its decision and that the committee had not taken into account matters other than those brought to W's attention. Therefore it was not necessary to express a final decision on the question whether natural justice applies to applications for membership. If it does it may well be true, as was pointed out in the Court of Appeal, that the remedies available may differ from those where someone's existing proprietary rights have been infringed.

The rights of applicants seeking membership of organisations or other "privileges" are, of course, in many instances now protected by the Sex Discrimination Act 1975 and the Race Relations Act 1976. Both Acts, for example, forbid discrimination in admitting members to unions on the grounds of race or sex; Sex Discrimination Act 1975, s. 12; Race Relations Act 1976, s. 11. Membership of social clubs falls within the Race Relations Act, although discrimination is permissible in some cases on the ground of race but not of colour; sections 25 and 26. The Sex Discrimination Act 1975 does not, on the other hand, apply to social clubs.[15]

Expulsion from an organisation or club comes, in Lord Pearce's words quoted above, in a different category from refusals of admission to membership. Natural justice will apply, as was seen in the previous chapter, where expulsion involves interference with property rights. In other cases the right to a hearing before an impartial tribunal will depend on contract and, possibly, considerations of public policy. Where the courts construe the relevant contract as expressly conferring a right to a fair hearing there will be no difficulty: *Stevenson* v. *United Road Transport Union* [1977] 2 All E.R. 941. A contract may, however, be silent on the right to a hearing or may expressly provide for expulsion from an organisation without a hearing. In the former case it is hard to see why silence should be of any great importance in deciding whether a right to a hearing exists. As in the case of a statute[16] it is the very gravity of the dispute which imports a right into a document which is silent about the right. Difficulties may arise if the question is treated as one of implying a term into a contract, as was done in *Lawlor* v. *Union of Post Office Workers* [1965] Ch. 712, where Ungoed Thomas J. accepted counsel's contention that

> "the rules of natural justice can only be implied in a contract (i) if they are not inconsistent with what is expressed in the contract and (ii) if they are necessary to carry out and therefore must have been intended by the parties, and not merely if the rules of natural justice make the carrying out of the contract more convenient and might have been included if the parties had thought about it."

Although the learned judge in *Lawlor's* case did feel able to imply a right to a hearing the danger of this narrow approach is illustrated by the refusal of the majority of the Court of Appeal in *Abbott* v. *Sullivan* [1952] 1 K.B. 181, to imply a term that a disciplinary committee of a union would not expel a member without a hearing. The rules of natural justice should not be regarded as rules whose incorporation into a contract has to be proved but as "terms implied by the law" which can be implied "although it is by no means clear that the parties would have agreed to incorporate them in their contract . . . [they] are, in truth, simply duties prima facie imposed by law on the parties to particular kinds of contracts."[17]

Recognition that the implication of a right to a fair hearing is a matter of public policy and does not have to satisfy the strict tests normally applied to implied terms is important when the converse question arises, can the rules of natural justice be excluded by express contractual terms. As the writer quoted in the previous paragraph says, following his comments on the nature of terms implied by law, "a term implied in law can sometimes be excluded by a definite contrary agreement."[18] It does not follow that courts must, or should, allow parties the same freedom to exclude the rules of natural justice as to settle the purchase price or delivery date of a motor car. Whether ultimately public policy does allow the waiving of a right to a fair hearing the contract must be construed "and in the process of construction, the court will be slow to conclude that natural justice has been excluded"; *per* Megarry J. in *John* v. *Rees* [1970] Ch. 345, 400. If, however strictly construed, a contract does purport to exclude the rules of natural justice the question of public policy arises, a question to which so far the courts have not had to give a final answer. In *Russell* v. *Duke of Norfolk* [1949] 1 All E.R. 109 all members of the Court of Appeal held that the hearing conducted by the stewards of the Jockey Club before they withdrew Russell's licence accorded with the rules of natural justice. Denning L.J., nonetheless, discussed the validity of contractual terms purporting to exclude natural justice and concluded that they were probably contrary to public policy, at least in some cases.[19] Tucker L.J., on the other hand, was prepared to hold that under the rules the stewards could withdraw R's licence without a hearing while Asquith L.J. refrained from expressing a view. More recently, in *Edwards* v. *SOGAT* [1971] Ch. 354, where the Court of Appeal was concerned with the damages to which a workman who had been, admittedly, wrongfully expelled from his union was entitled, Lord Denning denied that a union "can give itself by its rules an unfettered discretion to expel a man or to withdraw his membership. The reason lies in the man's right to work" (p. 695).[20] Sachs J.J. expressed similar views, relying by analogy on cases in which the courts have "protected a man against any unreasonable restraint on his right to work even if he has bargained that right away" (p. 700). The dicta of Lord Denning and Sachs L.J. have been criticised as an "extraordinary revival of the judicial desire to control union rule books."[21] Other writers have taken a different view of Lord Denning's frequently expressed view about the impossibility of excluding the rules of natural justice by a contractual term.[22] In terms which might have been regarded as unexceptional, the Industrial Relations Act 1971, s. 65(8) and (9) removed any doubt about the possibility of trades unions and associations of employers expelling members without a fair hearing. But subsequent legislation has ensured that in these cases, as in those of other bodies whose jurisdiction is based on contract—however nominally—the position is governed by the common law, whatever it may be.[23] In addition the TUC has established an Independent Review Committee to which individuals who have been expelled from unions (or refused admission) may have recourse. The committee only deals with complaints where membership of a union is a condition of employment, *i.e.* where a closed shop operates. As Sir Otto Kahn-Freund had pointed out,[24] this arrangement is defective first in that expulsion where there is no closed shop may equally be a serious matter for a worker and secondly in that the impartiality of the committee is, however wrongly, likely to be doubted by those who have recourse to it.

Professional expertise

The courts cannot usefully be expected to interfere where the issue is one of professional expertise, for example, a doctor deciding a question of treatment or a university examiner assessing the merit of a thesis.[25] In such cases, in the words of Megarry J. quoted earlier, the safeguard for the parties is to be found in "the position of independence and skill" of the decision maker; *Hounslow London Borough Council* v. *Twickenham Garden Developments* [1971] Ch. 233,

259. Moreover, as the learned judge also pointed out, an architect (or doctor, or lawyer) has to take a large number of decisions daily, at short notice, many of them trivial. It would be impossible, he said, to distinguish between trivial decisions where natural justice did not apply, and important ones where it did.

Nonetheless, in a sense, the law does, and must do, this on occasions. Not every decision taken by a doctor is purely a medical one, not every decision taken by a university an academic one. Which, for example, of two patients ought to be allowed to take advantage of the only kidney machine in a particular hospital: the mother of a large family or a distinguished scientist? If time allows in such a case it is arguable that the final decision can and should be "judicialised." In the field of mental health there exists a precedent in the Mental Health Review Tribunals, created by the Mental Health Act 1959. These bodies owe their existence to the feeling that deprivation of liberty is too serious a matter to be left entirely in the hands of the doctors. Recent government proposals have even suggested that treatment of mentally sick patients should, in certain circumstances, be undertaken only after consulting a "multi-disciplinary panel," including a layman among its members.[26] Medical decisions may affect the financial rights of individuals too as well as the right to freedom. In *R.* v. *Kent Police Authority, ex p. Godden* [1971] 2 Q.B. 622, G, a police officer had been examined by the medical officer of his force who concluded that G was mentally ill. A consultant reached the same diagnosis after examining G and taking into account the report of the police doctor and the report on G prepared by a senior police officer. G's own consultant found no evidence of insanity. The local authority took steps to have G certified as permanently disabled under the police pensions regulations, choosing for that purpose the police doctor who originally examined G. The Court of Appeal held, *inter alia*, that mandamus should issue to compel the production to G's medical advisers of the reports which the consultant nominated by the police force had seen. The court, not surprisingly, assumed that natural justice does not apply to the doctor–patient relationship but, in the words of Lord Denning M.R.,

> "The decisions leading to compulsory retirement are of a judicial character and must conform to the rules of natural justice. When

a medical practitioner is making a decision which may lead to a man being compulsorily retired, he must act fairly. He is not acting simply as doctor to patient.... He is doing something which affects the man's whole future" (p. 669).[27]

Disciplinary proceedings

In a number of cases the courts have suggested that the rules of natural justice do not apply to decisions taken in the course of disciplinary proceedings. The limits of this concept are unclear and it has found favour with the courts at times when they have been reluctant generally to invoke natural justice.[28] In *Buckoke* v. *G.L.C.* [1971] Ch. 655, which was concerned with the availability of the injunction as a remedy against a domestic tribunal, and not directly with natural justice, the Court of Appeal expressed doubts about the correctness of cases on disciplinary proceedings which had been decided before *Ridge* v. *Baldwin*. More recently, in *R.* v. *Hull Prison Board of Visitors, ex p. St. Germain* [1979] 2 W.L.R. 42, a prisoner successfully sought leave to apply for certiorari to quash a decision of the board of visitors on the ground of breach of natural justice. The Divisional Court had held that certiorari did not lie to such a body, a decision in keeping with judicial reluctance to interfere in the running of prisons.[29] The reason for that is, no doubt, largely to be found in the fear expressed by Lord Denning M.R.: "If the courts were to entertain actions by disgruntled prisoners, the governor's life would be made intolerable"; *Becker* v. *Home Office* [1972] 2 Q.B. 407, 418. However, in *Ex p. St. Germain* the Court of Appeal emphasised the gravity of the matters dealt with by the board of visitors and the severity of the punishment they could award. Their function could easily be distinguished from the disciplinary role of the prison governor—on which matter the court refrained from expressing a final view. Shaw L.J. emphasised that the rights of a citizen, however circumscribed by a penal sentence or otherwise, must always be the concern of the courts unless their jurisdiction was clearly excluded by some statutory provision. The courts were in general the ultimate custodians of the rights and liberties of the subject whatever his status and however attenuated those rights and liberties might be as the result of some punitive or other process.

Master and servant, unfair dismissal

Whatever the uncertainty of the applicability of natural justice in some areas "the law regarding master and servant is not in doubt": *Ridge* v. *Baldwin* [1964] A.C. 40, 65 *per* Lord Reid. At common law the servant can "in the ordinary course of things"[30] be validly dismissed at any time without a hearing.[31] If the dismissal is in breach of contract the master is liable in damages in an action in contract. The position is thus the reverse of that discussed above in connection with contractual terms regulating membership of association where, at common law, expulsion without a hearing may well be invalid even if the contract has provided for such summary expulsion. Here dismissal is effective even if the contract has provided for dismissal only after a hearing as is shown by *Taylor* v. *National Union of Seamen* [1967] 1 W.L.R. 532. T was both a member and servant of the union. He was dismissed from his position and expelled from the union after a hearing which, contrary to the rules of his union, was not held in accordance with the principles of natural justice. Ungoed-Thomas J. granted a declaration that the expulsion from membership of the union was invalid but held that he could not grant a declaration with regard to T's dismissal from his paid post. Where, however, a servant is dismissed not by his employer but by a third party to whom that power has been delegated then a dismissal in breach of natural justice will be a nullity if that third party has failed to observe the required procedure: *Stevenson* v. *United Road Transport Union* [1977] 2 All E.R. 941.

While the law is in no doubt as to the rights of a servant it shows considerable doubt in deciding who is a servant. The existing case law has been described by Lord Wilberforce as "illogical and even bizarre"; *Malloch* v. *Aberdeen Corporation* [1971] 1 W.L.R. 1578, 1595. Thus a consultant has been held to be a servant dismissible without a hearing,[32] while a junior doctor employed in a hospital has been entitled to a hearing.[33] Professors, as servants, have been held dismissible without a hearing[34] while, as will be seen later in Chapter 7, students, because of the gravity of the consequences, at least in some cases, may be entitled to a hearing before being required to withdraw from a university.[35] The exclusion of a right to a hearing is, in Lord Wilberforce's words in *Malloch's* case, to be confined to "'pure master and servant cases' ... cases in which there is no element of public employment or service, no support by statute, nothing in the nature of an office or a status which is capable of protection." The most important modern decision to apply this distinction is *Vine* v. *National Dock Labour Board* [1957] A.C. 488 where the House of Lords granted a declaration that the dismissal of a docker in a manner not authorised by the statutory provisions regulating the employment of dockers was invalid. Viscount Kilmuir expressly distinguished what he called "the ordinary master and servant case" where a wrongful dismissal, whether summarily or after insufficient notice, is effective to terminate the contract.[36]

The difficulty inherent in distinguishing "pure master and servant cases" from those involving some element of an office or status is illustrated by *Malloch's* case itself. M, a schoolmaster, had been dismissed without a hearing by Aberdeen Corporation. Under the relevant statutory provisions he could be dismissed at pleasure.[37] Nonetheless, three members of the House were able to imply into the legislative scheme a right to a hearing before dismissal.[38] Of the three, Lord Wilberforce alone expressly recognised that the case was "to be tested broadly on arguments of public policy and not to be resolved on narrow verbal distinctions." Such an approach can hardly be criticised on the ground that it will increase uncertainty when the law as it stands has been described as endowed "with a kaleidoscopic unpredictability."

Even where an employee could, normally, be dismissed without the rules of natural justice being observed, the courts will require a hearing if the dismissal also involves interference with a proprietary interest of the worker such as forfeiture of pension and superannuation rights; *Fullbrook* v. *Berkshire Magistrates' Courts Committee* (1971) 69 L.G.R. 75.

The dismissal of a servant without a hearing will not be invalidated by the rules of natural justice but it will almost certainly be "unfair" under legislative provisions which trace their origins to the Industrial Relations Act 1971, s. 22, and are now to be found in the Employment Protection (Consolidation) Act 1978, s. 54. There is no express reference to the need for a hearing in any of the relevant statutes. The current law, contained in section 57 of the 1978 Act requires that the employer satisfies certain requirements if he is to discharge the burden of showing that the dismissal was fair and then provides that

> "the determination of the question whether the dismissal was fair or unfair, having regard to the reason shown by the employer, shall depend on whether the employer can satisfy the tribunal that in the circumstances (having regard to equity and the substantial merits of the case) he acted reasonably in treating it as a sufficient reason for dismissing the employee."

To suggest that such a provision imports the right to a hearing before dismissal might be thought to involve an extremely strained interpretation of the words. The section seems to envisage simply reasonableness in relation to the gravity of the conduct. However, the Code of Practice issued by the Secretary of State under section 3 of the 1971 Act[39] includes a right to a hearing in its elaborate rules regulating the procedure to be followed in dismissing an employee and the right has been recognised, and its limits defined in a number of decisions in the last seven years.

The importance of the right to be heard before dismissal was established by the decision of *Earl* v. *Slater & Wheeler* (*Airlyne*) *Ltd.* [1972] I.C.R. 508. Despite dicta which have suggested that "whatever the circumstances, whatever the employee is alleged to have done ... it is always necessary that he should be afforded some opportunity of explaining himself,"[40] it is now clearly established that there are circumstances justifying dismissal without a hearing, for example where an employee's conduct was of such a nature that whatever the explanation his continued employment was not in the interests of the business or where an employee was so clearly incapable of performing his duties that warnings and opportunities to improve would be of no benefit to the employee and might constitute an unfair burden on the business; *James* v. *Waltham Holy Cross U.D.C.* [1973] I.C.R. 398; approved by the Court of Appeal in *Retarded Children's Aid Society Ltd.* v. *Day* [1978] I.C.R. 437. In such circumstances it is irrelevant to inquire about the adequacy of an inquiry or hearing which may, in fact, have preceded dismissal; *Alidair Ltd.* v. *Taylor* [1978] I.C.R. 445. In that case, which concerned the dismissal of an airline pilot on the ground of incompetence, Lord Denning quoted with approval from the judgment of Bristow J. in the Employment Appeal Tribunal,

> "There are activities in which the degree of professional skill which must be required is so high, and the potential consequences of the smallest departure of that high standard are so serious, that one failure to perform in accordance with those standards is enough to justify dismissal. The passenger-carrying airline pilot, the scientist operating the nuclear reactor, the chemist in charge of research into the possible effect of, for example, thalidomide, the driver of the Manchester to London express, the driver of an articulated lorry full of sulphuric acid, are all in the situation in which one failure to maintain the proper standard of professional skill can bring about a major disaster. In this context, even though it is easy to criticise the way in which the inquiry was held and the contents of the letters which preceded and followed it, taking all the circumstances into consideration, and having regard to equity and the substantial merits of the case, we do not consider Captain Dadd, on behalf of the employers, acted unreasonably in treating Captain Taylor's error of judgement as a sufficient reason to dismiss him" ([1977] I.C.R. 446, 453).

The fairness of the dismissal is not determined by whether any necessary hearing slavishly followed the letter of the Code of Practice; *Lewis Group* v. *Wiggins* [1973] I.C.R. 335. Nor, since natural justice is, *ex hypothesi* inapplicable, can the fairness of the dismissal be determined by whether the procedure followed before dismissal corresponded to what, in other circumstances, natural justice would require. Nonetheless reference is sometimes expressly made to these requirements, for example in *Bentley Engineering Co. Ltd.* v. *Mistry* [1978] I.R.L.R. 436 where Slynn J. discussed in terms of natural justice the adequacy of the hearing given to an employee before dismissal and held that a tribunal was entitled to hold unfair a dismissal which followed a hearing at which the employee had had no chance to cross-examine the person whose complaint initiated the dismissal procedure. In *Ellis* v. *Inner London Education Authority*, *The Times*, November 7, 1978 a number of teachers alleged that their dismissal had been unfair because, contrary to natural justice, the same official had initiated the proceedings before the disciplinary tribunal and acted as adviser to the tribunal. Kilner Brown J., however, referred to *Ward* v. *Bradford Corporation* (1972) 70 L.G.R. 27 and held that the tribunal had acted with scrupulous fairness so that there was no merit in the teachers' case. Clearly a dismissal procedure which accorded fully with natural justice would, in any event, be fair. To argue, however, that a dismissal after a procedure which does not so agree is necessarily unfair is to confuse two distinct legal concepts.

II. Practical Considerations

Of all the grounds for excluding the rules of natural justice none is more vague than that of "practical considerations." Apart from any question of whether applicants are seeking a "licence" or a "privilege," the number of applicants may preclude a hearing on the ground of practical impossibility as, for example, in the case of applications for places in universities.[41] But even in such situations would the courts, in the light of *Nagle* v. *Feilden* (*supra*), refuse to intervene if, for instance, a student alleged a particular university automatically rejected all applicants from public schools? Might the courts not hold that "fairness" or public policy required that each case was properly examined on its merits and even, in extreme cases, that a fair decision could only be reached after interviewing a particular applicant? In *Central Council for Education and Training in Social Work* v. *Edwards*, *The Times*, May 5, 1978, Slade J. held that an educational institution, in considering an application for admission as a student, was under no obligation to act judicially. Such an institution was not bound to give a student a hearing or to assign reasons for refusing to admit him. He also held that, whether or not there was a general duty to act fairly if an institution decided to interview a student, there *was* such a duty on the facts before him because the polytechnic was a publicly-funded educational establishment; the inability to obtain a certificate of qualification in social work would seriously affect the applicant's professional career and the polytechnic had published details of its selection procedures, a copy of which had been supplied to him when he applied for the course.

Again the large numbers involved may explain why the courts

have assumed that local authorities are under no duty to grant a hearing before deciding to grant or withhold planning permission; *Gaiman* v. *National Association for Mental Health* [1971] Ch. 317, 333 *per* Megarry J.[42] On the other hand, natural justice, or fairness, applies to such decisions to the extent that a party with an interest in the granting or withholding of permission must not participate in the decision; *R.* v. *Hendon R.D.C., ex p. Chorley* [1933] 2 K.B. 696.

Practical considerations involving numbers and the nature of the cases are given as the explanation for, and justification of, the procedure followed by the Parole Board which has been subject to criticism by writers.[43] The number of prisoners whose cases have to be considered results in a rather attenuated right of hearing. Prisoners are interviewed by a member of the appropriate local review committee. The person conducting the interview is not necessarily present at the meeting of the committee which prepares the report which goes to the Parole Board. The Board itself makes its decisions on the basis of the papers before it. In the view of the Board, other considerations make the giving of reasons for decisions difficult or inexpedient. The Board has considered the question of giving reasons at length in its annual reports and explained what it sees as the practical problems. According to the Board, it might be impossible to give honest reasons to a prisoner, for example, where they related to matters beyond his control; "the truth could sometimes be damaging." A statement of reasons could lead to demands for further hearings to challenge the accuracy of the reasons. However, the Board is now attempting, internally, to draw up reasons for refusal of parole by the use of standardised "causes for concern." If it is shown to be possible to express the views of the Board on particular cases in a useful and succinct way, the possibility of conveying the "causes for concern" to prisoners will be considered.[44]

Practical considerations alone might also be thought sufficient to exempt referees, umpires and other officials in control of sporting events from a duty to give a hearing before ruling on disputes about scoring or sending players off the field for misbehaviour.[45] Dicta in *Machin* v. *Football Association, The Times*, July 21, 1973, suggest that, while natural justice does apply to disciplinary proceedings brought as a result of decisions of referees, the courts will be reluctant to interfere in such cases for fear of, indirectly, subjecting the actions of referees to judicial review.[46] Nonetheless there may be a distinction between a fairly minor penalty imposed to uphold the authority of a referee or umpire and a ban for a long period, or even life, from participating in a sport which, for the player concerned, may provide his, possibly extremely remunerative, livelihood. In such cases judicial interference might be entirely proper, particularly where the question is one of misconduct of a kind which the courts frequently deal with themselves, for example, allegations of drunkenness or violence off the field of play.

Judicial views on whether the urgency of a decision is a practical consideration which justifies excluding natural justice have varied. Lord Upjohn in *Durayappah* v. *Fernando* [1967] 2 A.C. 337, 345 thought that "... while great urgency may rightly limit such opportunity timeously, perhaps severely, there can never be a denial of that opportunity if the principles of natural justice are applicable." On the other hand, in *De Verteuil* v. *Knaggs* [1918] A.C. 557 the Privy Council, while of the opinion that the governor of a colony must normally give a hearing before exercising his powers under an ordinance (*infra*, p. 170), thought that this duty might be excluded in special circumstances, "*e.g.* an emergency when promptitude is of great importance or there might be obstructive conduct on the part of the person affected." Suggestions that "disciplinary powers" may be exercised without a hearing are perhaps explicable, as was seen earlier, on the basis of the need to act with speed. This, however, is not a plea likely to meet with favour after *Ridge* v. *Baldwin* and indeed was hardly adverted to in *Glynn* v. *Keele University* [1971] 1 W.L.R. 487, although the university vice-chancellor had justified his resort to summary action by reference to the need to take swift action before the students involved in the alleged incident had gone down for the long vacation. Pennycuick V.-C. held that a decision of exclusion from the university campus could only be made after a proper hearing. (*Glynn's* case will be discussed later in Chapter 7.) In *Gaiman* v. *National Association for Mental Health* [1971] Ch. 317, Megarry J., in holding that natural justice did not apply to expulsion from a company limited by guarantee, listed the need to act with great speed as a relevant factor among others which included the existence of statutory rules regulating the rights and duties of members of such organisations.

The necessity for speed may justify immediate action; it will, however, normally allow for a hearing at a later stage. The possibility of such a hearing—and the adequacy of any later remedy should the initial action prove to have been unjustified—are considerations to be borne in mind when deciding whether the need for urgent action excludes a right to rely on natural justice. Moreover, however the need to act swiftly may modify or limit what natural justice requires, it must not be thought "that because rough, swift or imperfect justice only is available that there ought to be no justice"; *Pratt* v, *Wanganui Education Board* [1977] 1 N.Z.L.R. 476, 485 *per* Somers J.

Perhaps the most tempting practical consideration to urge as a ground for excluding a right to a hearing—although, even so, hardly a reason for denying the right to an unbiased judge—is that there is no answer to the charge[47]; for example, because the alleged wrongdoer was caught in *flagrante delicto*. Streatfeild J. succumbed to this temptation in *Ridge* v. *Baldwin* [1961] 2 W.L.R. 1054, when, at first instance, he held that the chief constable had no right to be heard by the watch committee since "out of the [Chief Constable's] own mouth at the Central Criminal Court, for the purposes of his trial, for all the world as well as the watch committee to hear, the plaintiff convicted himself of unfitness to hold the office of chief constable" (p. 563). The House of Lords, however, reversed the trial judge on this point because, even if the chief constable could not have hoped in the disciplinary proceedings to persuade the watch committee that he ought to be allowed to continue in his position, the committee had open to it a number of courses and, if they had heard the chief constable, might have followed the most lenient course.

The same argument had found favour with the Court of Queen's Bench in the nineteenth century, when it issued mandamus ordering a vicar to restore to his office the parish clerk whom he had dismissed without a hearing although the misconduct justifying the dismissal, irreverent behaviour during divine service, had occurred in the vicar's presence; a hearing, it was held, might have allowed the clerk to raise mitigating factors such as the absence of criminal motives;

R. v. *Smith, ex p. Harris* (1844) 5 Q.B. 614. More recently, in *Fullbrook* v. *Berkshire Magistrates' Courts Committee* (1971) 69 L.G.R. 75, 97, John Stephenson J. pointed out that

> "There are, after all, degrees even of grave misconduct and explanations if not excuses for it. Suppose the plaintiff had told the committee a tale of blackmail, reducing him to financial and physical and mental exhaustion, or suppose he had urged upon them, as he wanted to urge upon me, that he was under abnormal pressure of work and mental strain and that there was no financial loss to public funds or none that he could not quickly repay. Or suppose he had persuaded the majority of the committee to take the lenient view that his conduct was negligence and folly—or more negligence and folly than deliberate misconduct. Knave or fool, for dismissal it did not matter which. The plaintiff might be either or neither but it did matter for forfeiture [of pension rights]. For that mere folly or even minor misconduct would not do and if folly diluted grave misconduct it might also temper forfeiture."

There are at least three justifications for requiring a hearing even where there appears to be no answer to a charge. First, experience shows that unanswerable charges, may, if the opportunity be given, be answered; inexplicable conduct be explained. Secondly, the party condemned unheard will feel a sense of injustice.[48] Thirdly, suspicion is inevitable that a body which refuses a hearing before acting does so because of the lack of evidence not because of its strength.[49]

It may be that there is no right to a hearing where "such hearing could only be a useless formality"[50] because the court or tribunal had no choice of sanction. Such cases will be rare. An example is provided by *Scott* v. *Aberdeen Corporation* 1976 S.L.T. 141. Scott argued that the corporation, although under a statutory duty to dismiss him, had an obligation to give him a hearing before doing so. Lord Avonside, in rejecting that claim, said

> "It cannot be a denial of 'natural justice' to refuse a man the right to attempt to persuade those entrusted with the administration of substantive law to breach the law which it is their duty to uphold" (p. 147).

In cases where there is a choice of action but a hearing might be described as a useless formality because there is no defence which could conceivably affect the outcome, the right to a hearing is, after *Ridge* v. *Baldwin*, an open question according to Lord Pearce in *Maradana Mosque Trustees* v. *Mahmud* [1967] 1 A.C. 13 Judicial dicta differ in the case of office holders dismissible at will.[51] In one sense, a hearing in such circumstances is a useless formality since the employer may dismiss, if he wishes, whatever the office holder might say. On the other hand, since the employer is free to dismiss or not his decision may be affected by what is said. In *Malloch* v. *Aberdeen Corporation* [1971] 1 W.L.R. 1578 the House of Lords took the view that there is a right to a hearing in such circumstances. That decision may, however, be applicable only to cases where the terms of appointment are governed by statutory provisions which may be regarded as creating something akin to a status.[52]

III. Necessity

Practical considerations equally dictate that the rule *nemo iudex in re sua* yield to necessity as if, for example, all available judges or members of a tribunal are, or may be thought to be, biased. The doctrine of necessity in this field of law is well recognised but "has been applied very sparingly is modern English law."[53] A curious example of the operation of the doctrine, although the question of bias was not in fact raised, is supplied by *O'Byrne* v. *Minister for Finance and Attorney-General* [1959] I.R. 1, where the High Court and Supreme Court of Ireland had to determine the question, posed by the executrix of a deceased judge, whether the state was entitled to tax judicial salaries. The right of the state was upheld in the High Court and in the Supreme Court by three judges out of five. In many cases, as will be seen, reliance on the doctrine can be avoided because of statutory provisions.

IV. Waiver

There is no doubt that a party, in circumstances where natural justice is normally applicable, may waive his right to object to a judge who is acting in his own cause[54] or who might be reasonably suspected of bias.[55] As was seen earlier, doubts have been expressed in some cases about the validity of contractual terms by which parties waive their rights to natural justice. The apparent inconsistency between these dicta and the certainty voiced on the right of a party to waive his right to an unbiased judge is explicable in a number of ways. First, different considerations of public policy may apply to an indefinite, continuing waiver of rights under a contract from those applicable to waiver on one specific occasion. Secondly, the cases where doubt has been expressed about waiver have involved circumstances where the party allegedly waiving rights has not been in a position to do otherwise; there has been an inequality of bargaining power. Thirdly, it may be that a distinction should be drawn between forgoing a right to a hearing and to an impartial tribunal. In the former case, it might be argued that the most conscientious tribunal cannot be relied on to reach the correct solution if it hears only one side of the case. In the latter case, what is waived is normally the right to object not to a biased judge but to one whom the reasonable man might suspect of bias. If the person affected is prepared to accept that a judge can be relied on to decide justly, despite the existence of some reason which could lead to a suspicion of a risk of prejudice, there can hardly be any reason for the law to intervene. The prospect of a party consenting to appear before a tribunal which in fact was biased can safely be dismissed as unreal. If, having waived a right to object on the ground of an appearance of bias, a party discovered that the tribunal was, in fact, biased there can be little doubt that the law, whether or not on the ground of public policy, would not hold him to his waiver.[56]

V. Exclusion by Statute

Finally, natural justice may, by express words, or by implication, be excluded by statute. Examples of express provisions are to be found in nineteenth-century statutes which authorised justices to hear cases although, as ratepayers, they may have had an interest in the outcome because of such litigation.[57] The Supreme Court of Judicature (Consolidation) Act 1925, s. 17(1) provides that a judge of the High Court or Court of Appeal shall not be incapable of acting in any proceeding by reason of his being as one of several ratepayers or as one of any other class of persons liable to contribute to or to be benefited by any rate or tax which may be in any way affected by that proceeding. It remains open in such cases for a litigant to object that, beyond the risk or appearance of bias dealt with by the statute a particular individual is disqualified by virtue of special facts which give rise to a real likelihood of bias.[58]

A curious instance of unintentional statutory exemption from the rule against bias is provided by *Tolputt* v. *Mole* [1911] 1 K.B. 87 and 836. The plaintiff sued Mole, a solicitor, alleging professional negligence, in the county court in which Mole was registrar. Tolputt lost his action and objected when Mole, as registrar, purported to tax the costs of the action. The Court of Appeal upheld the validity of the taxation. The legislation then in force[59] required costs in each county court to be taxed by the registrar of that court; "the only person who could tax the defendant's costs was of necessity the defendant himself"; *per* Cozens Hardy M.R. at p. 838.

Whether it is a question of a right to an impartial judge or to a hearing,

> "It is easier to imply procedural safeguards when Parliament has provided none than when Parliament has laid down a procedure, however inadequate its critics may consider it to be" (*Bates* v. *Lord Hailsham of St. Marylebone* [1972] 1 W.L.R. 1373, 1378, *per* Megarry J.).

Judicial views may, however, differ on the effect of particular statutory procedures. In *Furnell* v. *Whangarei High Schools Board* (*supra*), for example, the elaborate statutory code made no reference to a hearing at the preliminary stage before the sub-committee. Lord Morris relied on the detailed provisions relating to the giving of notice and the hearing of the teacher's reply at the later stages of an inquiry as proving that the absence of any such provisions at the preliminary stage must have been deliberate. Viscount Dilhorne, with whom Lord Reid concurred, thought, on the other hand, that the description in the code of the sub-committee's proceedings as an "investigation" implied "hearing both sides, allowing both sides to call witnesses and to cross-examine and allowing the teacher to give evidence if he wishes." An example of statutory procedure which can hardly leave room for any doubt is to be found in the Prevention of Terrorism (Temporary Provisions) Act 1974. Section 3 authorises the Secretary of State to make exclusion orders against persons whom he is satisfied are involved in the commission of acts of terrorism. Any argument that the Secretary of State should hold a hearing before making an order is clearly excluded by section 4, which provides that *after* the order is made notices of the making of the order shall be served on the person against whom it is made. If the person objects to the order he may, within 48 hours of receiving the notice, make written representations which the Secretary of State, unless he considers the ground of objection to be frivolous, is directed to refer to persons nominated by him for advice.

The absence of reference to a right to a hearing in one section of a statute may have special significance if other sections of that Act expressly recognise such a right. In *Jarvis* v. *Chief Constable of Strathclyde Constabulary* 1976 S.L.T.(Sh.Ct.) 66 the question was whether a chief constable, when revoking a firearm certificate under the Firearms Act 1968, s. 30(1), had to give the holder of the certificate advance warning of his intention and a chance to be heard. Under the section the chief constable may revoke a certificate if he "is satisfied that the holder is ... unfitted to be trusted with such a firearm." In holding that there was no right to a hearing the sheriff relied on the fact that other sections of the Act—for example section 38 which deals with the removal of names from the register of authorised dealers in firearms—expressly provided for a preliminary hearing.[60]

In some cases a statute should perhaps be considered not as excluding natural justice from a decision to which it would otherwise be applicable, but rather as providing an example of a statutory power or discretion of a kind not subject to natural justice, or possibly to any judicial review at all. Such it is suggested, is the best way to view ministerial powers of the kind mentioned in Chapters 5 and 8. Similarly in *Abergavenny* v. *Llandaff* (1888) 20 Q.B.D. 460

the court refused to interfere with the exercise by a bishop of his discretion to refuse to appoint not because the statute took away a right to a hearing but because the bishop's discretion fell outside the range of decisions within the ambit of natural justice.

Notes

[1] It is doubtful, therefore, if the English courts would regard as correctly decided the recent Irish case of *The State* (*Shannon Atlantic Fisheries*) v. *McPolin* [1976] I.R. 93 where Finlay P. held that natural justice applied to the "preliminary inquiry" which, under the Merchant Shipping Act 1864, s. 465, may be held "where a shipping casualty has occurred."

[2] See *Hoffman La Roche* (*F.*) *& Co.* v. *Secretary of State for Trade and Industry* [1975] A.C. 295, 368 *per* Lord Diplock quoted *supra*, p. 81.

[3] *Supra*, pp. 104–105. I.C.F. Spry. *Equitable Remedies* (1971) The Law Book Co. Ltd. Melbourne, pp. 459 *et seq.*

[4] *Cf. Lewis* (*A.H.*) v. *Lewis* (*R.W.F.*) [1978] Fam. 60 (C.A.).

[5] Customs Consolidation Act 1876, s. 42; Customs and Excise Act 1952, s. 275.

[6] For these, and other examples, of the bizarre behaviour of the Customs see Harry Street, *Freedom, The Individual and the Law* (4th ed., 1977), Penguin Books, pp. 149–151. For an account of a successful attempt to recover material seized by the Customs see *David Hockney*, by David Hockney (1976) Thames and Hudson, p. 193. United Kingdom membership of the EEC has not affected the statutory provisions concerned; *R.* v. *Henn*; *R.* v. *Darby*, *The Times*, July 12, 1978.

[7] Post Office Act 1953, s. 11 (as amended). See *R.* v. *Stamford* [1972] 2 Q.B. 391 (C.A.). See also *R.* v. *Arndel* (1906) 3 C.L.R. 557; *R.* v. *Randolph* (1966) 56 D.L.R. (2d) 283.

[8] *Nakkuda Ali* v. *Jayaratne* [1951] A.C. 66; *R.* v. *Metropolitan Police Commissioner, ex p. Parker* [1953] 1 W.L.R. 1150.

[9] "The Court has fully and finally rejected the wooden distinction between 'rights' and 'privileges' that once seemed to govern the applicability of procedural due process rights"; *Board of Regents* v. *Roth* 408 U.S. 564, 571 (1972) *per* Stewart J. *Cf. Banks* v. *Transport Regulation Board* (1968) 119 C.L.R. 222.

[10] A case which has the rare, if not unique, distinction of being criticised for its "sterile conceptualism" by one writer (W. Birtles, "Natural Justice Yet again" (1970) 33 M.L.R. 559, 560) and praised by another for setting the law "on a better course" and sweeping away "a jumble of confusion": see H. W. R. Wade, "Licensing and Natural Justice" (1970) 86 L.Q.R. 309. Lord Denning in *Breen* v. *AEU* [1971] 2 Q.B. 175, 190, regarded *Ex p. Benaim and Khaida* as extending rather than restricting the scope of judicial review.

[11] *Supra*, p. 71.

[12] At p. 693; see also Salmon L.J. at pp. 698–700.

[13] At p. 694. See R. W. Rideout, "Admission to Non-Statutory Associations Controlling Employment" (1967) 30 M.L.R. 389.

[14] A right not to be arbitrarily excluded from membership of a trade union was recognised by the Industrial Relations Act 1971, s. 65(2) but the position is, now, governed again by common law (subject to a right of recourse to a non-statutory

body set up by the TUC); Trade Union and Labour Relations Act, 1974, s. 5; Trade Union and Labour Relations (Amendment) Act 1976, s. 1(*a*); *infra*, p. 117.

[15] See further, O. Hood Phillips and Paul Jackson, *op. cit.* pp. 451 *et seq.*

[16] *Supra*, pp. 15 and 110.

[17] G. H. Treitel, *The Law of Contract* (4th ed., 1975) Stevens, pp. 131–132. See also at p. 133, "In *Abbott* v. *Sullivan* use of the implied term terminology obscured the vital question what standard of behaviour should, as a matter of law, be required of members of disciplinary bodies." In *Gaiman* v. *National Association for Mental Health* [1971] Ch. 317, 336. Megarry J. said that "the Courts are ready to imply a term that natural justice is to be observed, even in cases where this cannot be said to be necessary in order to enable the contract to be carried out ... but I do not think that the courts will do this in the teeth of sufficient indications that the principle of natural justice are not to apply."

[18] *Op. cit.* p. 131.

[19] See also *Lee* v. *Showmen's Guild of Great Britain* [1952] 2 Q.B. 329, 342; *John* v. *Rees* [1970] Ch. 345, 400. *Citrine's Trade Union Law* (ed. M. A. Hickling) (3rd ed., 1967) Stevens, supports the view that the rules of natural justice may be expressly or impliedly excluded; *contra* C. Grunfeld, *Modern Trade Union Law* (1966) Sweet & Maxwell, p. 194.

[20] See also *Enderby Town F.C.* v. *The Football Association* [1971] Ch. 591.

[21] K. W. Wedderburn, *The Worker and the Law* (2nd ed., 1971) Penguin, p. 459.

[22] *e.g.* R. W. Rideout, *Right to Membership of a Trade Union* (1963) London, Athlone Press, p. 102. It should, in fairness to the courts, be pointed out that their interest in protecting the rights of individuals against powerful organisations extends beyond trade unions; *Nagle* v. *Feilden* (*supra*). *Pharmaceutical Society of Great Britain* v. *Dickson* [1967] Ch. 708; [1970] A.C. 403. In the case of the professions it is thought entirely appropriate that discipline should be regulated by statute, with rights of appeal to the ordinary courts.

[23] Trade Union and Labour Relations Act 1974, s. 6(13); Trade Union and Labour Relations (Amendment) Act 1976, s. 1(*b*).

[24] *Labour and the Law* (2nd ed., 1977) Stevens, pp. 190–193.

[25] *Thorne* v. *University of London* [1966] 2 Q.B. 237, *infra*, p. 157.

[26] Review of the Mental Health Act 1959. Cmnd. 7320 (1978).

[27] See also *R.* v. *Post-master General, ex p. Carmichael* [1928] 1 K.B. 291 and *R.* v. *Boycott, ex p. Keasley* [1939] 2 K.B. 651.

[28] *e.g. R.* v. *Metropolitan Police Commissioner, ex p. Parker* [1953] 1 W.L.R. 1150; *Ex p. Fry* [1954] 1 W.L.R. 730.

[29] *Lewis* v. *Morgan* [1943] 1 K.B. 376 (absentee sailor); *R.* v. *Hogan* [1960] 2 Q.B. 513, 519 (C.A.) (prison discipline); *Becker* v. *Home Office* [1972] 2 Q.B. 407, 418. (The Prison Rules, made under the Prison Act 1952, are regulatory only and do not confer rights. However the right to have a proper opportunity of presenting a case, if charged with an offence under the Prison Rules, stems from the Prison Act 1952 itself; see s. 47(2).) In a case reported briefly in *The Times*, May 3, 1977 Cantley J. held that a prisoner had no right to know why he had been classified as a high security risk; natural justice is "inappropriate" to the classification of prisoners. See further M. L. Friedland, *Double Jeopardy* (1969) Oxford University Press, p. 317.

[30] *Hill* v. *Parsons* (*C.A.*) *& Co.* [1972] 1 Ch. 305, 314 *per* Lord Denning M.R.

[31] See also *Pillai* v. *Singapore City Council* [1968] 1 W.L.R. 1278.

[32] *Barber* v. *Manchester Regional Hospital Board* [1958] 1 W.L.R. 181.

[33] *Palmer* v. *Inverness Hospitals Board* 1963 S.L.T. 124.

[34] *Vidyodaya University of Ceylon* v. *Silva* [1965] 1 W.L.R. 77, a decision of the

Privy Council on which Lord Wilberforce cast considerable doubt at p. 1295 of his speech.

[35] *R.* v. *Aston University, ex p. Roffey* [1969] 2 Q.B. 538; *Glynn* v. *Keele University* [1971] 1 W.L.R. 487.

[36] At p. 500. See also *Barnard* v. *National Dock Labour Board* [1953] 2 Q.B. 18; *The State (Gleeson)* v. *Minister for Defence* [1976] I.R. 280. (Members of the Irish Army hold an office from which they cannot be dismissed without a hearing under the provisions of the Defence Act 1954.) The element of public employment may be the explanation of the decision of the House of Lords in *McClelland* v. *NIHRB* [1957] 1 W.L.R. 594; otherwise that decision must have the result of rendering invalid a dismissal in breach of natural justice even in a "pure master and servant case" if the contract of employment provides that no dismissal will take place without a hearing. See further I. Zamir, *The Declaratory Judgement* (1962) Stevens & Sons, pp. 146–148.

[37] Education (Scotland) Act 1962, s. 82(1): "... Every appointment shall be during the pleasure of the authority." This section substantially re-enacted the Education (Scotland) Act 1872 before which teachers had been appointed *ad vitam aut culpam*. A subsequent Act, the Public Schools (Scotland) Teachers Act 1882, s. 3, re-enacted in the 1962 Act s. 85, requires that teachers should have three weeks' notice of a meeting to consider dismissing a teacher.

[38] Malloch's victory was short-lived; the law was changed with retrospective effect; *Malloch* v. *Aberdeen Corporation (No. 2)* 1974 S.L.T. 253.

[39] And continued in effect by the Trade Union and Labour Relations Act 1974, s. 1(2) and Sched. 1, Pt. 1. Like the Highway Code the Code of Practice does not have direct legal effect but its provisions may be taken into account in any proceedings before an industrial tribunal.

[40] *Budgen & Co.* v. *Thomas* [1976] I.C.R. 344, 348 *per* Phillips J.

[41] *R.* v. *Aston University Senate, ex p. Roffey* [1969] 2 Q.B. 538, 554 *per* Donaldson J.; *Central Council for Education and Training in Social Work* v. *Edwards, The Times*, May 5, 1978 *per* Slade J.

[42] J. E. Alder, "Planning Decisions and Natural Justice" [1973] J.P.L. 216.

[43] Criminal Justice Act 1967, ss. 59–62; K. Hawkins, "Parole Procedure, An Alternative Approach" (1973) 13 B.J.Crim. 6; J. E. Hall Williams, "Natural Justice and Parole" [1975] Crim.L.R. 82 and 215.

[44] Annual Reports of the Parole Board for 1975 and 1977; H.C. 432, paras. 19–25 and H.C. 497, paras. 18–20.

[45] The refusal to interfere might also be based on an express or implied consent to the summary jurisdiction of the referee; "He claims that by the rules of the game he was entitled to be declared the winner, while he at the same time declines himself to abide by the rules"; *Cipriani* v. *Burnett* [1933] A.C. 83, 90 *per* Lord Macmillan.

[46] For an example of interference see *Sadler* v. *Smith* (1869) L.R. 5 Q.B. 40 where the court held itself entitled to decide whether a race had begun, since the commencement of the event was a condition precedent to the operation of the term agreed between the parties that the decision of the referee should be final.

[47] See D. H. Clark, "Natural Justice, Substance and Shadow" [1975] P.L. 27.

[48] *John* v. *Rees* [1970] Ch. 345, 402; quoted *supra*, p. 87.

[49] *Cf.* Macbeth's killing of the, apparently, guilty pages: Act II, sc. 4.

[50] *Malloch* v. *Aberdeen Corporation* [1971] 1 W.L.R. 1578, 1599 *per* Lord Simon.

[51] *Supra*, p. 16.

[52] See further G. Ganz, "Public Law Principles Applicable to Dismissal from Employment" (1967) 30 M.L.R. 288, 292 *et seq.*

[53] H. H. Marshall, *op. cit.*, p. 38; de Smith, *op. cit.*, p. 244.

[54] *Matthew* v. *Ollerton* (1693) 4 Mod. 226. "Debt upon an award, and a verdict for the plaintiff; and it was now moved in arrest of judgement. The exception taken was, that the matter in difference was referred to the plaintiff himself who made an award. Sed non allocatur. And the case of Serjeant Hards was remembered by Dolben Justice, viz. the serjeant took a horse from my Lord of Canterbury's bailiff for a deodand, and the archbishop brough his action; and it coming to a trial at the assizes in Kent, the serjeant, by rule of Court, referred it to the archbishop to set the price of the horse, which was done accordingly; and the serjeant afterwards moved the Court to set aside the award for the reason now offered; but was denied by Lord Hale and per totam Curiam."

[55] *R.* (*Giant's Causeway etc. Tramway Co.*) v. *Antrim JJ.* [1895] 2 I.R. 603; *supra*, p. 43.

[56] *Cf.* Arbitration Act 1950, s. 24.

[57] *e.g. R.* v. *Recorder of Cambridge* (1857) 8 E. & Ḃ. 637; *supra*, p. 134.

[58] *R.* v. *Handsley* (1881) 8 Q.B.D. 383; *R.* v. *Barnsley Licensing JJ. ex p. Barnsley & District Licensed Victuallers' Association* [1960] 2 Q.B. 167.

[59] County Courts Act 1888, s. 118. See now, C.C.R., Ord. 47, r. 3. In most circumstances such a problem will no longer arise since C.C.R. Ord. 2, r. 12(1) directs that an action should not be commenced against a registrar in his own court. In any event the judge may, and at the request of a party, must direct that a trial involving a court officer take place at some other convenient court; C.C.R., Ord. 16, r. 3.

[60] The question of a right to a hearing was not raised in *Kavanagh* v. *Chief Constable of Devon and Cornwall* [1974] Q.B. 624. For an earlier Scottish decision requiring a right to a hearing see *Cunning* v. *Chief Constable of Fife* 1975 S.L.T.(Sh.Ct.) 18. See also *Day* v. *Williams* (1969) 46 T.C. 59 (C.A.).

Chapter 7

FOUR EXAMPLES

In the previous chapters the factors affecting the application of the rules of natural justice were discussed, as were the contents of those rules in various circumstances. In this chapter it is intended to consider in some detail how the courts have dealt with four types of situation: arbitrations; educational institutions; ministerial powers and planning inquiries; and, lastly, judgments and decrees of foreign courts. Each of these classes of case has been the subject of considerable litigation which illustrates various aspects of the difficulties of applying the general principles of natural justice to specific problems. In arbitrations, for example, it will be seen that the courts, while emphasising the importance of an impartial judge and a full and fair hearing, have recognised that arbitrators are eligible to hear disputes although more closely involved with one of the parties than would be normally acceptable. Such deviation from the general rule may be explained by recognition of the necessity of obtaining the services of a judge with the necessary professional knowledge and by the belief that the professional standing and reputation of such a judge is the guarantee that he will deal fairly with the parties before him. The informality of hearing which has been allowed in these cases may be attributable again to necessity—as evidenced by the general resort to such hearings in commercial matters—and acceptable both because of the standing of the arbitrators and because the parties, who may usually be regarded as of roughly equal power and at arm's length, have freely consented to it. In the case of educational institutions, the application of natural justice raises different questions. Is it inappropriate to attempt to "judicialise" procedures in schools, colleges and universities? Can some decisions be identified as "academic" and beyond the limits of natural justice while others are "non-academic" and subject to judicial review? If the courts are prepared to interfere, what standards do they, or should they, require? Attempts to invoke natural justice against ministers may raise questions of constitutional importance. Should the courts, for example, attempt to control ministerial acts or is that the duty of Parliament? Can the courts take account of the increasing unreality of control by the doctrines of ministerial responsibility and accountability to Parliament? To what extent should the traditional rules of natural justice apply to inquiries held by inspectors and, even more difficult, to what extent do they apply after the inquiry has closed and before the minister announces his decision? The case law on natural justice, in its application to foreign judgments, is interesting in two ways. First, as will be seen, the English courts are, in this field, still more inclined than elsewhere to give a wide meaning to "natural justice" extending beyond minimum procedural safeguards to the content of the rules of foreign legal systems. Secondly, the courts must reconcile their idea of a desirable standard of procedural fairness against the difficulties that may arise in practice if judgments or decrees pronounced in one jurisdiction are not recognised in another.

I. Arbitrators and Quasi-Arbitrators

Whether someone should be described as an arbitrator, or quasi-arbitrator, may be important for various reasons. In two recent cases, for example, *Sutcliffe* v. *Thackrah* [1974] A.C. 727 and *Arenson* v. *Arenson* [1977] A.C. 405 the House of Lords had to consider who is entitled to claim the immunity which arbitrators, like judges, enjoy from legal actions arising from their decisions. For this purpose "arbitrator" was defined as a person to whom there is a submission of a specific dispute or of present points of difference or of defined differences that may in future arise, the parties concerned agreeing to accept his decision as binding and the agreement being within the terms of the Arbitration Act 1950. Where two or more parties agree, in circumstances not falling within that Act,[1] to refer a dispute to a third party for decision he can be described, in the view of Lord

Morris, as a "quasi-arbitrator" and may well enjoy the immunity from liability of an arbitrator *stricto sensu.*[2] Doubt remains, however, as to exactly what is meant by "quasi-arbitrator" after the decision in *Sutcliffe*[3] and the term is, perhaps, best avoided for the future. It is certainly inappropriate to describe the position of a professional man such as an engineer,[4] architect[5] or valuer[6] when, often under a standard form of contract,[7] he discharges such duties as "certifying" or "approving" work done for his client or employer by a third party or values an item to be bought or sold. On the other hand it has been used and, no doubt, will be used again with some justification to describe the position of experts such as architects when discharging the additional duty cast on them by contract of arbitrating, although they are interested parties in the case of disputes arising under the contract.[8]

Although there cannot be an arbitration without a dispute, it does not follow that everyone deciding a dispute is a judge or arbitrator and so required to conform to the rules of natural justice as to bias or to deliberate together before giving judgment. There is nothing in the speeches in *Sutcliffe* v. *Thackrah* or *Arenson* v. *Arenson* to cast doubt on decisions such as *Ellis* v. *Hopper* (1858) 28 L.J.Ex. 1; 3 H. & N. 766, and *Parr* v. *Winteringham* (1859) 29 L.J.Q.B. 123; 1 El. & El. 394, which held that stewards at a race meeting are not acting as arbitrators when they decide disputes over which horse won a race. The principle in these cases would, no doubt, extend to all referees and umpires in sports and to, for example, editors or similar people whose decisions in competitions of one kind or another are made "final" by the relevant rules.[9]

An arbitrator or quasi-arbitrator, in the sense those terms seem to have been used in *Sutcliffe* v. *Thackrah* and *Arenson* v. *Arenson*, must observe the rules of natural justice in reaching a decision.[10] The expert, assessing valuing or certifying is equally clearly not so bound, but he must act "fairly and impartially; he must hold the balance between his client or employer and any relevant third party."[11] Before considering what these requirements mean in this context it should be pointed out that "natural justice" is nowhere mentioned in the Arbitration Act 1950 as a ground for setting aside an arbitrator's award.[12] Section 24 deals with the removal of an arbitrator where there is reason to believe he is not, or may not, be impartial[13] but in other cases allegations of breach of natural justice are normally raised under section 23 which provides for the removal of an arbitrator, or the setting aside of an award, where the arbitrator "has misconducted himself."[14] Section 22(1) provides that "In all cases of reference to arbitration the High Court or a judge thereof may from time to time remit the matter referred, or any of them, to the reconsideration of the arbitrator or umpire." Under this subsection the courts have remitted awards where there has been any doubt whether justice has been done, or been seen to be done; *The "Aristides Xilas"* [1975] 2 Lloyd's Rep. 402, 410 *per* Donaldson J.; *The "Yperagia"* [1977] 1 Lloyd's Rep. 29.

In attempting to ascertain what the courts expect of arbitrators if they are to satisfy the demands of natural justice a number of general points must be borne in mind. First, the attitude of the courts towards arbitrations has changed since the nineteenth century when decisions such as *Harvey* v. *Shelton* (1844) 7 Beav. 455 and *Re Brook and Delcomyn* (1864) 16 C.B.(N.S.) 403 appeared to require a hearing in the presence of both parties.[15] It is now easier to convince the court that a less formal, "rough and ready way of getting at the truth" suffices; *W. Naumann* v. *Edward Nathan & Co. Ltd.* (1930) 37 Ll.L.R. 249, 250 *per* Scrutton L.J. The modern judicial view is clearly shown by the words of McNair J. in *Henry Bath & Son Ltd.* v. *Birgby Products* [1962] 1 Lloyd's Rep. 389, 399;

> "Great care has to be used in reading the decisions of a century or half a century ago as to the powers of arbitrators today.... The growth of commercial arbitrators in the City has been so wide and, as a whole, so beneficial that the Courts show increasing reluctance to interfere with the manner in which these trade bodies carry out their important functions and only interfere in the very rare case where it has been shown that some real impropriety has been committed."

A similar view was expressed, more briefly, by Devlin J. as he then was, in *F. E. Hookway & Co. Ltd.* v. *Alfred Isaacs & Sons* [1954] 1 Lloyd's Rep. 491, 515; "An arbitrator is not to be removed because he does not display all the judicial qualities which many of us only begin to acquire after a lifetime of application." Secondly, the courts are prepared to distinguish between arbitrations involving disputed questions of law or fact, or both, and quality arbitrations where the only question is one for an expert; are these goods of the standard required or recognised as appropriate by the trade concerned? The case for some formality, for hearing and even legal representation[16] is clearly stronger in the first instance. On the other hand, in quality arbitrations it may suffice for the arbitrator to "go down at his own convenience to a warehouse, inspect a sample of merchandise displayed to him by the foreman and return his opinion on its quality or value"; *Arenson* v. *Arenson* [1977] A.C. 405, 431 *per* Lord Kilbrandon. Thirdly, judges have emphasised that the fairness of the procedure followed by arbitrators should be assessed in the light of the customs and practices of the particular trade concerned; *Star International (U.K.) Ltd.* v. *Bergbau Handel GmbH* [1966] 2 Lloyd's Rep. 16, 19 *per* Mocatta J.[17]

Arbitrators, like judges, must be impartial. The test of bias, however, is somewhat different in the two cases. The parties have themselves chosen the particular person to whose jurisdiction they have submitted. Practical considerations justify—and require—the determination of disputes by arbitrators who in one form or another, might be regarded as having an interest in their outcome. In *Bright* v. *River Plate Construction Co.* [1900] 2 Ch. 835, 839, Cozens Hardy J. said:

> "In case of a named arbitrator all those considerations which affect the qualification of a person who may be suspected, though unreasonably suspected, of bias in a judicial position must be laid aside, unless it can be shewn that the arbitrator has prejudged the case, or has actual bias."[18]

This difference can be illustrated by a case such as *Ranger* v. *G.W.R.Co.* (1854) 5 H.L.C. 72, where the House of Lords distinguished *Dimes* v. *Grand Junction Canal* (1852) 3 H.L.Cas. 759 and held that the chief engineer of the railway company was not disqualified from acting as arbitrator under a contract because he held some shares in the company. The contractors should have realised such a person might well have shares in the company for which he worked. Mere indebtedness of an arbitrator to a party is not a disqualification although "It is certainly a matter of suspicion"; *Morgan* v. *Morgan* (1832) 1 Dowl. 611. In *Drew* v. *Drew* (1855)

2 Macq. 1, the House of Lords refused to hold that an arbitrator was disqualified because one of the parties had certain trust monies in his hands, of which the arbitrator was one of the trustees. It was argued that a beneficiary who was indebted to the arbitrator would be less solvent if the award went against that party. If it went in that party's favour the beneficiary would be better placed to pay the arbitrator his debt. Lord Cranworth said:

> "I do not hesitate to say, that that is a sort of interest, if you call it interest, with which it is quite impossible for your Lordships to deal. If partics choose to appoint a person arbitrator without making inquiry into those minute circumstances, they must abide by the result. It is not suggested that there was any fraud in concealing from the parties any existence of interest. The interest, therefore, seems to be a question entirely out of the case" (p. 7).

On the other hand an arbitrator will be disqualified if his financial interest is of an unusual kind which the party objecting could not have foreseen. An arbitrator, for example, who had bet on the outcome of the arbitration in which he was acting would normally, like a magistrate, be disqualified from acting; *R.* v. *Farrant* (1887) 20 Q.B.D. 58. In *Ellis* v. *Hopper* (1858) 28 L.J.Ex. 1; 3 H. & H. 766, however, as was seen earlier in Chapter 2, the fact that one of five stewards had bet against the defendant's horse was held not to disqualify him from adjudicating on a dispute as to whether a race had been won by the plaintiff's horse or the defendant's. The stewards were not arbitrators in the legal sense, and the likelihood of an interest of this kind must have been foreseen by the parties. Nor was there any evidence that the decision had been affected by the interest. On the other hand, in *Kimberley* v. *Dick* (1871) L.R. 13 Eq. 1 Lord Romilly M.R. held that a builder was not bound to submit to the arbitration of an architect when it was discovered that by virtue of an agreement between the architect and his client, the architect had a financial interest in ensuring that the cost of the house in question did not exceed a certain price.[19] In *Blanchard* v. *Sun Fire Office* (1890) 6 T.L.R. 365 it emerged after an award had been made in a dispute betwween the defendant company and a policy-holder that the latter had, before the meeting of arbitrators and umpire, assigned his interest in the policy to one of the arbitrators for value. In setting aside the award Willis J. said that it was "positively immoral that the case should be heard and decided under such circumstances."

Where an arbitrator—or an expert who is merely required to act fairly—is employed by one of the parties to the arbitration—or by one of the parties interested in the valuation or certification—the courts will interfere if the arbitrator or expert has allowed himself to take instructions from his employer, for example to delay making a decision or "to reduce the account as much as possible on account of the heavy expenses we have already had"; *Hickman* v. *Roberts* [1913] A.C. 229.[20] The courts will also interfere if there is a real likelihood of bias arising from the fact that earlier events have been such that an employee who is also an arbitrator would, in effect, in a dispute, have to be not only judge but also witness. A similar rule applies if earlier events are such that the arbitrator is in a position where a finding in favour of one of the parties would require him to deny the correctness of his own professional decisions in the carrying out of the contract; *Nuttall* v. *Manchester Corporation* (1892) 8 T.L.R. 513; *Bristol Corporation* v. *John Airds Co.* [1913] A.C. 241. In *Blackwell* v. *Derby Corporation* (1911) 75 J.P. 129 the arbitrator was an engineer employed by the corporation. The builder objected that it was the arbitrator's unreasonable behaviour in his capacity as engineer which had led to delays of which the corporation were complaining. The Court of Appeal upheld the builder's claim that he was not required to submit the dispute to arbitration. Buckley L.J. said:

> "The worst possible referee on the question of unreasonable conduct is the person who is accused of being unreasonable.... It is not human nature to suppose that he can properly determine that he himself is an unreasonable person" (p. 132).

Again, the relationship between the arbitrator and the person appointing him may be such that the court will regard the likelihood of bias as sufficiently serious to merit removal of the arbitrator. In *Burkett Sharp* v. *Eastcheap Dried Fruit* [1961] 2 Lloyd's Rep. 80; [1962] 1 Lloyd's Rep. 267, the defendant company appointed as its arbitrator P, a man who was "wholly or partially managing its business." Diplock J., as he then was, and the Court of Appeal, held that P, in view of the closeness of his association with the defendant company, "was manifestly not a suitable arbitrator." In *Veritas Shipping Corporation* v. *Anglo Canadian Cement* [1966] 1 Lloyd's Rep. 76, the defendant appointed its managing director as an arbitrator. In removing him from that position McNair J. said "Arbitrators must not only act judicially and show no bias at all but must also appear to be in a position to act judicially and without any bias" (p. 77).

Usually the suggestion that an arbitrator is likely to be biased because he is employed in some capacity by one party to the dispute is likely to be raised by the other party. However, the employer himself may wish to object as is illustrated by the Scottish decision, *Edinburgh Magistrates* v. *Lownie* (1903) 5 F. 711. A dispute had arisen between the town council and Lownie. A Mr. Ormiston agreed to act as arbitrator but a few months later he was elected to an office which entailed *ex officio* membership of the town council. The latter body objected that Ormiston was no longer eligible to determine such disputes. It was held that Ormiston was disqualified, not merely while he held office but after he relinquished office. Such a decision is defensible on a number of grounds. First the arbitrator, consciously or unconsciously, may, in trying to establish his impartiality, lean against the party to whom he is, or was, in some way related. Secondly, he may have obtained information which affects his view and which an outsider would not have. Thirdly, particularly after a relationship has terminated, an arbitrator might take the opportunity to pay off old scores which he wishes to settle with his former employer.

The fact that an arbitrator, or umpire, has acted as witness for one of the parties in other, earlier proceedings dealing with, for example, the value of land adjacent to that the subject-matter of the arbitration in question, is not sufficient to disqualify him. Day J. said in one such case, "It is within the knowledge of us all that surveyors are constantly acting either as umpires or as witnesses in cases of this description"; *Re Haigh and London & N.W. and G. W. Rys.* [1896] 1 Q.B. 649, 650.[21] The fact that an arbitrator or umpire has been treated to lunch or dinner by one party, in the absence of the other, has similarly been held insufficient to justify setting awards aside: *Re Hopper* (1866) L.R. 2 Q.B. 367[22]; *Moseley* v. *Simpson* (1873) L.R. 16 Eq. 226.

Arbitrators may disqualify themselves by conduct or statements which show or suggest a real likelihood of bias. In *Beddow* v. *Beddow* (1878) 9 Ch.D. 89 an arbitrator had misappropriated funds given to him to meet a cheque drawn by him in favour of one of the parties as part of an arrangement between the parties to the arbitration. It was held that such conduct justified the arbitrator's removal because of the likelihood of his favouring the party he had wronged. In *Bonnim* v. *Neame* [1910] 1 Ch. 732, Swinfen-Eady J. refused to allow an arbitration to proceed because of the vigour with which each arbitrator had expressed his support for the rights of the party appointing him; "Arbitrators should be persons who are prepared to exercise an independent judgment on the matter, free from partiality or bias, and not mere advocates of the parties" (p. 740). In *Catalina (Owners)* v. *Norma (Owners)* (1938) 61 Ll.L.Rep. 360 a dispute between the owners of a Portuguese and a Norwegian ship had been submitted to arbitration. The arbitrator, a distinguished King's Counsel, said in the course of the hearing, "The Italians are all liars in these cases and will say anything to suit their book. The same thing applies to the Portuguese. But the other side here are Norwegians and in my experience the Norwegians generally are a truthful people." The English-speaking managing director of the Portuguese company who heard these remarks applied, successfully, to have the award set aside.

The nature and form of the hearing which must take place before arbitrators reach a decision has been the subject of many cases and, as has been seen earlier, the attitude of the courts has changed since the middle of the nineteenth century. Judges now are quite prepared to accept that in quality arbitrations no hearing is required; *Arenson* v. *Arenson* [1977] A.C. 405, 431; *supra*, p. 150. In the absence of any express provision requiring a formal, oral hearing or of any request by the parties or one of them for such a hearing, the courts will expect the parties to accept the procedure customary in the particular trade or type of arbitration. In *Amram Ltd.* v. *Bremar Company Ltd.* [1966] 1 Lloyd's Rep. 464 Megaw J. refused to set aside an arbitral award which had been reached without, it was alleged, the parties being given the opportunity to appear before the arbitrators and call witnesses. The learned judge said (at p. 499),

> "They properly and judicially investigated the matters in dispute which had been referred to them. There was in the circumstances no reason why they should have required the presence of the parties. They indicated that they proposed to hold a meeting, and it would have been fully open to either of the parties had they so desired to ask to be heard and, if they wished, to produce additional evidence over and above what appeared in the correspondence or to explain that correspondence.... It appears from the joint affidavit of the arbitrators that the applicants did, in fact, provide the arbitrators with a file of correspondence, and had they desired to provide any additional documentary evidence or to call any witnesses, there was nothing to stop them from indicating that they would do so. The course followed by the arbitrators was the usual course in accordance with an arbitration of this sort."[23]

The courts will not, however, assume that the parties have impliedly assented to a custom or trade practice which is contrary to the rules of natural justice; *London Export Corporation Ltd.* v. *Jubilee Coffee Roasting Co.* [1958] 1 W.L.R. 271 and 661.

Although arbitrators may proceed informally and rely on documentary evidence in many cases, the courts may interfere in the interests of justice. Thus, if there is an oral hearing the parties must be heard together in each other's presence and witnesses cannot be examined behind the backs of the parties; *Drew* v. *Drew* (1855) 2 Macq. 1, 3 *per* Lord Cranworth L.C.[24] Nor can evidence be taken from one party, in the absence of the other, after the hearing has ended.[25] An arbitrator may not communicate to the umpire evidence which he has withheld from the other arbitrator; *Re Brook and Delcomyn* (1864) 16 C.B.(N.S.) 403. An arbitrator should not inspect property which he is to value in the presence of one party to the dispute; *Re Brien and Brien* [1910] 2 I.R. 84.[26] An inspection in the absence of both parties may, equally, be unsatisfactory; "The premises might almost tell their own tale yet there might be other facts which should be inquired into..."; *Anon.* (1814) 2 Chitt. 44. Arbitrators may, exceptionally, see one party in the absence of another, for example to inquire if that party admits certain items in the accounts; *Anderson* v. *Wallace* (1835) 3 Cl. & F. 26. They may also, in the absence of one or both of the parties, consult for advice "men of science in every department where it becomes necessary"; *Caledonian Railway Co.* v. *Lockhart* (1860) 3 Macq. 808, 823 *per* Lord Wensleydale; or lawyers; *Rolland* v. *Cassidy* (1888) 13 App.Cas. 770.[27] In such situations it might be argued that the question to be asked is not whether justice has been done but has been seen to be done. The answer must, obviously, depend on the circumstances. Other cases establish that a decision will be set aside if there was a hearing, of which one party had not been informed; *The Warwick* (1890) 15 P.D. 189; or, if the decision was reached on the basis of written submissions, the arbitrators had failed to take proper steps to ensure that one of the parties did not wish to put a case before them; *Montrose Canned Ltd.* v. *Eric Wells Merchants Ltd.* [1965] 1 Lloyd's Rep. 597. Decisions must not be based on points taken by arbitrators or umpires but not put to the parties; *The Seistan* [1960] 1 W.L.R. 186.[28] Like others entrusted with the power of deciding disputes arbitrators cannot delegate that function[29] and one case at least requires them to exercise that power jointly.[30]

Even where arbitrators have not acted in a way which amounts to a denial of the right to a hearing or misconduct the courts have recently indicated that they will interfere in the interests of justice and remit an award for reconsideration if, without anyone's fault there has been a "procedural mishap," that is if something has gone wrong with the procedural side of an arbitration which has or may have caused injustice to one of the parties. In *The Aros* [1978] 1 Lloyd's Rep. 456, Brandon J. remitted an award on this ground where a party had not had a full hearing but, on the facts, the arbitrator had been fully entitled to assume that the party in question had produced all the evidence which he wished to and had no further submissions to make.[31]

II. Students

The rights, if any, of students applying for admission to an institution have been discussed earlier, in Chapter 6. Here it is intended to discuss the relationship between an educational body and those students who have been admitted to membership of it. Whether, and if so, in what circumstances, educational institutions must observe the rules of natural justice has been the subject of litigation on a number of occasions in the last 10 years. It is intended here to discuss the matter as one of principle and then to consider and comment on recent cases in the light of older authorities.

Educational institutions range from schools for the very young to universities for students, most of whom in the eyes of the law are adults, of above average intelligence, pursuing academic and professional studies at the highest level. In all such bodies it is perhaps possible to distinguish between decisions on academic matters, that is, for example, success in examinations and non-academic, or disciplinary matters. In the former situation the rules of natural justice clearly do not apply, in the normal sense at any rate. A student has no right to be heard before he is failed—except to the extent that the student's script or performance of some other academic task could be regarded as his presentation of his case. Normally there will in any educational institution be provision for calling into question the correctness of such decisions and the words of Megarry J. will no doubt apply, whether or not a university is the body concerned:

> "To say that the requirements of natural justice do not apply is not, of course, to say that the university is free to trample on the student's rights: for he is entitled to have his application duly considered by whatever bodies have the power of decision" (*Leary* v. *National Union of Vehicle Builders* [1971] Ch. 34, 52).

The unspoken assumption behind most judicial discussions of the law relating to disputes over examination results is that the plaintiff is challenging the subjective judgment of the examiners perhaps, for example, because, as alleged in *Thorne* v. *University of London* [1966] 2 Q.B. 237, they performed their task negligently. It remains to be seen what would be the attitude of the courts if it could be shown that examiners were motivated by conscious bias or prejudice, for example, if examiners could be shown to have said that they would fail all Jewish students.

In the case of Oxford and Cambridge colleges, universities other than Oxford and Cambridge,[32] and other charitable, educational (or eleemosynary) corporations,[33] the courts may refuse to interfere with academic decisions for the further ground that they are within the exclusive jurisdiction of the visitor.[34] The extent of the jurisdiction of the visitor is unclear.[35] Support for the view that it at least extends to all questions of disputed membership is to be found in the recent decision of Megarry V.-C. in *Patel* v. *University of Bradford* [1978] 3 All E.R. 841, 849. On that ground the learned Vice-Chancellor refused to entertain an action alleging arbitrary expulsion from a university by a former student.

In dealing with disputes the visitor must observe the rules of natural justice. He must grant a hearing although not necessarily an oral one; *R.* v. *Bishop of Ely* (1788) 2 T.R. 290, 338; *R.* v. *Bishop of Lincoln* (1788) 2 T.R. 338n. Nor can a visitor, as seen in Chapter 2, be a judge in his own cause; *R.* v. *Bishop of Chester* (1791) 2 Str. 797. (There is no reason to doubt that he would be disqualified by any other form of bias recognised by the law, whether arising from financial interest or favour.) Although the visitor's jurisdiction is exclusive and his determinations "final and conclusive" (*Att.-Gen.* v. *Talbot* (1747) 3 Atk. 662, 673), the courts can and will interfere to supervise the correct use of that jurisdiction, for example, by mandamus to compel a hearing.

Disputes about non-academic or disciplinary matters may range from the right of a teacher to administer a swift blow to a misbehaving infant to the expulsion of a student from a university on a charge which will ensure that he is unlikely ever to be admitted to the profession for which he had been training. Different considerations may, not unreasonably, be thought to apply to such a variety of cases. Circumstances may dictate the application of force before a hearing, for example to persuade two youngsters wrestling in the classroom to desist. The administration of corporal punishment in a more formal sense is likely to be governed by local authority rules. The teacher who infringes such rules is liable to various sanctions. Excessive punishment may constitute a tort or crime or both. In other circumstances the attitude of the English courts is no doubt correctly expressed by Pennycuick V.-C. in *Glynn* v. *Keele University* [1971] 1 W.L.R. 487, 494:

"The context of educational societies involves a special factor which is not present in other contexts, namely the relation of tutor and pupil ... there exists a wide range of circumstances in which the body or individual (acting on behalf of the society) is concerned to impose penalties by way of domestic discipline. In these circumstances it seems to me that the body or individual is not acting in a quasi-judicial capacity at all but in a magisterial capacity.... No doubt there is a moral obligation to act fairly, but this moral obligation does not, I think, lie within the purview of the court in its control over quasi-judicial acts. Indeed, in the case of a schoolboy punishment the contrary could hardly be argued."

A similar view has recently been expressed by the American Supreme Court which considered the matter at length in *Ingraham* v. *Wright*, 430 U.S. 651 (1977). The court held, four of the nine justices dissenting, that due process does not require prior notice and a hearing before corporal punishment is administered in schools. Suspension, or expulsion, from a school or university on the other hand, is a process where it is not unreasonable to require formal procedural safeguards, the complexity of which should obviously vary with the circumstances. In *Goss* v. *Lopez*, 419 U.S. 565 (1975), for example, the Supreme Court held by five to four that in the case of a suspension from school for a period of 10 days there must, before the decision was taken, be "at least an informal give-and-take between student and disciplinarian" (p. 584). It was not necessary that there should be a delay between the time "notice" was given and the "rudimentary hearing" took place.[36] It is difficult to envisage the English courts being prepared to require a hearing, however rudimentary, before suspension or expulsion from a school.

In the nineteenth century it was suggested that there might be a remedy in damages for breach of an implied contract—that there should be reasonable grounds for expulsion.[37] Nowadays the position is likely to be governed by regulations made under statutory authority. In the case of a school maintained by the local education authority, for example, expulsion may only be effected by the authority, or the managers or governors of the school, and an appeal lies to the Secretary of State.[38] The courts, it is suggested, would not wish to interfere in this process at the first stage although they might be prepared to intervene to require that the Secretary of State in hearing an appeal observed natural justice or, at least, acted fairly.

Expulsion from a university, polytechnic or similar institution can hardly fail to be regarded as a matter sufficiently serious, prima facie, to require the observance of natural justice. The only exception is where membership is terminated automatically on academic grounds, where, as we have seen, the courts do not interfere. Even in cases of expulsion on non-academic grounds it could be argued that the jurisdiction of the courts is excluded in the case of institutions possessing visitors. This point has not been argued (or, more correctly, in the case of *Herring* v. *Templeman* (*supra*), decided) in the cases discussed in this and the following paragraphs. The exclusive jurisdiction of the visitor has, however, been asserted in *Patel* v. *University of Bradford* [1978] 3 All E.R. 841 where Megarry V.-C. suggested that in other modern cases "the visitatorial jurisdiction seems to have been forgotten or overlooked" (p. 852). Assuming the correctness of the decision in *Patel*, decisions such as the *Aston University* case and *Herring* v. *Templeman* remain important where an institution is not subject to the jurisdiction of a visitor. The need for academic bodies to observe natural justice when deciding, in the light of non-academic as well as academic factors, the fate of students who had failed to pass their examinations, was affirmed by the Divisional Court in *R.* v. *Aston University Senate, ex p. Roffey* [1969] 2 Q.B. 538. In that case the committee in question was empowered to take into account "a wide range of extraneous factors some of which by their very nature, for example personal and family problems might only have been known to the students themselves' (*per* Donaldson J. at p. 554). However, in *Herring* v. *Templeman* (*supra*) the Court of Appeal emphasised that everything in the judgments of Donaldson and Blain JJ. was *obiter* since the court unanimously refused the relief sought. Also it appeared that the university had conceded that natural justice applied. The argument for requiring compliance with natural justice which is still stronger in cases involving expulsion, or indeed other punishment, for alleged misconduct, was accepted in *Glynn* v. *Keele University* [1971] 1 W.L.R. 487 by Pennycuick V.-C. The facts, as alleged in the affidavit of the vice-chancellor of the university were that a number of students "had appeared naked in the area of the Students' Union . . . causing offence to many members and employees of the University, and residents on the campus." Because there was no time before the end of term to summon a meeting of the university disciplinary panel the vice-chancellor decided to act summarily. He wrote to Glynn, whom he regarded as having been identified as one of the nudists, to inform him that he was being fined £10 and was to be excluded from residence on the campus for the following session. The letter pointed out that an appeal against the decision lay to the university council. The plaintiff wrote to the registrar of the university on July 3, 1970 and, at the end of that month, went abroad. On August 10 a letter was written to him informing him that the council would hear his appeal on September 2. Unfortunately Glynn was abroad and did not return home until after the date fixed for the hearing. The council by then had upheld the decision of the vice-chancellor. Pennycuick V.-C. held that the disciplinary powers of the university vice-chancellor were, under the university statutes, so extensive and far-reaching in their consequences that, when exercising them, he was acting judicially and was required to observe the rules of natural justice. It would not be right, said the learned judge, "to treat those powers as merely matters of internal discipline." The failure to hear Glynn before deciding to punish him was clearly a breach of natural justice. Nonetheless, in the exercise of his discretion, Pennycuick V.-C. refused to grant an injunction restraining the university from excluding him from the campus. There was no question of fact, as the proceedings stood, and the court had to assume Glynn had acted as alleged, the offence merited a severe penalty "according to any standards current even today." If the student had had a hearing he could only have put forward a plea by way of mitigation:

> "But I do not think the mere fact that he was deprived of throwing himself on the mercy of the vice-chancellor in that particular way is sufficient to justify setting aside a decision which was intrinsically a perfectly proper one."

Before considering what natural justice requires in the context of educational societies, it is necessary to consider the distinction drawn in the case law between academic and non-academic matters. The classification of a degree based purely on examination scripts or other written work clearly falls into the former class. Equally, a committee which is entitled to allow a student, despite failure in an examination, to repeat a year, or proceed to the next year of his course, because of extraneous factors such as the health of his relatives, is dealing with non-academic matters. Are, however, the personal, moral qualities of a student academic or non-academic matters; his, or her, ability to mix with colleagues; his, or her, personal hygiene? The answer, it is suggested, varies with the subject or discipline in question. In many instances they are extraneous factors; to take them into account might be considered inappropriate in any circumstances. To make them the ground for expulsion or refusal of permission to repeat a year, whether or not following academic failure, without a hearing must surely be contrary to natural justice or, at least, "unfair." But certain "personal qualities" may be generally accepted requirements in the case, for example, of a particular profession. Thus in *Herring* v. *Templeman* the Court of Appeal distinguished between "extraneous factors" in the wide sense in which that phrase had been used in the *Aston* case and, on the other hand, matters other than examination results, which were relevant to an assessment of the candidate's likely success as a teacher. In the latter case a decision could be properly reached without first hearing the student. In *Herring*'s case these matters were individual assessments by members of the college and external assessors of the quality of his teaching practice and his lack of capacity for self-criticism. More recently in *Board of Curators of the University of Missouri* v. *Horowitz* 55 L.Ed. 2d 124 (1978) the Supreme Court of America considered the claim of a medical student that she had been dismissed from medical school without due process. The court, in a unanimous judgment referred to

> "the significant difference between the failure of a student to meet academic standards and the violation by a student of valid rules of conduct. This difference calls for far less stringent procedural requirements in the case of an academic dismissal" (p. 132).

In the case of a medical student the views of her clinical teachers that her performance in "clinical patient orientated settings" was below the required standard and that "she lacked a critical concern for personal hygiene" were academic judgments, not subject to the stringent procedural requirements.

What does natural justice require in those circumstances where it applies to an educational body? The first difficulty concerns the rule against bias. Often the same individual will sit on a number of committees dealing with a case, in various capacities; perhaps as an examiner, then as dean of a faculty board and, possibly, as a member of senate or even as a member of a final appeal board or disciplinary committee. A number of decisions show the courts paying regard to practical realities. In *King* v. *University of Saskatchewan* [1969] S.C.R. 678, for example, the Supreme Court of Canada refused to quash a university decision merely on the ground of overlapping membership in the various university bodies which had dealt with King's case, holding such duplication inevitable in the light of the organisation of universities. In *Herring* v. *Templeman* (*supra*) it was alleged that it was a breach of natural justice for the principal of the college to sit both on the academic board which recommended the student's expulsion and on the governing board which accepted that recommendation. That complaint failed because the trust deed under which the College operated expressly provided that the principal should be a member of both bodies. In *Ward* v. *Bradford* (1972) 70 L.R.G. 27 the facts, according to Lord Denning M.R., were that the principal of a college of education had been informed by someone outside the college that a man had, for some weeks, been living in the room of one of the women students. He was believed to be involved in the illegal use of drugs. At 4.00 a.m. one morning the girls' rooms were searched. The gravity with which the matter was viewed is shown by the fact that the police were asked, and were prepared, to be at hand in case of trouble. A man was discovered in W's room. There was no evidence of any illegal use of drugs during the two months he had been living in the room.

The principal, who was the only person able to refer matters to the disciplinary committee of the college, was unwilling to do so. The governing body thereupon retrospectively amended the rules of the college and referred W's case to the committee under the new power which it had conferred upon itself. When the committee met, there were present three governors among its nine members and three non-members, N, the assistant education officer, the clerk to the governing body and the assistant town clerk. The minutes of the committee, which recommended W's expulsion from the college, showed that the assistant education officer participated in its deliberations. The Court of Appeal held, perhaps surprisingly, that the governors who sat on the committee and had participated in the retrospective alteration in the rules were not within the rule which prohibits a man from being both prosecutor and judge in the same cause.[39] Nor, in the view of the court, did N's presence at the meeting fall within the general prohibition against a person who is not a member of a committee participating in its deliberations when it is making a decision.[40] His position was comparable to that of magistrates' clerks who retire with the justices to advise them although, as Lord Denning M.R. admitted, it "came very near the line" (p. 34).

Another problem which often occurs in large organisations, educational as well as administrative, is the extent to which it is possible to delegate powers of deciding cases to a small committee. As was seen in Chapter 3, the question is first one of fact; has the power been delegated or merely the duty of collecting and forwarding evidence, perhaps with recommendations. In certain cases delegation of the power to make the decision may be possible, for example, because it is expressly provided for in the statute, charter or other document establishing the institution in question. The problem of delegation in universities was discussed in *Ex p. Forster*; *Re University of Sydney* (1963) S.R.(N.S.W.) 723. The senate of the university delegated to each faculty the right to decide whether to allow a student who had failed an examination to repeat a year of his course. From the decision of the faculty there was a right of appeal to the senate. In upholding the validity of that delegation the court said:

> "Without the most ample facility for delegation the affairs of a university could not be carried on at all. It is a matter of common knowledge, and illustrated by the by-laws which are in evidence in the present case, that the affairs of a university are for the most part carried on under authority delegated from its governing body, by its officers, both executive and academic,

and by a multitude of subordinate bodies—faculties, boards, committees or by whatever other name called. The importance of the subject-matter may have a bearing upon the permissibility of delegation or upon the appropriateness for the purpose of the body or person to whom the delegation is made. Thus the question whether a candidate has passed or failed in an examination in a particular subject is commonly delegated to the individual examiner in that subject with perhaps, some supervision over the result by a board of examiners; but the question whether a professor should be removed from his office would be quite another matter" (p. 733).

Where a student has a right to a hearing the first question is whether the right is to an oral hearing. Only in exceptional cases does natural justice require an oral hearing. Thus, inside educational bodies it is likely that a committee dealing with appeals to continue a course despite failure in examinations, would satisfy natural justice by allowing only written submissions. Certainly, Blain J. in the *Aston University* case (*supra*) expressly indicated that he was not suggesting that natural justice necessarily required a personal interview (p. 558). But such a committee deciding whether to expel a student for alleged dishonesty might well be required to allow an oral hearing. In *Brighton Corporation* v. *Parry* (1972) 70 L.G.R. 576, 585 Willis J. emphasised that each case must depend on its own facts. In that case there was a prolonged argument between Parry, who had been elected president of his college's student union, and the authorities of the college about whether he was carrying out his academic duties. There had been correspondence and meetings between the principal and Parry. Finally, at a meeting which Parry was not allowed to attend, the relevant committee decided to recommend his expulsion. The learned judge found that Parry knew the contents of the reports on his work which were before the committee and that everything he wanted to say was known to the committee. In the circumstances, Willus J. thought the *audi alteram partem* rule had been complied with by the defendant being allowed to make written representations for the committee's consideration.

In *Herring* v. *Templeman* (*supra*), the aspect of a fair hearing which was at issue was the extent to which the body before which a student had a right to appear was required to reconsider the decision reached on academic grounds by a body which was not required to grant a hearing. The governing body of the college to which Herring belonged received from its academic board recommendations based on the board's academic assessments and had the right, in deciding whether to act on those recommendations to take into account what, in the *Aston* case, were called "extraneous factors." Russell L.J., giving the judgment of the court, held that the governing body was not a court of appeal from the academic board. The duty of the governing body was to act fairly in deciding how to exercise its discretion whether to expel or not. The plaintiff was not entitled to a rehearing with witnesses and discovery of documents and the reasons for, and the evidence leading to, the academic board's assessment. He could advance such excuses as illness, parental or family problems, emotional difficulties and so on; he could not reopen the examiners' decision.

If a student has a right to, or is granted, an oral hearing he is entitled to cross-examine any witnesses, if he wishes; *University of Ceylon* v. *Fernando* [1960] 1 W.L.R. 223; *supra* p. 74. Whether there is a right to legal representation has not been considered at length in any modern case. In *R.* v. *Oxford University, ex p. Bolchover*, *The Times*, October 7, 1970, the denial of a right to legal representation before a committee of the University of Oxford which sat to hear appeals from decisions of the proctors formed one of the grounds on which Bolchover sought certiorari to quash the committee's decision for a breach of natural justice. The Divisional Court refused the application in a very brief judgment which, as reported, made no express reference to this point. In the nineteenth-century case, *Ex p. Death* (1852) 18 Q.B. 647 the right to legal representation was claimed by a Cambridge tradesman who had been summoned to appear before the vice-chancellor and heads of colleges to show cause why, for breach of a rule requiring tradesmen to inform college authorities whenever an undergraduate had incurred debts of £5 or more, undergraduates should not be forbidden to deal with him. The Court of Queen's Bench refused to grant prohibition to restrain the proceedings before the vice-chancellor. Lord Campbell C.J. said that to say "that before such a domestic forum a party is entitled to come attended by counsel or attorney is a proposition not tenable" (p. 659). As the members of the court pointed out, the university was concerned with protecting undergraduates from running up debts, not with punishing tradesmen for misbehaviour. This decision is not, necessarily, a reliable authority should a university wish to send down a student on the basis of an alleged act of serious misconduct.

None of the cases involving the rights of students has clearly established the basis of the court's jurisdiction. Does it rest on contract or status? The question may have practical implications. The remedies available to a litigant may differ, depending on the answer. If the student's rights arise from contract then, subject to what was said in Chapter 6 about public policy, they can be waived. Support for the contract theory may be found in remarks of Russell L.J. in *Herring* v. *Templeman* (*supra*). On the other hand Kindersley V.-C. in *Thomson* v. *University of London* (1864) 33 L.J.Ch. 625, 638 said that it was a misnomer to describe the relationship between a university and student as one of contract.[41] Two points may be made in favour of the status theory. First, even if there is originally a contract between a student and an educational institution, that is not inconsistent with the existence of a status.[42] A contract may give rise to a status. Secondly, it does not follow that a contract exists whenever one person provides services for another, whether for payment or on other terms. There is, for example, no contract between the sender of a letter and the Post Office.[43]

Despite the recognition, in modern cases, of a duty on universities and other bodies, to observe the rules of natural justice, one writer has complained that "when it comes to natural justice students appear to have had a very raw deal."[44] Another suggests that the courts see students

> "essentially as children and sometimes very unpleasant children —above all, as very undisciplined children. And universities and colleges are institutions of the state and so to be upheld. . . . The student cases indeed are excellent examples of the judicial obsession with, as they see it, the necessity to protect and preserve the structures of constitutional authority without

undue concern for the rights of those who wish to challenge that authority."[45]

Views about individual cases may, of course, vary. Both critics would probably admit that inside universities the decisions to which they refer have been seen very differently and a great amount of time and effort has been devoted to improving the procedures for dealing with matters of discipline and problems arising from academic failure. Moreover even if it were granted that the judiciary—or certain judges, which, in any case, is not the same thing—were consciously or unconsciously unsympathetic to students it would not follow that such a view was a reflection of an attitude of mind peculiar to a small group of middle-aged and elderly men. It might be indeed that by virtue of their judicial background their level of tolerance far exceeded that of the majority of people living in the United Kingdom. Nor does it follow that because a particular view is unpopular in some academic circles or among a group of people affected by a decision it does not command popular support.

III. Ministerial Decisions: Inquiries

The extent to which ministerial decisions are, or should be, subject to judicial review is a matter of constitutional law and theory raising questions of which the applicability of the rules of natural justice is but one. It is this latter question, however, with which this book is directly concerned. Examples were given in Chapter 5 of ministerial decisions with which the courts would be unlikely to seek to interfere. Other examples might include the choice by the Prime Minister of the date for a general election or a decision by the Cabinet to accede to a treaty.[46] Decisions taken by particular ministers which directly affect specific individuals may not, on the other hand, seem to be so self-evidently beyond the scope of judicial review. But the courts, even in such cases, may be reluctant to interfere. For example, in the case of powers derived from the Royal Prerogative, the courts may refuse to interfere on the ground that the applicant has not been deprived of any legal right. Thus in *De Freitas* v. *Benny* [1976] A.C. 238 the Privy Council held that a minister could not be required to disclose the evidence on which he based his advice on the exercise of the Royal Prerogative of Mercy because "Mercy is not the subject of legal rights. It begins where legal rights end"; at p. 247 *per* Lord Diplock.[47] A similar reluctance to interfere has been shown in the exercise of statutory powers in areas originally within, or believed to be within, the scope of the Prerogative, for example, the admission and deportation of aliens. In *R.* v. *Leman Street Police Station Inspector, ex p. Venicoff* [1920] 3 K.B. 72 the Divisional Court refused to hold that an alien was entitled to a hearing before deportation. The Earl of Reading C.J. said:

> "The Home Secretary is not a judicial officer for this purpose, but an executive officer bound to act for the public good, and it is left to his judgment whether upon the facts before him it is desirable that he should make a deportation order" (at p. 80).

This reluctance to interfere is particularly marked where questions of national security are involved. Lord Denning M.R. succinctly expressed this judicial attitude in *R.* v. *Secretary of State for the Home Department, ex p. Hosenball* [1977] 1 W.L.R. 766, 778; "The rules of natural justice have to be modified in regard to foreigners here who prove themselves unwelcome and ought to be deported."

There is no doubt that a Minister, or any other body, in *making* legislation, for example, by statutory instrument or by-law, is not subject to the rules of natural justice—*Bates* v. *Lord Hailsham of St. Marylebone* [1972] 1 W.L.R. 1373[48]—any more than is Parliament itself; *Edinburgh and Dalkeith Ry.* v. *Wauchope* (1842) 8 Cl. & F. 710, 720 *per* Lord Brougham; *British Railways Board* v. *Pickin* [1974] A.C. 765. (In the case of Parliament such a conclusion follows inevitably from the inability of the courts, as illustrated in these and other authorities, to interfere with the procedure followed by the two Houses in the course of enacting legislation.) Whether a minister is required to observe the rules of natural justice when *exercising* legislative powers is a question of statutory construction. In answering it the courts will be influenced by the factors discussed in Chapter 5 as well as others such as whether the legislation has been passed to deal with a temporary emergency, whether it provides a specific procedure to be followed, or whether it provides a statutory right of appeal. In addition, decisions will be influenced by the views of the courts at a particular time on the desirability, or otherwise, of extending judicial review of ministerial powers. Nothing would be gained by attempting to deal at length with the many reported cases dealing with individual statutes; one or two examples must suffice. In *De Verteuil* v. *Knaggs* [1918] A.C. 557, the Privy Council thought that the governor of a colony was normally[49] required to hold a hearing before exercising his power under an ordinance which provided that he could order the removal of immigrants from a plantation if he thought "on sufficient ground shown to his satisfaction" that they ought to be removed. On the other side of the line, in *Laffer* v. *Gillen* [1927] A.C. 886 the Privy Council held that a minister was entitled to determine a lease without a hearing where a clause in the lease provided that he could determine it at any time within 10 years if "satisfied on such evidence as he deems sufficient" that the tenant was incapable of farming the demised land. In *Patterson* v. *District Commissioner of Accra* [1948] A.C. 341, the Privy Council held that a district commissioner was not required to hold a hearing before assessing the liability of inhabitants to contribute towards the cost of special security measures under an ordinance which entitled him "after inquiry, if necessary [to] assess the proportion in which [the cost] is to be paid by the said inhabitants according to his judgment of their respective means."

The application of the rule against bias to ministerial decisions raises special problems because of the interest which a minister inevitably has in almost any decision which he makes. The Committee on Ministers' Powers recognised the danger of what it called departmental bias, painting a slightly fanciful picture of "an easy-going and cynical Minister rather bored with his office and sceptical of the value of his Department [who] would find it far easier to apply a judicial mind to purely judicial problems connected with the Department's administration than a Minister whose head and heart were in his work"; Cmd. 4060 (1932), p. 78. It was the misfortune of the objectors in *Franklin* v. *Minister of Town and Country Planning* [1948] A.C. 87 to encounter such an enthusiastic minister. At a public meeting the minister had said he had a duty to carry out and he would carry it out even if people were fractious and unreasonable. When the minister later made an order relating to the public inquiry which had been the subject of his remarks at the meeting certain householders unsuccessfully applied to have the order quashed on the grounds of bias. Lord Thankerton said:

> "No judicial duty is laid on the respondent in discharge of these statutory duties . . . the only question is whether he has complied with the statutory directions to appoint a person to hold the public inquiry, and to consider that person's report" (at p. 102).

"Bias," according to Lord Thankerton, was a term to be confined to those who hold judicial or quasi-judicial office. *Franklin* may be explicable as turning purely on a point of statutory interpretation, or simply as another example of the judicial attitude of non-intervention which prevailed for a period after the Second World War. In the latter event, changes in judicial attitudes[50] may have made *Franklin* an unsafe guide for the future. If it could be shown that a minister might be reasonably thought to be biased because of some private financial interest he had in a decision the courts might be prepared to interfere, in the light of the right they regularly claim to exist, on the ground of bad faith.[51]

Statutes dealing with such matters as compulsory purchase of land, planning controls or the building of roads commonly provide for an inquiry or a hearing[52] to be held by an inspector whose report must be considered by the minister before he makes his decision. In such cases a number of questions relating to the requirements of natural justice arise quite apart from that of "departmental bias."

Many inquiries are governed by rules contained in statutory instruments which recognise and apply the normal requirements of natural justice such as adequate notice of the case an objector has to meet.[53] The House of Lords, in *Fairmount Investments* v. *Secretary of State for the Environment* [1976] 1 W.L.R. 1255 held that it was a breach of natural justice for an inspector to make recommendations on the strength of considerations which the objector had not known were in the inspector's mind and had had no chance to deal with. This was an application to planning cases of the principle discussed earlier in Chapter 3.[54] Neither those cases not the *Fairmount Investments* case must be taken to mean that an inspector can make no comment or express no view without first putting it to the parties. He may draw inferences from what was argued before him; what he must not do is introduce into his report entirely novel points; *General Accident Fire and Life Assurance Co.* v. *Secretary of State for the Environment* (1977) 241 E.G. 842. It is a breach of natural justice for an inspector to receive evidence in the absence of one of the parties, for example, by visiting a site after an inquiry and speaking to the residents to ascertain their views on the matter at issue, whether to demolish or improve their houses; *Hibernian Property Co. Ltd.* v. *Secretary of State for the Environment* (1974) 27 P. & C.R. 197.[55] Departure from the strict rules of evidence observed in the courts is, of course, no more a breach of natural justice in the case of inquiries than in the case of other administrative or domestic tribunals.[56] In *Bushell* v. *Secretary of State for the Environment*, *The Times*, December 10, 1977, for example, Sir Douglas Frank, Q.C., sitting as a deputy judge, held that hearsay evidence was admissible before an inspector provided only that the other side was given an opportunity to comment on it. Documents might be put in evidence and relied on by witnesses without being proved as they would have to be in the High Court.'[57]

Authority for the view that a right to cross-examine witnesses forms part of the right to a hearing was discussed in Chapter 3. Here it is only necessary to refer to *Nicholson* v. *Secretary of State for Energy and National Coal Board* (1977) 76 L.G.R. 693, where Sir Douglas Frank, Q.C., sitting as a deputy judge, held that the right to cross-examine was a rule of natural justice and hence might be asserted even by parties appearing before an inspector who had no express statutory right under any of the inquiries procedure rules laid down by statutory instrument. In the view of the learned deputy judge any applicable statutory rules do not in general exclude the rules of natural justice but are supplemental to them. Whatever the correctness of that proposition in the light of the particular facts in *Nicholson's* case it must be remembered that normally the courts will assume that legislature provisions governing procedure are intended to replace the rules of natural justice.[58] Support for that approach in the case of inquiries is to be found in *Lake District Special Planning Board* v. *Secretary of State for the Environment*, *The Times*, February 18, 1975 where Kerr J. said, with respect correctly, that "a complainant inevitably faced a heavy burden in seeking to establish a breach of the rules of natural justice when the allegation related to something comprised within the scope of statutory procedure when no breach of the procedure had been established." In *Bizony* v. *Secretary of State for the Environment* [1976] J.P.L. 306 Bridge J. expressed a similar view when he said that where a statute prescribed the grounds on which a decision could be challenged it might be that it is not open to the court to introduce the wider concept of natural justice. The learned judge, however, thought that, in any event, the hearing accorded to Bizony satisfied the requirements of natural justice.

Apart from the adequacy of the hearing, a dissatisfied objector may wonder about the impartiality of inspectors. Are they, as judges are, free even from the risks of bias which might arise from a concern for their own future careers? Are they too closely connected with the departments for which they hold inquiries to be able to bring a genuinely impartial mind to their work? This question was considered by the Franks Committee which emphasised that it had received "virtually no criticism of the qualifications of inspectors or of the manner in which they conduct enquiries."[59] Nonetheless the Committee finally decided to recommend that inspectors should be put under the control of the Lord Chancellor rather than being employed as full-time members of particular departments or being appointed from time to time by a department to conduct a particular inquiry. That recommendation was not accepted by the Government. However, the Departments of the Environment and Transport have recently agreed that highway inquiries should in future be conducted by inspectors nominated by the Lord Chancellor.[60]

Another important aspect of public confidence in the operation of inquiries is the right to know the contents of the inspector's report. There is likely to be suspicion about a system which grants a hearing and, as will be seen later, requires ministers in some cases to reopen inquiries or allow further representations if the report at the centre of the procedure is withheld from the parties. The courts gave no right to see the report but the Franks Committee recommended publication on the ground that "fair play for the citizen" required that he should know what the inspector said to the minister.[61] This recommendation has been accepted and is specifically included in the statutory rules of procedure governing various classes of inquiries. The report is not, however, made available until the minister has made his decision.

A point which should not be overlooked is that not all inquiries are held because of a statutory duty to do so. Ministers sometimes hold inquiries to better inform themselves although there is no legal obligation to do so. In such cases parties cannot object that the hearing did not satisfy the standards required by natural justice. If they have no legal right to any bread at all they must accept a half loaf if it is offered; *Essex County Council* v. *Minister of Housing and Local Government* (1967) 18 P. & C.R. 531.

To what extent, if at all, does natural justice apply to the minister himself? In a series of cases the courts have distinguished between the judicial or quasi-judicial role of a minister which arises once an objection or an appeal has brought into existence a *"lis"* or justiciable issue between the complainant and a public authority and, on the other hand, the minister's administrative role before the *"lis"* comes into existence. In the latter case the minister may quite properly communicate with a local authority, discussing and commenting on their plans.[62] Once an objection is lodged such communications—unless both parties are involved—constitute a breach of natural justice; *Errington* v. *Minister of Health* [1935] 1 K.B. 249. The courts themselves were perfectly well aware of the unsatisfactory and artificial nature of attempts to separate the "judicial" and "administrative" functions of ministers. Lord Greene M.R., for example, referred to attempts "to force this very curious procedure, with its curious obligations into the straight jacket of the formulae of ordinary litigation by the use in ambiguous senses of such words as 'lis,' 'quasi-judicial' and so forth"; *B. Johnson & Co.* (*Builders*) *Ltd.* v. *Minister of Health* [1947] 2 All E.R. 395, 402. The courts were trying to produce a balance between ensuring that a particular objector knew enough to be able to make an effective presentation of his case and, on the other hand, the recognition that behind every dispute lay general political, economic and social considerations which every minister must have in mind and, in the light of which the local authority reached the decision which led to the inquiry. As Lord Greene M.R. said in *B. Johnson & Co.* (*Builders*) *Ltd.* v. *Minister of Health* [1947] 2 All E.R. 395, 401,

"It is obvious to anyone who has any familiarity with the operations of government departments that matters of high public policy, such as this, are, or may be under constant consideration and review by the necessary Minister. The problem does not, so to speak, arrive suddenly out of the blue by the putting forward by the local authority of a compulsory purchase order for confirmation."

Once the inspector has concluded his hearing and produced his report the rights of the ministers and objectors are now largely governed by statutory rules. The Franks Committee had been concerned about the extent to which a minister might take into account new evidence received after an inquiry had concluded. The committee suggested a distinction between new factual evidence and advice on policy, which the Government accepted. A minister is, in many cases, now required to notify all the parties concerned if (i) he intends to differ from an inspector on a finding of fact or (ii) he is likely to disagree with the inspector's recommendations because he has taken into consideration new evidence (which includes expert evidence on a matter of fact) or any new issue of fact (which does not include questions of government policy). Where the minister is differing on a finding of fact the parties have 21 days in which to make written representations. In the other cases the parties have 21 days within which to ask for the reopening of the inquiry.[63] An example of the rules being successfully invoked to invalidate a ministerial decision is to be found in *French Kier Developments Ltd.* v. *Secretary of State for the Environment* [1977] 1 All E.R. 296. In making his report, an inspector disregarded a document put before him but the minister relied on that document to justify a refusal to accept the inspector's recommendations. Willis J. held that to attach any weight to the contents of the document in the circumstances amounted to the taking into consideration of new evidence and the parties should therefore have had the opportunity to reopen the inquiry. The difficulty which may arise in interpreting the new rules is illustrated by *Murphy (J.) and Sons Ltd.* v. *Secretary of State for the Environment* [1973] 1 W.L.R. 560. An inspector had recommended against allowing a site to be developed for residential use because of the amount of noise coming from the plaintiff company's adjoining premises. The minister, however, granted permission for the development and the plaintiff's company claimed that, in doing so, he had differed from the inspector on a finding of fact. Ackner J. held that the minister had not differed from the inspector on a finding of fact but from the inspector's expression of opinion on the planning merits, which did not give the plaintiff the right to make further representations.[64] In the case of inquiries governed by these or similar rules the right to make further representations or to reopen the inquiry only arises if the minister differs from his inspector. Hence the receipt by the minister of new evidence from one side which strengthens his decision to agree with the inspector's recommendations does not give the parties a right to be notified and make representations or seek a reopening; *Bushell* v. *Secretary of State for the Environment*, *The Times*, December 10, 1977; [1978] J.P.L. 310. Nor, according to *Lake District Special Planning Board* v. *Secretary of State for the Environment*, *The Times*, February 18, 1975, is there a right to be notified where the minister decides not to accept the inspector's recommendations if that decision would have been taken despite the receipt of further evidence from one party. Such a view may be a correct interpretation of the statutory rules but it ignores the importance of justice being seen to be done.

The extent to which a minister is bound by the rules of natural justice after a hearing is completed is unlikely to be further elucidated in the future because of the statutory rules discussed in the previous paragraphs. In a case that falls outside those rules, the position has not been the subject of a decision, as opposed to dicta, in the courts.[65] Should the matter arise in the future it is to be hoped that the courts would resort to the concept of "fairness" rather than reviving the distinction between administrative and judicial functions. In defining fairness they would no doubt be influenced by the distinction drawn by the Franks Committee, and subsequently given statutory recognition, between matters of fact and questions of policy.

IV. Conflict of Laws and Natural Justice

Natural justice has often been referred to by English courts when considering the effect to be given to decisions of foreign courts.[66]

In most cases the phrase has been used in a narrow sense to refer to the rights discussed in the preceding chapters. Bramwell B. said, in *Crawley* v. *Isaacs* (1867) 16 L.T. 529, 530, "The term 'natural justice' which has been used in reference to foreign judgments refers rather to the form of procedure than to the merits of the particular case." A similar view was expressed by Channell J. when he said, in *Robinson* v. *Fenner* [1913] 3 K.B. 835, 842,

> "Whatever the expression 'contrary to natural justice,' which is used in so many cases means (and there really is very little authority indeed as to what it does mean), I think it is not enough to say that a decision is very wrong, any more than it is merely to say that it is wrong.... So far as I can see, all the instances given of what is 'contrary to natural justice' for the purpose of preventing a foreign judgment being sued on here are instances of injustice in the mode of arriving at the result, such as deciding against a man without hearing him or without having given him any notice or the like."[67]

In *Richardson* v. *Army Navy and General Assurance Association* (1925) 21 Ll.L.R. 345, the defendant company raised the interesting argument that a foreign judgment violated natural justice if the relevant foreign court had knowingly and perversely disregarded the rights given to an English subject by English law. Sankey J. did not think that the judgment under attack revealed such disrespect for English rights and thus he did not have to decide whether such a fault amounted to a breach of natural justice. However, having commented on the difficulty, and undesirability of defining natural justice the learned judge went on to say, "One has sometimes thought that the only certain thing is where a person has had no notice at all of the proceedings against him and gets a judgment against him under those circumstances" (p. 348). Nonetheless there is authority, particularly in connection with the recognition of foreign decrees of nullity and divorce, for the view that natural justice extends to a consideration of the substance of the rules applied by foreign courts. When used in this wide sense justice is liable to be described as "substantial" either instead of, or in addition to "natural." An example of the use of the two adjectives in the same judgment where they were clearly intended as synonymous is to be found in *Middleton*

v. *Middleton* [1967] P. 62. In the following paragraphs the position at common law will be discussed first before considering the effect of some important statutory provisions.

The requirement of a hearing if a foreign judgment or decree is to be enforceable in England was clearly stated in *Buchanan* v. *Rucker* (1807) 1 Camp. 63 when Lord Ellenborough said that "It is contrary to the first principles of reason and justice that either in civil or criminal proceedings a man should be condemned upheld." In that case the defendant to an action brought against him in Tobago had never been to that country and was unaware that proceedings had been taken against him: service of process was satisfied under local law by nailing the summons to the door of the court house. The judgment was held to be ineffective in England. Later cases have emphasised that even these words relating to the right to be heard must be read carefully in their context. They must not, for example, be taken to forbid judgment in default of appearance or service of process by advertisement, which the defendant fails to see, if, unlike the case in *Buchanan* v. *Rucker*, the defendant is subject to the jurisdiction of the foreign court, for example by residence in the relevant country; *Schibsby* v. *Westernholz* (1870) L.R. 6 Q.B. 155. In matrimonial cases breach of the *audi alteram partem* rule has been successfully pleaded in cases where the foreign court lacked jurisdiction under English conflict of law rules. In *Rudd* v. *Rudd* [1924] P. 72, for example, although Horridge J. was prepared to hold that the decree of a court in Washington would not be recognised because the wife had had no notice of the proceedings, the first ground of his judgment was that the husband was not domiciled in Washington and hence, under the law at that time, the American court had no jurisdiction over the marriage.[68] Where the foreign court does have jurisdiction the English courts are prepared to recognise a decree provided that notice of proceedings has been given in accordance with the requirements of the local law even if the respondent did not in fact receive notice; *Igra* v. *Igra* [1951] P. 404.[69] However, if the petitioner has been guilty of fraud to ensure that notice, although formally served as required by the local law, is not received by the respondent the English court will not recognise the foreign decree; *Macalpine* v. *Macalpine* [1958] P. 35; *Middleton* v. *Middleton* [1967] P. 62. It is possible that the English courts would refuse to recognise a foreign judgment if the rules for service were such that, for example, they afforded no real opportunity to prepare a defence even if notice were received before the hearings. This question was briefly discussed in the recent case of *Law* v. *Gustin* [1976] Fam. 155. W had left her husband, H, who was domiciled in England, to follow her lover to Kansas. After a period of residence there she obtained a decree of nullity. Advertisements of the proceedings were placed in the local newspaper, according to the law of Kansas, and a letter was sent to H by W's American solicitors which was received by H five days before the expiry of the time limit for defending the proceedings. The decree of nullity was pronounced a week after that date. Bagnall J. held that the procedure satisfied the requirements of natural justice. That finding is not, perhaps, surprising since H was seeking a declaration that the Kansan decree was valid. There is no doubt that at common law a party who agreed to accept a particular method of receiving notification of legal proceedings could not complain if that resulted in him not receiving notice in time to participate in proceedings which did in fact ensue.[70]

The fact that a foreign court has refused to allow the giving of evidence which would be admissible in an English court does not amount to a denial of natural justice; *Scarpetta* v. *Lowenfeld* (1911) 27 T.L.R. 509. Conversely it is not a breach of natural justice to admit evidence which is inadmissible under English law; *De Cosse Brissac* v. *Rathbone* (1861) 6 H. & N. 301. Nor, under a plea of natural justice, can the English court be asked to decide on the reliability of the evidence before the foreign court. In *Jacobson* v. *Frachon* (1928) 138 L.T. 386, for example, the plaintiff claimed—with some apparent justification—that the expert witness on whom the French court relied was biased in favour of the other party. The French court had rejected that argument and the Court of Appeal refused to consider it as a ground for not recognising the French judgment. It is possible that the rules of evidence and procedure of a foreign tribunal might be such that a party, despite notice and appearing before the tribunal, had no real chance to put his case. If that were so, it might be argued that the requirements of natural justice had not been satisfied. Atkin L.J. in *Jacobson* v. *Frachon* expressly referred to the possibility of holding a foreign judgment invalid if the court concerned had refused a "substantial hearing."

The application of the rule against bias to a foreign court is illustrated by *Price* v. *Dewhurst* (1837) 8 Sim. 279. Under Danish law executors were entitled to constitute themselves into an executors court of dealing and determine questions of testamentary law. Two executors, appointed under a Danish will, exercised their powers to declare that will to be valid and a later English will invalid. The executors and their relatives were entitled under the Danish will to a large part of the deceased estate. In refusing to recognise their judgment Shadwell V.-C. said that it was "contrary to the common course of justice that anything should be called a judgment, or be allowed to have any effect where the persons to decide are the interested persons" (p. 305).

The view that in the context of recognition of foreign judgments natural justice extends beyond the requirements of a fair hearing and an impartial tribunal largely rests on the use by Lindley M.R. of the phrase "substantial justice" in *Pemberton* v. *Hughes* [1899] 1 Ch. 781, 790. It may be doubted whether the learned Master of the Rolls intended his words to bear the wide meaning subsequently given to them. Vaughan Williams L.J., for instance, in the same case, spoke of natural justice in what might be described as the narrow sense (at p. 796). Nor does other judicial usage suggest that "substantial" means something wider than natural justice in the procedural sense; see, for example, the reference to "the substantial requirements of justice" by the Earl of Selborne L.C. in *Spackman* v. *Plumstead District Board of Works* (1885) 10 App.Cas. 229, 240. However, in *Gray* v. *Formosa* [1963] P. 259[71] the Court of Appeal quoted the words of Lindley M.R. as justifying the refusal to recognise a decree of nullity pronounced by a Maltese court because, in the view of the English court, a rule of law which invalidated the marriage of a Maltese Catholic which had been celebrated in a register office in England was contrary to "the simple principles of justice"; *per* Lord Denning M.R. at p. 422. In *Lepre* v. *Lepre* [1965] P. 52 Sir Jocelyn Simon P. applied *Gray* v. *Formosa*, basing his decision on "natural justice" (p. 63). Even if it is desirable that the courts should have a wide discretion to refuse to recognise foreign decrees or judgments there is no need to give an unusually wide meaning to substantial or natural justice since the courts have always asserted an entirely separate right to refuse to recognise decisions of foreign courts which are contrary to public policy.

Foreign judgments could not be enforced at common law in England except by resorting to a further action in the English courts. Statutes have, however, provided for the direct enforcement of foreign judgments which have been registered in accordance with their provisions. The importance of adequate notice of proceedings has been recognised in two such Acts, the Administration of Justice Act 1920 and the Foreign Judgments (Reciprocal Enforcement) Act 1933.[72] In the former case a judgment obtained anywhere in the Commonwealth could be registered if the court thought registration just and convenient. Registration was, however, expressly forbidden if the defendant in the original proceedings had not been served with process and did not appear in the original proceedings. The Foreign Judgments (Reciprocal Enforcement) Act 1933, which is intended, ultimately, to supersede the 1920 Act, is not confined to Commonwealth territories. Registration is of right. Registration may, however, be set aside if the defendant, whether or not he was duly served with process in accordance with the foreign law, did not receive notice of the proceedings in sufficient time to prepare his defence and did not appear in court, (s. 4(1)(*a*)(iii)). Neither statute refers to the effect of bias on the part of the foreign tribunal.

Further statutory recognition of the importance of the right to a hearing is contained in the Arbitration Act 1975 under which foreign arbitral awards may be enforced in the English courts. Section 5 provides that a foreign arbitration within the terms of the Act may not be enforced if proper notice of the appointment of the arbitrator or of the arbitration proceedings had not been given to the party against whom the award is invoked or if that person was otherwise unable to present his case.

In the case of the recognition of foreign divorce decrees, the relevant statutory provisions are not in addition to but replace the common law rules. The Recognition of Divorces and Legal Separations Act 1971, s. 8(2) provides that an English court may refuse to recognise the validity of a divorce or legal separation obtained outside the British Isles if (*a*) it was obtained by one spouse—

(i) without such steps having been taken for giving notice of the proceedings to the other spouse as having regard to the nature of the proceedings and all the circumstances, should reasonably have been taken;

(ii) without the other spouse having been given (for any reason other than lack of notice) such opportunity to take part in the proceedings as having regard to the matters aforesaid, he should reasonably have been given.

(*b*) its recognition would manifestly be contrary to public policy.

By implication, the exclusion from the terms of subsection 2 of decrees granted elsewhere in the British Isles is clearly intended to mean that they are open to challenge only on the ground set out in section 8(1), namely that such a decree was obtained at a time when according to English law there was no subsisting marriage between the parties.

The meaning of section 8(2)(*a*)(ii) was considered by Rees J. in *Newmarch* v. *Newmarch* [1977] 3 W.L.R. 832. The wife alleged that she had not been able to defend a petition brought in New South Wales because of the failure of her Australian solicitors to comply with instructions from her English solicitor. The learned judge held that the subsection gave a discretion to the court which, in the circumstances, he was not prepared to exercise. On the facts there was little doubt that the husband would have obtained the decree even if the Australian solicitors had carried out the wife's instructions. Recognition of the Australian decree did not affect her chance of obtaining maintenance in the Australian courts and was, in the judge's view, in the wife's best interests.[73]

The meaning of section 8(2)(*b*) was considered in the earlier decision of *Kendall* v. *Kendall* [1977] 3 All E.R. 471 where a wife challenged the validity of a decree of a Bolivian court. At her husband's request she had signed a form which she did not realise was a power of attorney authorising the commencement of divorce proceedings in her name. The learned judge thought that since the wife was, on the face of the decree, the person who brought the proceedings, she could not rely on the provisions of subsection 8(2)(*a*). Whether that view was correct or not is immaterial since he held that recognition would be manifestly contrary to public policy.

It may be presumed that in future cases the courts will, in interpreting these provisions, pay regard to the decisions prior to the Act which have been discussed earlier. Nor can there be any doubt that the reference to public policy will allow the courts to take account of bias in a tribunal, which is not expressly mentioned in the Act, and, as in *Gray* v. *Formosa*, the injustice of a foreign rule according to English notions of justice.

Notes

[1] In one sense all arbitration agreements are within the Arbitration Act 1950 but in view of the added powers possessed by the courts where arbitration agreements are in writing it is possible to describe the latter as alone falling within the Act.

[2] *Sutcliffe* v. *Thackrah* [1974] A.C. 727, 752; see further, Enid A. Marshall, "When the Architect is not a Quasi-Arbitrator" (1974) 37 M.L.R. 566.

[3] *Arenson* v. *Arenson* [1977] A.C. 405, 422 *per* Lord Simon.

[4] *Hatrick* (*N.Z.*) *Ltd.* v. *Nelson Carlton Con.* [1964] N.Z.L.R. 72.

[5] *Hickman* v. *Roberts* [1913] A.C. 229; *Hounslow LBC* v. *Twickenham Developments* [1971] Ch. 233; *Sutcliffe* v. *Thackrah* (*supra*).

[6] *Jenkins* v. *Bentham* (1855) 15 C.B. 168; *Turner* v. *Goulden* (1873) L.R. 9 C.P. 57; *Arenson* v. *Arenson* (*supra*).

[7] See, *e.g.* I. N. Duncan Wallace, *Hudson's Building and Engineering Contracts* (10th ed., 1970) Sweet & Maxwell; *Building and Civil Engineering Standard Forms* (1969) Sweet & Maxwell; *Further Building and Engineering Standard Forms* (1973) Sweet & Maxwell; D. Keating, *Building Contracts* (4th ed., 1978) Sweet & Maxwell.

[8] As was the case in *Sutcliffe* v. *Thackrah*. See also *Nuttall* v. *Manchester Corporation* (1892) T.L.R. 513; *Bristol Corporation* v. *John Aird & Co.* [1913] A.C. 241.

[9] See also *Sadler* v. *Smith* (1869) L.R. 5 Q.B. 40; *Cipriani* v. *Burnett* [1933] A.C. 83 (P.C.).

[10] *Harvey* v. *Shelton* (1844) 7 Beav. 455; *Re Brook and Delcomyn* (1864) 16 C.B.(N.S.) 403; *supra*, p. 17.

[11] See the cases cited *supra*, n. 5.

[12] For the Arbitration Act 1975 see *post*, p. 181. On arbitration generally see A. Walton, *Russell on Arbitration* (18th ed.) Stevens; C. M. Schmitthoff, *The Export Trade* (6th ed., 1975) Stevens, Chap. 26.

[13] "Where an agreement between any parties provides that disputes which may arise in the future between them shall be referred to an arbitrator named or designated in the agreement, and after a dispute has arisen any party applies, on the ground that the arbitrator so named or designated is not or may not be impartial, for leave to revoke the authority of the arbitrator or for an injunction to restrain any other party or the arbitrator from proceeding with the arbitration, it shall not be a ground for refusing the application that the said party at the time when he made the agreement knew, or ought to have known, that the arbitrator, by reason of his relation towards any other party to the agreement or of his connection with the subject referred, might not be capable of impartiality."

[14] Since the arbitrator may have acted in complete good faith the word misconduct is inappropriate and unfortunate; *Re Fuerst and Stephenson* [1951] 1 Lloyd's Rep. 429, 431 *per* Croom-Johnson J.; *Wildhandel N.V.* v. *Tucker & Cross* [1976] 1 Lloyd's Rep. 341, 343 *per* Kerr J.

[15] Some earlier dicta are, it is suggested, explicable in the light of the particular cases. They occur not in cases where the parties had agreed to waive a right to a hearing but where the question was precisely whether they had so agreed or, assuming that they had not agreed, whether the hearing conducted by the arbitrator complied with the minimum requirements for such a hearing.

[16] *F. E. Hookway & Co. Ltd.* v. *Alfred Isaacs & Sons* [1954] 1 Lloyd's Rep. 491; *Henry Bath & Son Ltd.* v. *Birgby Products* [1962] 1 Lloyd's Rep. 389; *supra* p. 74.

[17] See also *W. Naumann* v. *Edward Nathan & Co. Ltd.* (1930) 37 Ll.L.R. 249; *London Export Corporation Ltd.* v. *Jubilee Coffee Roasting Co. Ltd.* [1958] 1 W.L.R. 271 and 661.

[18] Similarly *Eckersley* v. *MDHB* [1894] 2 Q.B. 667 (C.A.).

[19] See also *Sellar* v. *Highland Ry.* 1919 S.C.(H.L.) 19.

[20] See further *Panamena Europea Navigacion* (*Compania Limitada*) v. *Frederick Leyland & Co. Ltd.* (*J. Russell & Co.*) [1947] A.C. 428.

[21] In *Re Elliot and S. Devon Ry.* (1848) 12 Jur.(o.s.) 445 Knight Bruce V.-C. held that the plaintiff had waived any right to object to the railway company's arbitrator who had been their agent in earlier attempts to buy the plaintiff's land by agreement. The vice-chancellor refused to set aside the arbitral award on the ground that the umpire was a surveyor for the G.W.R. which had an interest in the S. Devon Ry. although he thought that "in point of delicacy" he ought not to have been appointed.

[22] "At that dinner so far as the umpire is concerned, there appears to have been some excess, and he is afterwards found to be intoxicated, and obliged to remain in the inn."

[23] See also *Wessanen's Koninklijke Fabrieken N.V.* v. *Isaac Modiano* [1960] 1 W.L.R. 1243 [1960] 2 Lloyd's Rep. 257; *M. V. Myron* (*Owners*) v. *Tradax Export S.A.* [1970] 1 Q.B. 527; [1969] 1 Lloyd's Rep. 411.

[24] See also *Oswald* v. *Earl Grey* (1855) 24 L.J.Q.B. 69; *Bache* v. *Billingham* [1894] 1 Q.B. 107; *W. Ramsden & Co.* v. *Jacobs* [1922] 1 K.B. 640.

[25] *Walker* v. *Frobisher* (1801) 6 Ves. 70; *Dobson* v. *Groves* (1844) 14 L.J.Q.B. 17; *Re Camillo Eitzen and Jewson & Sons* (1896) 40 S.J. 438; *Re Fuerst and Stephenson* [1951] 1 Lloyd's Rep. 429; *Eastcheap Dried Fruit Co.* v. *N. V. Gebroeders Catz* [1962] 1 Lloyd's Rep. 283.

[26] See similarly, *Re Gregson and Armstrong* (1894) 70 L.T. 106.

[27] Similarly *Giacomo Costa Fu Andrea* v. *British Italian Trading Co. Ltd.* [1961] 2 Lloyd's Rep. 392; [1963] 1 Q.B. 201.

[28] See also *Re Tidswell* (1863) 33 Beav. 213; *Andrews* v. *Mitchell* [1905] A.C. 78; *Societe Franco Tunisienne D'Armement Tunis* v. *Govt. of Ceylon* [1959] 1 W.L.R. 787.

[29] *Haigh* v. *Haigh* (1861) 5 L.T. 507; *Eastern Counties Ry.* v. *Eastern Union Ry.* (1863) 3 De G.J. & S. 610; *Cerrito* v. *North Eastern Timber Importers* [1952] 1 Lloyd's Rep. 330; *Giacomo Costa Fu Andrea* v. *British Italian Trading Co. Ltd.*, *supra*.

[30] *Re Hawley and N. Staffordshire Ry.* (1848) 12 Jur. 389. *Cf. Parr* v. *Winteringham* (1859) 28 L.J.Q.B. 123, 125; 1 El. & El. 394, 397 *per* Lord Campbell C.J., *supra* p. 91 and p. 148.

[31] See also *GKN Centrax Gears Ltd.* v. *Matbro Ltd.* [1976] 2 Lloyd's Rep. 555, 581, *per* Bridge L.J.

[32] The two ancient universities, as opposed to their constituent colleges, are regarded as civil corporations which are not subject to visitorial jurisdiction: Blackstone, Comm.i.471; *R.* v. *Vice-Chancellor of Cambridge* (1765) 3 Burr. 1647. Hence the

willingness of the courts to intervene in Dr. Bentley's case, *R.* v. *Cambridge University* (1723) 1 Stra. 557; *supra*, p. 14.

[33] *Eden* v. *Foster* (1725) 2 P.Wms. 325 (King Edward VI School, Birmingham); *Att.-Gen.* v. *Price* (1744) 3 Atk. 108 (King Edward VI School, Barkhamstead); *Herring* v. *Templeman* [1973] 3 All E.R. 569 (Church of England College for the training of teachers).

[34] *Thomson* v. *University of London* (1864) 33 L.J.Ch. 625; *Thorne* v. *University of London* [1966] 2 Q.B. 237.

[35] See J. W. Bridge, "Keeping Peace in the Universities: The Role of the Visitor" (1970) 86 L.Q.R. 531. In *Herring* v. *Templeman*, *supra*, the Court of Appeal refused to strike out the plaintiff's claim on the ground that it was subject to the visitor's jurisdiction precisely because of doubt about the extent of his authority.

[36] See also *Carey* v. *Piphus* (U.S.) 55 L.Ed. 2d 252 (1978).

[37] *Fitzgerald* v. *Northcote* (1865) 4 F. & F. 656, 685 *per* Cockburn C.J. But see the doubts as to the contractual nature of the action expressed in *Wood* v. *Prestwich* (1911) 104 L.T. 388.

[38] Pupils Registration Regulations 1956, S.I. No. 357. Articles of Government or Rules of Management usually give a head teacher power to suspend a pupil for adequate cause while requiring that he immediately report the suspension to the managers or governors of the school and the local education authority.

[39] *Supra*, p. 37.

[40] *Lane* v. *Norman* (1891) 66 L.T. 83; *Leary* v. *National Union of Vehicle Builders* [1971] Ch. 34. 54 *per* Megarry J.; *supra* p. 88.

[41] *Cf.* the similar doubts about the contractual nature of the right of a schoolchild not to be expelled without reasonable cause expressed by Ridley and Avory JJ. in *Wood* v. *Prestwich supra*, n. 37.

[42] J. F. Garner, "Students—Contract or Status?" (1974) 90 L.Q.R. 6; reply by H. W. R. Wade, 90 L.Q.R. 157.

[43] See Paul Jackson [1972] P.L. 97; *Stephen & Co.* v. *The Post Office* [1977] 1 W.L.R. 1172, 1177 *per* Lord Denning M.R. See also *D'Mello* v. *Loughborough College of Technology*, *The Times*, June 17, 1970.

[44] A. Samuels, "The Student and the Law" (1973) 12 J.S.P.T.L. 252, 255; B. Schwartz and H. W. R. Wade, *Legal Control of Government* (1972) O.U.P., 245.

[45] J. A. G. Griffith, *The Politics of the Judiciary* (1977) Fontana, pp. 170, 197.

[46] *Cf. Blackburn* v. *Att.-Gen.* [1971] 1 W.L.R. 1037 (C.A.); *McWhirter* v. *Att.-Gen.* [1972] C.M.L.R. 882 (C.A.).

[47] See also *Hanratty* v. *Lord Butler of Saffron Walden* (1971) 115 S.J. 386 (C.A.). (The courts will not inquire whether a Home Secretary has been negligent in advising the Sovereign on the exercise of the Prerogative of Mercy.)

[48] See also *R.* v. *Legislative Committee of the Church Assembly, ex p. Haynes-Smith* [1928] 1 K.B. 411. The English and Irish courts have differed on where to draw, the line between legislative proceedings with which they will not interfere and proceedings which are subject to natural justice; compare *Re Local Government Board, ex p. Kingstown Commissioners* (1884) 16 L.R.Ir. 150; (1886) L.R.Ir. 509 with *R.* v. *Electricity Commissioners* [1924] 1 K.B. 171.

[49] For a possible exception, see *supra*, p. 135.

[50] See *Padfield* v. *Minister of Agriculture* [1968] A.C. 997; *Congreve* v. *Home Office* [1976] Q.B. 629 (C.A.); *Laker Airways Ltd.* v. *Department of Trade* [1977] Q.B. 643 (C.A.). But *cf. Gouriet* v. *Union of Post Office Workers* [1978] A.C. 435.

[51] *e.g. R.* v. *Governor of Brixton Prison, ex p. Soblen* [1963] 2 Q.B. 243, 302.

[52] See Wade *op. cit.* Chap. 24; R. E. Wraith and G. B. Lamb, *Public Inquiries as an Instrument of Government* (1971) George Allen & Unwin.

[53] For example, the Compulsory Purchase by Ministers (Inquiries Procedure) Rules 1967, S.I. 1967 No. 720; Compulsory Purchase by Public Authorities (Inquiries Procedure) Rules 1976, S.I. 1976 No. 746; The Highways (Inquiries Procedure) Rules 1976, S.I. 1976 No. 721.

[54] *Supra*, p. 65. [55] See also *Errington* v. *Minister of Health* [1935] 1 K.B. 249.

[56] *Supra*, p. 73.

[57] See also *Miller (T.A.)* v. *Minister of Housing and Local Government* [1968] 1 W.L.R. 992 (C.A.).

[58] For a discussion of the extent to which the rights of a party may vary with the terms of the relevant statute see *Magistrates of Ayr* v. *Lord Advocate* 1950 S.C. 102.

[59] Report of the Committee on Administrative Tribunals and Enquiries, Cmnd. 218 (1959), para. 292.

[60] Report on the Review of Highway Inquiry Procedures, Cmnd. 7133 (1978), para. 27.

[61] Cmnd. 218, para. 329. [62] *Frost* v. *Minister of Health* [1935] 1 K.B. 286.

[63] See *supra*, n. 53. See M. Purdue, "Natural Justice and the Post Inquiry Procedure" [1975] J.P.L. 445; [1976] J.P.L. 146.

[64] See also *Lord Luke of Pavenham* v. *Minister of Housing and Local Government* [1968] 1 Q.B. 172.

[65] See *B. Johnson & Co. (Builders) Ltd.* v. *Minister of Health* [1947] 2 All E.R. 395, 399–401; *Darlassis* v. *Minister of Education* (1954) 52 L.G.R. 304. In *Bushell* v. *Secretaries of State for the Environment and Transport* (*supra*) the suggestion was made that the position of the minister might vary, depending on whether he was dealing with a quasi-*lis* involving two parties, such as a local authority and an objector, or, on the other hand, with a scheme which he himself had initiated.

[66] See generally, Dicey and Morris, *The Conflict of Laws* (General ed. J. H. C. Morris) (9th ed., 1973) Stevens & Sons Ltd., pp. 324–326, 370 and 1018–1036.

[67] Similarly Lord Hanworth M.R., in *Jacobson* v. *Frachon* (1928) 138 L.T. 386, 390.

[68] See also *Shaw* v. *Att.-Gen.* (1870) L.R. 2 P. & D. 156.

[69] See also *Maubourquet* v. *Wyse* (1867) I.R. 1 C.L. 471; *Wood* v. *Wood* [1957] P. 254; *Hornett* v. *Hornett* [1971] P. 255.

[70] *Vallee* v. *Dumergue* (1849) 4 Exch. 290, 303; *Bank of Australasia* v. *Nias* (1851) 16 Q.B. 717, 734; *Jeannot* v. *Fuerst* (1909) 25 T.L.R. 424.

[71] Criticised, L. J. Blom-Cooper, "Temptation or Sophistry?" (1963) 26 M.L.R. 94.

[72] Judgments of Northern Irish and Scottish courts are registrable in England under the Judgments Extension Act 1868 and the Inferior Judgments Extension Act 1882, which contain no provisions for challenging the validity of the judgments of those courts.

[73] See also the brief report of *Hack* v. *Hack* (1976) 6 Fam. Law 177.

Further Developments: Foreign Judgments (pp. 181–182)

The State Immunity Act 1978 which gives effect to the European Convention on State Immunity provides by s. 18 for enforceability in U.K. courts of judgments given against the U.K. in courts of other parties to the Convention. S.19 (1)(*a*), however, provides that a court need not give effect to section 18 "if to do so would be manifestly contrary to public policy or if any party to the proceedings in which the judgment was given had no adequate opportunity to present his case."

CHAPTER 8

BREACH OF NATURAL JUSTICE AND REMEDIES

IN this chapter three topics will be discussed: first what is the effect of a decision reached in violation of natural justice? Secondly, must domestic remedies be exhausted before recourse to the courts is possible? Thirdly, what remedies are available in the courts to the litigant who has been denied natural justice?

I. THE EFFECT OF A BREACH OF NATURAL JUSTICE

Are all decisions affected in the same way when vitiated by a failure to observe the rules of natural justice, where they are applicable? And, if so, should such decisions be characterised as void or voidable? One writer has suggested that administrative law has suddenly been complicated by what he describes as this "new question"[1] although it might be better to say that it is only recently that the question has been discussed rather than to suggest that there used to be a clear rule which has been unsettled by the case law of the last few years. The problem, if there be one, extends beyond the bounds of administrative law, however that may be defined.

Before trying to state the law some preliminary points must be made. In the first place it is impossible to discuss, much less answer, the question unless the term "void" and "voidable" are clearly defined. It remains true, as was said in an earlier edition of a leading textbook, that to a large extent "analysis of [this question] is bedevilled by terminological inconsistencies, in particular by the bewildering use of the terms 'void' and 'voidable' "[2] Secondly, unless the outcome of a particular case will be affected by whether a breach of natural justice renders a decision void or voidable the question is little more than meaningless. The conflict between dicta in different cases is explicable, it is suggested, on this very basis, that often it does not really matter how a court characterises an offending decision. Thus in *White* v. *Kuzych* [1951] A.C. 585, the Privy Council refused to express a view on whether a decision reached by a biased tribunal was void or voidable because it was able to decide the case simply on the construction of the relevant union rule book.[3] But such judicial self-restraint is rare. Thus Megarry J. in *Hounslow L.B.C.* v. *Twickenham Garden Developments* [1971] Ch. 233, 258 could not help saying, although he had decided that natural justice was not applicable to the case before him:

> "A decision reached by a tribunal wholly outside its jurisdiction and in complete defiance of natural justice is about as void as anything can be; but if nobody who is entitled to challenge or question it chooses to do so, it remains in being. Yet to describe such a decision as being 'voidable' is to use that word in a sense that is not only very special but also liable to mislead."

It might be objected that it is equally misleading to describe a decision as "void" which is only void at the instance of certain parties, by resort to particular remedies. Thirdly, in the field of administrative law, at least, both terms may be equally inapplicable. That was clearly the view of Lord Diplock in *Hoffman La Roche* [1975] A.C. 295, 366, where, speaking of delegated legislation alleged to be invalid because of a failure to follow the correct procedure in its making, he said, "It leads to confusion to use such terms as 'voidable,' 'voidable ab initio,' 'void' or 'a nullity.' These are concepts developed in the private law of contract which are ill-adapted to the field of public law."[4] Fourthly, it is possible that the law is not yet settled. If, for example, as one writer maintains, the correct answer—that a breach of natural justice makes a decision void—is so clearly established by *Ridge* v. *Baldwin* [1964] A.C. 40, it is curious that the Privy Council in *Durayappah* v. *Fernando* [1967] 2 A.C. 337 and the House of Lords in *Anisminic Ltd.* v. *Foreign Compensation Commission* [1969] 2 A.C. 147 should reach conflicting views on what *Ridge* v. *Baldwin* decided. Similarly it is strange, if the law was explained by the House of Lords with "perfect clarity" in *Anisminic*, that confusion still prevails, on the same writer's admission, in the Court of Appeal.[5] De Smith has to admit to the continued existence of "nagging doubts whether breach of natural justice really does render an order or determination void."[6] Fifthly, to classify decisions reached in breach of natural justice as voidable, as opposed to void, would not constitute a unique exception to a general principle underlying judicial review that that jurisdiction extends only to void decisions. It is beyond doubt that decisions of tribunals quashed for error of law on the face of the record are voidable not void—a principle which Professor Wade describes, understandably, as an "awkward piece of doctrine."[7] Sixthly, it is misleading to use "void" when the voidness in question is admitted to be "relative not absolute."[8] It is similarly, with respect, misleading to say that "There is no such thing as voidness in an absolute sense for the whole question is, void against whom? It makes no sense to speak of an act being void unless there is some person to whom the law gives a remedy."[9] Without invoking analogies from the law of nullity of marriage or the law of contract which might be argued to be unreliable evidence in such a different sphere,[10] there are examples in administrative law of decisions which can be described as void in an absolute sense: in *Re Daws* (1838) 8 Ad. & El. 936 a coroner's clerk held an inquest in the absence of the coroner and purported to sign the inquisition in the coroner's name. Denman C.J. refused certiorari to quash the decision; "It is a mere nullity and because of that does not necessitate certiorari." Professor Wade regards this case as an example of the "short-lived fallacy" that certiorari would not lie "to quash nullities."[11] However, it is precisely this "fallacy" which best explains a case like *R.* v. *Barnstaple Justices, ex p. Calder* [1938] 1 K.B. 385 where certiorari was refused to quash a "decision" made by justices who were purporting to exercise a jurisdiction to licence plans of cinemas before they were built, in the absence of any statutory power.[12] In *Craig* v. *Kanssen* [1943] 1 K.B. 256 Lord Greene M.R. said that a judgment of the High Court was a nullity which could be disregarded without the need for an appeal where there had been a fundamental breach of the rules relating to the service of process on the defendant. On the other hand, less serious defects in service result in a voidable judgment which is valid unless set aside on appeal; *Dryden* v. *Dryden* [1953]

1 W.L.R. 952. Seventhly, it is suggested that decisions relating to the remedies available to a person aggrieved by a failure to observe natural justice do not provide reliable evidence with which to answer the question, void or voidable? Such decisions are inconsistent; they often make no reference to the controversy and in many cases can be used to support either view. For example, it is argued that since a declaration merely declares the law it can only issue where the action in question is void. Voidable acts must be quashed by certiorari. Since the House of Lords granted a declaration in *Ridge* v. *Baldwin* (*supra*) the dismissal of the chief constable without a hearing must have been void. But it is still far from being generally accepted that declarations cannot be granted where the act or judgment complained of is merely voidable.[13] Similarly mandamus has in some instances issued without certiorari to quash a decision complained of irrespective of whether the decision was void or voidable.[14] A final difficulty, or, at any rate, peculiarity, about classifying as void decisions reached in breach of natural justice is that the party adversely affected may waive his or her right to a fair hearing before an impartial tribunal. The possibility of waiver does not, of itself, establish that breach of the rules of natural justice does not go to the jurisdiction of the court or tribunal—in which case its decision would be void—but it is a factor to be taken into consideration with others already mentioned.[15]

It has been suggested that terms such as "void" and "voidable" are freely used by the courts when quashing decisions vitiated by a breach of natural justice because often nothing turns on how the defect is classified. In some instances, however, the distinction may have, or may be treated as having, important legal consequences. First, the courts, in interpreting restrictively statutory provisions which aim at ousting their powers of review, have relied on the void–voidable distinction. A void determination, it has been argued, is not a determination at all and its invalidity can be declared by the courts in the face of a section which seemingly protects a tribunal's findings from judicial questioning. In *Anisminic Ltd.* v. *Foreign Compensation Commission* [1969] 2 A.C. 147, for example, the House of Lords held that a decision of the Commission, based on a misconstruction of an Order in Council, involved an excess of jurisdiction. The Foreign Compensation Act 1950 which established the Commission had expressly provided that determinations of the Commission were not to be questioned in any court of law; s. 4(4). The House of Lords, however, said that such a clause did not apply to a void decision such as that before their Lordships; such a decision was not a determination at all. The sequel to *Anisminic* was the Foreign Compensation Act 1969 which in certain circumstances creates a right of appeal to the Court of Appeal from decisions of the Commission. Section 3(10) preserves "any right of any person to bring proceedings questioning any determination of the Commission on the ground that it is contrary to natural justice." Such wording, of course, does nothing to settle whether such a right exists or, more generally, the effect of a breach of natural justice. *Anisminic* itself contained dicta that decisions reached in breach of natural justice are void as being in excess of jurisdiction; Lord Reid at p. 171, Lord Pearce at p. 197. Lord Pearson expressed his concurrence with the views of Lords Reid and Pearce on the courts' supervisory function (at p. 215); Lord Wilberforce, while recognising that it must be taken to follow from *Ridge* v. *Baldwin* that a failure to apply natural justice "may be equivalent to a departure from the remitted area" (that is, amount to excess of jurisdiction) expressly adverted to the dangers of the use of the word "nullity"—"if it draws with it the difficult distinction between what is void and what is voidable . . . I certainly do not wish to be taken to recognise that this distinction exists or to analyse it if it does" (at pp. 207–208). Secondly, the right of a plaintiff to challenge a decision reached in breach of natural justice might well depend on whether it was categorised as void or voidable since in particular cases the appropriate remedy may depend on whether the decision impugned is void or voidable and, with the remedy, the right of the aggrieved person to seek relief.[16] As will be seen in the second part of this chapter it is sometimes thought that the right to a judicial remedy after exhausting domestic appellate procedures depends on the initial decision complained of being void rather than voidable. This, it is suggested, is the reason why, in *Ridge* v. *Baldwin* [1964] A.C. 40, Lord Reid and Lord Hodson were concerned to describe a breach of natural justice as rendering a decision void. (Lord Morris seemed to agree with Lord Reid and Lord Hodson, although he has been claimed as an adherent of the voidable school by the Privy Council in *Durayappah* v. *Fernando* [1967] 2 A.C. 337, 354. Lord Evershed and Lord Devlin both preferred to describe such a decision as voidable.) It will be suggested later that it is possible to maintain the right of resort to the courts after exhausting domestic remedies without having to define the original decision complained of as void.

Professor Wade has suggested a third significance in how the courts classify the effect of a breach of natural justice. His concern is that the courts, if they hold such decisions merely voidable, will be claiming for themselves a discretion of immense significance:

> "Judicial discretion plays an indispensable part in the law. But it ought not to be allowed to undermine constitutional fundamentals. One of these, surely, is that the citizen may resist unlawful governmental action as of right. If this were made a matter of discretion, the court would be taking upon itself the power to dispense public authorities from observance of the law. Every lawyer will understand the implications of this."[17]

If the courts claimed such a discretion they would, the learned author argues elsewhere, be introducing "dangerous uncertainty . . . palm-tree injustice."[18] This fear is perhaps somewhat misplaced. A decision may be voidable without the courts thereby having a discretion whether to set it aside or not. Conversely, whatever the effect of a breach of natural justice a court may, in its discretion, refuse to grant, for example, an injunction or declaration because of unmeritorious behaviour on the part of the plaintiff.

The case law, on the effect of a failure to observe the rules of natural justice has been described as affording a "spectacle of anarchy upon which order can hardly be superimposed."[19] In this, and the following paragraphs, it will be attempted, so far as possible, to minimise the anarchy by distinguishing between various types of courts, bodies and tribunals. In the case of the ordinary courts it is generally agreed, even by Professor Wade, that a breach of natural justice renders a decision of the superior courts voidable. This was the view of the judges who advised the House of Lords, in the case of a decree of the Lord Chancellor which was vitiated by financial interest; *Dimes* v. *Grand Junction Canal* (1852) 3 H.L.C. 759. The same principle applies, it is submitted, to all courts including magistrates' courts.[20] Support for this proposition is found in the criminal law. An acquittal secured in breach of natural justice before magistrates is sufficient to prevent a second trial.[21] If such a verdict is void, the refusal of the courts to allow a second trial is an illogical and unadmitted exception to the general rule that earlier *void* proceedings are no bar to a subsequent trial on the same charge.[22]

There is authority for the proposition that decisions of arbitrators reached in breach of natural justice are voidable, not void. Under the Friendly Societies Act 1875 justices had jurisdiction to determine disputes between such societies and claimants in default of a decision by arbitrators. In *Bache* v. *Billingham* [1894] 1 Q.B. 107 the question was whether justices could act where arbitrators had heard a complaint but had reached a conclusion in breach of natural justice. The Court of Appeal held that a "decision" existed; the behaviour of the arbitrators did "not make the decision void. It only [gave] ground for a Court to set it aside or for an appeal"; *per* Lord Esher M.R. at p. 110.[23]

In the case of decisions of administrative bodies there are a number of recent dicta, to which attention has been drawn in preceding paragraphs, to the effect that a breach of natural justice renders such decisions void—in a relative sense.[24] As Buckley L.J. said in *Stevenson* v. *United Road Transport Union* [1977] 2 All E.R. 941, 951, having referred to *Ridge* v. *Baldwin*, "Any distinction between such a decision being 'voidable' and its being 'void' (*i.e.* a nullity) can only reside in the degree of freedom which the court may feel itself entitled to enjoy in the exercise of its discretion." (The learned Lord Justice on the other hand objected to the use of the term "voidable" which, he said, implied an act which could be set aside by the unilateral act of one party). But, as has also been seen, the Privy Council in *Durayappah* v. *Fernando* [1961] 2 A.C. 337, thought a breach of natural justice rendered a decision "voidable" at the instance of the party affected, as opposed to being "truly a 'nullity.'" Lord Denning M.R. has recently expressed a similar view; *R.* v. *Secretary of State, ex p. Ostler* [1977] Q.B. 122, 135. As de Smith points out, neither view is free from difficulties.[25] It is, perhaps, better to admit that the law here is still unsettled rather than to attempt to assert that the case law is all explicable on the light of conclusions which follow inevitably from certain axioms which are taken to underlie all judicial review.

The type of case in which a breach of natural justice has most frequently been described as rendering a decision as "void" is that dealing with domestic tribunals, where the power of the tribunal is dependent on the terms of a contract. In *Wood* v. *Woad* (1874) L.R. 9 Ex. 190, an action for damages for loss arising from wrongful expulsion from a society, the plaintiff was non-suited because the expulsion was void and his membership was therefore unaffected. From the point of view of the plaintiff the result can hardly be regarded as particularly satisfactory. Amphlett B. recognised that the plaintiff could only be restored to the enjoyment of his rights by obtaining an injunction. In other words, the Court of Exchequer denied the plaintiff the choice of either accepting as effective a wrongful expulsion or challenging it by seeking an injunction. To attempt to assert a right of membership of an organisation whose other members have made it clear that they will not accept your membership is not necessarily an attractive or a wise undertaking. Nor, as will be seen later, will the courts, in their discretion, always grant the injunction, without which a large institution is likely to adhere to its original decision.

It is possible that the correct explanation of the case law is that a breach of the rule against bias renders a decision merely voidable, in other words *Dime's* case applies to all tribunals, not merely courts. On the other hand a failure to grant a hearing renders a decision void in all cases. Such a distinction between breaches of the two rules of natural justice is, however, rejected by writers as arbitrary and unjustifiable. Nonetheless it is as consistent with the authorities as any other view.

II. Exhaustion of Domestic Remedies

In many cases discussion of the effect of a breach of natural justice has arisen in connection with problems relating to resort to domestic remedies. Understandably the courts have wished to retain a jurisdiction to declare, for example, expulsion from a union to be invalid even although the original tainted decision has been confirmed by the appropriate appellate body inside the union.[27] In such cases it is first necessary to decide whether the aggrieved person must resort to domestic remedies before turning to the courts. In *White* v. *Kuzych* [1951] A.C. 585 the Privy Council held that everything turned on the rules of the association. K sought a declaration that his expulsion from a union was invalid because of bias on the part of the members of the disciplinary committee. The union rules provided that any member found guilty of an offence who "feels that the decision is unfair ... may ... file an appeal in writing." Members of the union had to swear an oath including a promise not to become a party to any suit at law or in equity against the union until they had exhausted all remedies allowed under the union's constitution and bylaws. The Privy Council refused to issue the declaration. The argument that a decision vitiated by breach of natural justice was not in any real sense a decision and therefore fell outside the rule was met with the common-sense reply from Lord Simon that:

> "The refinement which lawyers may appreciate between a tribunal's 'decision' and a conclusion pronounced by a tribunal which though within the tribunal's jurisdiction may be treated ... as no decision at all and therefore incapable of being subject to appeal cannot be attributed to the draftsmen of these byelaws or to the trade unionists who adopted them as their domestic code" (p. 600).

The Privy Council's decision has been described as "an isolated example ... contrary to the trend [of the case law]"[28] and in subsequent cases the courts have certainly shown less reluctance to interfere before exhaustion of domestic remedies. Thus in *Annamunthodo* v. *Oilfield Workers' Trade Union* [1961] A.C. 945, a case in which the worker had first exhausted domestic remedies, the Privy Council was of the opinion that the worker had had a choice whether to appeal within the union or to go straight to the courts where the relevant rule provided "any member so fined, suspended or expelled shall have the right of appeal to the annual conference of delegates whose decision shall be final and binding" (p. 956).

Similarly in *Lawlor* v. *Union of Post Office Workers* [1965] Ch. 712 Ungoed-Thomas J. distinguished *White* v. *Kuzych* on the ground that the constitution of the Post Office Workers' Union did not, like that of Kuzych's union, provide for any stay of expulsion pending the appeal so that if the court were to refuse relief until all domestic remedies had been exhausted the remedy might be quite inadequate and substantial injustice might be suffered. In *Leigh* v. *National Union of Railwaymen* [1970] Ch. 326, 334, Goff J. summed up the effect of earlier cases in two propositions:

> "The first is that even where there is an express provision in the rules that the plaintiff must first exhaust his domestic remedies, the court is not absolutely bound by that because its jurisdiction cannot be ousted, but the plaintiff will have to show cause why it should interfere with the contractual position.... The second proposition is largely the converse of the first, namely, that in the absence of such a provision the court can readily, or at all events, more readily, grant relief without prior recourse to the domestic remedies, but may require the plaintiff to resort first to those remedies."

If, then, an expelled member of an association resorts to the courts prematurely he may be refused a remedy. But if he has resorted to domestic remedies without obtaining relief the courts may refuse help on the ground that by using the domestic appeal he has approbated the original vitiated decision—a dilemma which would hardly be taken seriously had it not been raised in the courts. Lord Denning, at p. 956, rejected such an argument in *Annamunthodo* (*supra*) because, he said, an appeal, far from being an act of affirmance is a disaffirmance—a complaint. In *Ridge* v. *Baldwin* the majority of the House of Lords held that the chief constable had not, by appealing to the Home Secretary, lost his right to apply to the courts. The original decision, it was argued, was void and subsequent appellate proceedings could not breathe life into them. With respect, however, the reasoning is not entailed by the conclusion. It is not necessary to go further than Megarry J.'s dictum in *Leary* v. *National Union of Vehicle Builders* [1971] Ch. 34, 48;

> "If the rules and the law combine to give the member the right to a fair trial and the right of appeal why should he be told that he ought to be satisfied with an unjust trial and a fair appeal? Even if the appeal is treated as a hearing de novo the member is being stripped of his right to appeal to another body from the effective decision to expel him."[29]

Although the learned judge went on to describe the original decision as "a mere nullity" (at p. 49) his reasoning would remain convincing whether the original decision was regarded as void or voidable and he himself, at p. 52, stated that "for the purposes of the case before me I do not find it necessary to explore the use of the terms 'void' and 'voidable'. . . ."

III. Remedies in the Courts

A wide range of remedies is available to the individual who claims that he will be, or has been, prejudiced by a breach of natural justice. Before discussing these remedies in outline, it must be pointed out that in some circumstances where there can be no doubt that a body is under a duty to observe natural justice the courts may, because of a lacuna in the law, be unable to intervene. Such a situation occurred in *R.* v. *Smith* (*Martin*) [1975] Q.B. 531. Under the Courts Act 1971, s. 10, the supervisory jurisdiction of the High Court is excluded when the Crown Court is hearing indictable offences, as it was in this case. Appeals against criminal convictions lie to the criminal side of the Court of Appeal. Mr. Smith, however, was not a convicted person but a solicitor ordered, without being given a chance to defend himself, to pay the costs of a trial because the circuit judge thought that he was at fault in asking at the last minute for the adjournment of a case. The Court of Appeal had no doubt that the judge was in breach of natural justice but was unable to intervene. Another type of disappointed litigant is the one who fails because he applied for an inappropriate remedy although, had he chosen differently, he would have succeeded. *Hannam* v. *Bradford Corporation* [1970] 1 W.L.R. 937; *supra* p. 26 illustrates this shortcoming in the law. The Court of Appeal had no doubt that the decision of the relevant committee was vitiated by bias. Unfortunately Mr. Hannam had chosen to sue in contract when, in the view of the court, there was no contractual link between the parties. Had he sought a different remedy, for example, a declaration, he might well have succeeded in having the decision set aside.

It is not possible here to examine in detail the law relating to the remedies available to a person denied the impartial hearing to which he is entitled.[29] In the case of the superior courts the remedy, if there is one, is normally by way of appeal as, for example, *Dimes* v. *Grand Junction Canal* (1852) 3 H.L.Cas. 759. However, *R.* v. *Smith* (*Martin*) (*supra*), shows that the right of appeal does not necessarily cover every situation.

In the case of "inferior courts" and officials and bodies "acting judicially," in the exercise of a power derived from common law or statute, the prerogative orders of certiorari and prohibition are available; the former to quash a defective order after it has been made, the latter to restrain a body from proceeding to reach a decision in breach of natural justice or to act on a decision already taken. Certiorari is commonly used to challenge the decisions of magistrates, for example, *R.* v. *Birmingham JJ., ex p. Chris Foreign Foods* [1970] 1 W.L.R. 1428[30]; *R.* v. *Thames Magistrates' Court, ex p. Polemis* [1974] 1 W.L.R. 1371. The same remedy is available against administrative tribunals such as the rent assessment committee in *Metropolitan Properties* v. *Lannon* [1969] 1 Q.B. 577. The extent of the limits within which certiorari is available is unclear. It does not lie to a domestic tribunal[31] but in *R.* v. *Aston University Senate, ex p. Roffey* [1969] 2 Q.B. 538 the Divisional Court assumed that it was available against universities. The correctness of that decision was doubted subsequently in *R.* v. *Post Office, ex p. Byrne* [1975] I.C.R. 271 by another Divisional Court. A tendency to widen the scope of certiorari can be seen in cases such as *R.* v. *Criminal Injuries Compensation Board, ex p. Lain* [1967] 2 Q.B. 864 where certiorari was granted against the Board although it did not possess powers derived from the common law or statute.[32] Again in *R.* v. *Board of Visitors of Hull Prison, ex p. St. Germain* [1979] 2 W.L.R. 42, the Court of Appeal held that certiorari lay against a prison board of visitors, reversing the decision of the Divisional Court that the order was not available to quash decisions made in what were described as "private disciplinary proceedings." Prohibition may be used, for example, to restrain a magistrate from acting in a case if there is a suspicion of bias; *R.* v. *Emerson* [1913] 2 I.R. 377. Ecclesiastical courts may be restrained from acting in breach of natural justice; *R.* v. *North, ex p. Oakey* [1927] 1 K.B. 491.[33] Examples of the use of the order against local authorities, administrative bodies and similar public organisations are to be found in a number of cases discussed in earlier chapters; *R.* v. *Electricity Commissioners* [1924] 1 K.B. 171; *R.* v. *Liverpool Corporation, ex p. Taxi Fleet Operators Association* [1972] 2 Q.B. 299; *R.* v. *Kent Police Authority, ex p. Godden* [1971] 2 Q.B. 662.

A third prerogative order, mandamus, may lie to order a party to carry out a public duty, imposed by common law, statute or royal charter. Unlike certiorari and prohibition mandamus is not limited in its application to bodies acting judicially. The source of difficulty in the case of this order is, what is meant by "public duty." Often an application for mandamus ordering a defendant to carry out his duty in accordance with the law will be coupled with an application for certiorari to quash an earlier decision arrived at, for example, without a fair hearing. Examples of the use of mandamus range from Dr. Bentley's dispute with the University of Cambridge in the eighteenth century[34] to the recent leading case of *Padfield* v. *Minister of Agriculture, Fisheries and Food* [1968] A.C. 997.[35] In *R.* v. *Smith, ex p. Harris* (1844) 5 Q.B. 614 mandamus issued against a vicar ordering him to grant a hearing before dismissing the parish clerk from his freehold office. Modern cases illustrate the order enforcing duties against such bodies as country court judges,[36] statutory tribunals[37] and local authorities.[38]

The prerogative writ of habeas corpus is also available to challenge, on the ground of breach of natural justice, the validity of a decision under which anyone is being held in captivity against his will. This remedy is normally invoked in cases of extradition, deportation or immigration, areas of the law where the courts are reluctant to interfere with decisions of the executive.[39]

The declaration, or declaratory judgment,[40] and the injunction have been increasingly popular because they are not hedged about with the restrictions applicable to the prerogative orders. The declaration cannot be invoked to establish non-legal rights.[41] Nor will the court, in its discretion, grant a declaration if the granting would be of no practical use.[42] The declaration has been relied on against police authorities: *Cooper* v. *Wilson* [1937] 2 K.B. 309; *Ridge* v. *Baldwin* [1964] A.C. 40; trade unions: *Taylor* v. *National Union of Seamen* [1967] 1 W.L.R. 532; gentlemen's clubs: *Fisher* v. *Keane* (1878) 11 Ch.D. 353; the National Dock Labour Board: *Vine* v. *National Dock Labour Board* [1957] A.C. 488; and many other bodies of various kinds. The injunction is similarly available against a wide range of defendants, whether to restrain a threatened breach of natural justice or to prevent further reliance on an existing, invalid decision. An interlocutory injunction may restrain proceedings until it has been possible to establish by an action in the courts what natural justice requires in particular circumstances.[43] The injunction is not, however, necessarily available in all cases where a declaration would be. Thus, although a declaration may issue against a social club which seeks to expel a member without a hearing the court "will not grant an injunction to give a member the right to enter a social club, unless there are proprietary rights attached to it, because it is too personal to be specifically enforced"; *Lee* v. *The Showmen's Guild of Great Britain* [1952] 2 Q.B. 329, 342 *per* Denning L.J.

Other remedies available include statutory rights of appeal, for example, under planning legislation.[44] Recourse to the High Court against decisions of arbitrators who are alleged to be biased or to have failed to grant a full hearing is provided by sections 23 and 24 of the Arbitration Act 1950. Breaches of natural justice in educational institutions may be remediable by appeal to the visitor.[45]

Such a wide range of remedies has its own inherent defect: inevitably it leads to uncertainty as to which remedy is the correct one to pursue in a particular situation. No better comment on the English position could be found, at least until the reform to be discussed shortly, than that of an American writer who, describing his own legal system, has written that the present law could not in its complexity and unsatisfactoriness be rivalled by "an imaginary system cunningly planned for the evil purpose of thwarting justice and maximising fruitless litigation. . . ."[46] The courts may be tempted to concentrate not on the rights of the parties but on the remedies. The question the litigant is interested in is whether natural justice is applicable; the courts have often shown more interest in whether certiorari lies to the defendant before it.

This confusing, overlapping plethora of remedies cannot even justify itself as providing relief wherever a breach of natural justice has occurred. If, for example, there is no contractual link between an aggrieved party and a domestic tribunal which reaches a decision in violation of natural justice there is no right to damages; *Abbott*

v. *Sullivan* [1952] 1 K.B. 190. (Since the body in that case, the Committee of the Cornporters' Union was a domestic tribunal it was not subject to certiorari or prohibition.) Nor, according to *Byrne* v. *Kinematograph Renters' Society* [1958] 1 W.L.R. 762, is there a right to a declaration or an injunction in such circumstances.[47] In that case, Harman J., having decided that the plaintiff was not entitled to a remedy, went on to deny any obligation on the defendant to observe natural justice. Here is the reverse of the approach enshrined in the maxim *ubi ius ibi remedium*, reaffirmed recently as a "fundamental principle" by the Master of the Rolls.[48] This preferable approach is not unknown in the field of natural justice as is shown by the decision of Pilcher J. in *Davis* v. *Carew-Pole* [1956] 1 W.L.R. 833, 837, who recognised an obligation on the stewards of the National Hunt Committee not to warn off a person without a hearing and held that the jurisdiction to grant a declaration of injunction was not dependent on a contractual nexus.

One characteristic which all the remedies for a breach of natural justice share is that they are not available to anyone who wishes to challenge the validity of a decision but only to parties who can show that they possess the necessary *"locus standi"* or, in the phrase often used in statutes, that they are "persons aggrieved."[49] In the case of an action in tort or contract this restriction might be thought to go without saying. The class of qualified plaintiff is limited to those who can show such interference with a right as is normally required by the common law. Similarly an applicant for an injunction must establish an interference with a legal or equitable right, for example, the proprietary loss of an individual wrongfully excluded from a club; *Lee* v. *The Showmen's Guild of Great Britain* (*supra*). However, it is far less clear, in the case of the prerogative orders and the declaration, what interest the plaintiff must show if he is to be entitled to sue. Perhaps appropriately, in such a confused area of the law, the test of *locus standi* may well vary with the relief sought, or possibly, with the individual judge.[50]

These defects in the law have led to various suggestions for reform.[51] At first sight the solution is a new remedy to replace the existing rag-bag. To that suggestion there are two objections. First, whatever the uncertainties of the old law, a new remedy would inevitably produce uncertainties of its own, at least until a body of case law had built up. Secondly, the injunction and the declaration would continue to exist in the area of what might be called private law disputes. Inevitably the question would frequently arise; should the plaintiff alleging a breach of natural justice proceed by way of the statutory remedy or could he use the old, private law remedies? An attempt to minimise, or solve, the problems existing under the old law without creating the new problems which might follow from a complete reform of the law of remedies, has recently been made by the introduction, under the Rules of the Supreme Court, of a procedure called an application for judicial review.[52] In effect the new procedure enables the applicant to seek judicial review without confining himself to one remedy; he may apply for mandamus or certiorari or prohibition and the court shall grant the relief it considers appropriate. An injunction or a declaration may be granted on an application for judicial review if the court considers it would be just and convenient to do so having regard to—

(a) the nature of the matters in respect of which relief may be granted by way of an order of mandamus, prohibition or certiorari,
(b) the nature of the persons and bodies against whom relief may be granted by way of such an order, and
(c) all the circumstances of the case.

This provision is an attempt to distinguish the "public law" and "private law" use of the declaration and injunction. The wide discretion given to the court should avoid the problems of classification which would have arisen had a new statutory remedy been introduced. In accordance with the spirit of the Order there is no attempt to define, or clarify, *locus standi*. Rule 3(5) says simply "The Court shall not grant leave unless it considers that the applicant has sufficient interest in the matter to which the application relates." An applicant who would otherwise be entitled to sue for damages may include such a claim in his application for judicial review (r. 7). It remains to be seen how useful the new procedure is in the sphere of administrative law generally.[53] So far as natural justice is concerned, cases will, of course, continue to arise which lie outside the scope of Order 53 so that the litigant will still have to choose which remedy he wishes to pursue.

In addition to the remedies already discussed a person aggrieved by a decision which he alleges to have been reached in violation of natural justice may have an action for damages in tort or in contract. A local authority which destroys private property is liable in trespass if the decision under which it acts is vitiated by a failure to give a hearing; *Cooper* v. *Wandsworth Board of Works* (1863) 14 C.B.(N.S.) 180.[54] The application of force to exclude a man from a club from which he has been wrongfully expelled may be an assault; *Innes* v. *Wylie* (1844) 1 Car. & K. 257. To expel, without a hearing, in the face of a contractual obligation to grant a hearing is a breach of contract for which damages may lie; *Taylor* v. *National Union of Seamen* [1967] 1 W.L.R. 532. Is, however, the failure on the part of a body bound to observe the rules of natural justice to follow those rules in itself a tort which gives rise to a cause of action? In answering this question it is necessary to distinguish the possibility of tortious liability in the abstract from a failure of an action because of an immunity from suit. To varying degrees, judges and members of administrative tribunals possess immunity from liability for acts they commit which, in the case of other people, would constitute a tort. The law relating to judicial immunity is far from clear and only an outline can be attempted here. Judges of superior courts are immune from liability for any act done within their jurisdiction. Equally judges of superior courts are probably not liable to be sued for actions done in the course of their judicial duties either because there is no limit to their jurisdiction or it is presumed that such judges act within their jurisdiction.[55] In the case of inferior courts the law is even more unsettled,[56] especially since the decision of the Court of Appeal in *Sirros* v. *Moore* [1975] Q.B. 118. The argument for immunity for members of such courts for wrongful acts within their jurisdiction, even when committed maliciously, is strengthened by dicta in that recent case.[57] Judges of inferior courts are liable for wrongful acts committed outside their jurisdiction. It is possible that such liability only arises if the act results in a trespass to person or property.[58] Thus it is a matter of importance to determine whether a refusal to give a hearing is a wrongful exercise or jurisdiction, in which case there is immunity, or an act in excess of jurisdiction in which case there may be liability. This is the central question in the theory of judicial review and it is impossible to maintain that all the cases can be reconciled.[59] In the case of administrative tribunals the distinction is similarly between acts done within, and acts done in excess of, the jurisdiction. In the former case there is no liability in the absence of malice; *Partridge* v. *General Medical Council* (1890) 25 Q.B.D. 90. That decision also supports the view that a breach of natural justice is an error within a tribunal's jurisdiction rather than an act in excess of jurisdiction. The position of a domestic tribunal was considered in *Abbott* v. *Sullivan* [1952] 1 K.B. 189. Morris L.J. rejected the suggestion that the members of such a body should be personally liable in tort for mistakes which they had made "conscientiously and honestly." To hold otherwise, he said, would be to add new perils to certain forms of public service (p. 215). Where the "mistake" is malicious the argument against liability is weaker and should not necessarily be dependent on a contractual relationship between the tribunal and the party aggrieved. There is some support to be found in the case law for the existence of a tort of causing damage by the deliberate abuse of public office or authority but the limits of this new tort are far from clear.[60]

Even if a plaintiff has sought the appropriate remedy against a particular defendant and has satisfied the relevant test of *locus standi*, a third hurdle often requires to be surmounted. The prerogative orders, the injunction and the declaration all lie in the discretion of the court. As long ago as 1787 mandamus was refused to the holder of an office who had been suspended from office without a hearing because it appeared on the affidavits by which the application was made that his conduct had been "extremely reprehensible"; *R.* v. *Mayor etc. of London* (1787) 2 T.R. 177. Similarly, more recently, in *Fullbrook* v. *Berkshire Magistrates' Courts Committee* (1970) 69 L.G.R. 75, John Stephenson J. refused a declaration, despite holding that the committee was in breach of natural justice, because of what the judge regarded as the plaintiff's unreasonable behaviour generally in his dispute with the committee and his long history of dishonesty. In two cases involving students the courts have refused relief, although in both the universities concerned were found to have acted in breach of natural justice. In *R.* v. *Aston University Senate, ex p. Roffey* [1969] 2 Q.B. 538 a Divisional Court refused to issue orders of certiorari and mandamus because of delays in bringing proceedings. In *Glynn* v. *Keele University* [1971] 1 W.L.R. 487, 496 Pennycuick V.-C. refused to issue an injunction because, in the learned judge's view, there was no doubt about Glynn's guilt —at most a hearing would have provided an opportunity for a plea *ad misericordiam*; the university vice-chancellor's decision was "intrinsically . . . perfectly proper" so that the granting of an injunction would have resulted in a second disciplinary hearing with a similar conclusion to the first. It is easy to understand the unwillingness of the courts to assist plaintiffs whom they regard as being devoid of any merits. But in other contexts, judges have admitted the importance of giving a hearing although it would be unlikely to influence the final decision.[61] Apart from the plaintiff's sense of grievance which in itself is a legitimate matter of concern,[62] there is the need to ensure public confidence in the activities of courts, and tribunals, domestic and statutory. Glynn may have deserved what he got. But if vice-chancellors punish, or are allowed to punish, students without a hearing may they not occasionally err?

Notes

[1] H. W. R. Wade, "Unlawful Administrative Action: Void or Voidable?" (1967) 83 L.Q.R. 499. See also D. M. Gordon, "Certiorari and the Revival of Error in Fact" (1929) 45 L.Q.R. 459; "Observance of Law as a Condition of Jurisdiction" (1931) 47 L.Q.R. 386 and 557; A. W. Bradley, "A Failure of Justice and Defect of Police" (1964) C.L.J. 83, 100–104; M. B. Akehurst, "Void or Voidable?—Natural Justice and Unnatural Meanings" (1968) 31 M.L.R. 2 and 138; S. A. de Smith, *Judicial Review of Administrative Action* (3rd ed., 1973) Stevens & Sons, pp. 209 *et seq.* and 240 *et seq.*

[2] de Smith, *Judicial Review of Administrative Action* (2nd ed.), p. 223.

[3] Similarly *Kanda* v. *Government of Malaya* [1962] A.C. 322, 338.

[4] For other examples of recent references to the distinction between public and private law see *Ranaweera* v. *Ramachandran* [1970] A.C. 962, 972 *per* Lord Diplock; *Dorset Yacht Co.* v. *Home Office* [1970] A.C. 1004, 1067 *per* Lord Diplock; J. F. Garner, "Public Law and Private Law" [1978] P.L. 230.

[5] H. W. R. Wade, *Administrative Law* (4th ed., 1977) Oxford University Press, pp. 448–451.

[6] *op. cit.* p. 210.

[7] (1967) 83 L.Q.R. 499, 519.

[8] H. W. R. Wade (1969) 90 L.Q.R. 154, 155.

[9] (1969) 83 L.Q.R. 499, 512.

[10] See *De Reneville* v. *De Reneville* [1948] P. 100, 111 *per* Lord Greene M.R.; S. M. Cretney, *Principles of Family Law* (3rd ed., 1979) Sweet & Maxwell, pp. 31 *et seq.*

[11] *Administrative Law*, p. 543.

[12] See further A. Rubinstein, *Jurisdiction and Illegality* (1965), Clarendon Press, pp. 82 *et seq.* A similar view is expressed in *Halsbury's Laws of England* (4th ed.) i, para. 153.

[13] de Smith, *op. cit.* pp. 462 *et seq.*; Rubinstein, *op. cit.* p. 118; I. Zamir, *The Declaratory Judgment* (1962) Stevens & Sons, 160 *et seq.*; Akehurst, *supra*, note 1 at pp. 8–10.

[14] de Smith, *op. cit.* pp. 483 and 486.

[15] Akehurst, *supra*, note 1 at pp. 144–149. H. W. R. Wade, *op. cit.* p. 420; "There is no reason why the rule of law which says that a biased decision is void should not itself contain the qualification that it operates only if the right to object is not waived."

[16] *Supra*, p. 201.

[17] (1967) 83 L.Q.R. 499, 512.

[18] *Administrative Law*, p. 449.

[19] Rubinstein, *op. cit.* p. 220.

[20] See article by D. M. Gordon, *supra*, note 1. *Contra*, Wade, *op. cit.* p. 418.

[21] *R.* (*Giant's Causeway etc. Tramway*) v. *Antrim Justices* [1895] 2 I.R. 603; *supra* p. 43.

[22] Martin L. Friedland, *Double Jeopardy* (1969) Oxford, Chap. 4.

[23] But *cf. Hatrick* (*N.Z.*) *Ltd.* v. *Nelson Carlton Construction Co. Ltd.* [1964] N.Z.L.R. 72, 85 where Richmond J. refused to hold that an engineer, issuing certificates under a building contract, was bound to follow the rules of natural justice precisely because, if he were bound, "their non-observance would *ipso jure* invalidate a certificate." *Bache* v. *Billingham* (*supra*) was not referred to by the learned judge.

[24] See also *Cooper* v. *Wilson* [1937] 2 K.B. 309, 348 *per* Scott L.J.; *Kanda* v. *Government of Malaya* [1962] A.C. 322; *Malloch* v. *Aberdeen Corporation* [1971] 1 W.L.R. 1578.

[25] de Smith, *op. cit.* p. 210.

[26] Similarly, *Innes* v. *Wylie* (1844) 1 Car. & K. 257; *Blisset* v. *Daniel* (1853) 10 Hare 493.

[27] *e.g. Leary* v. *National Union of Vehicle Builders* [1971] Ch. 34.

[28] Citrine, *Trade Union Law* (3rd ed., 1967) (ed. M. A. Hickling) Stevens & Son, p. 317.

[29] Applied, *Pratt* v. *Wanganui Education Board* [1977] 1 N.Z.L.R. 476. But *cf. Pillai* v. *Singapore City Council* [1968] 1 W.L.R. 1278, 1286 *per* Lord Upjohn; *King* v. *University of Saskatchewan* (1969) 6 D.L.R. (3d) 120, 130 *per* Spence J.; *Giacomo Costa Fu Andrea* v. *British Italian Trading Co.* [1961] 2 Lloyd's Rep. 392; [1963] 1 Q.B. 201, 208 *per* Diplock L.J. Lord Parker C.J. in his briefly reported judgment in *Ex p. Bolchover*, *The Times*, October 7, 1970 seems also to assume that a breach of natural justice at one level may be made good by an appellate hearing.

[30] See also *R.* v. *Grimsby Borough Quarter Sessions, ex p. Fuller* [1956] 1 Q.B. 36 (certiorari to quash decision of recorder).

[31] *R.* v. *National Joint Council for the Craft of Dental Technicians, ex p. Neate* [1953] 1 Q.B. 704.

[32] For the extension of the scope of the order by the blurring of the distinction between "judicial" and "administrative" see *R.* v. *Liverpool Corporation, ex p. Liverpool Taxi Fleet Operators' Association* [1972] 2 Q.B. 299; *R.* v. *Barnsley Metropolitan Borough Council, ex p. Hook* [1976] 1 W.L.R. 1052. See also *R.* v. *Hillingdon London Borough Council, ex p. Royco Homes Ltd.* [1974] Q.B. 720.

[33] Certiorari, however, does not lie; *R.* v. *St. Edmundsbury and Ipswich Diocese* (*Chancellor*), *ex p. White* [1948] 1 K.B. 195.

[34] *R.* v. *University of Cambridge* (1723) 1 Str. 557.

[35] Although the order will lie against a minister charged with a statutory duty it will not lie against the Crown or Crown servants; de Smith, *op cit.* p. 494.

[36] *R.* v. *Pugh (Judge), ex p. Graham* [1951] 2 K.B. 623; *R.* v. *Briant (Judge)* [1957] 2 Q.B. 497.

[37] *Merchandise Transport* v. *British Transport Commission* [1962] 2 Q.B. 173.

[38] *R.* v. *Hereford Corporation, ex p. Harrower* [1970] 1 W.L.R. 1424. See also *R.* v. *Flintshire C.C. County Licensing (Stage Plays) Committee* [1957] 1 Q.B. 350.

[39] *e.g. R.* v. *Leman Street Police Station Inspector, ex p. Venicoff* [1920] 3 K.B. 72; *R.* v. *Secretary of State for Home Department, ex p. Hosenball* [1977] 1 W.L.R. 766. See further O. Hood Phillips and Paul Jackson, *op. cit.* pp. 476 *et seq.*

[40] See generally I. Zamir, *op. cit.*; *supra*, note 13.

[41] *Cox* v. *Green* [1966] Ch. 216; *Dickson* v. *Pharmaceutical Society of Great Britain* [1970] A.C. 403. Nor will the court grant declarations "in the air" about hypothetical questions; *Mellstrom* v. *Garner* [1970] 1 W.L.R. 603. There must be a "real and not a fictitious or academic" issue at stake between the parties; *Russian Commercial & Industrial Bank* v. *British Bank for Foreign Trade Ltd.* [1921] 2 A.C. 438, 452 *per* Lord Sumner.

[42] *e.g. Bennett* v. *Chappell* [1966] Ch. 391.

[43] *e.g. Pett* v. *Greyhound Racing Association (No. 2)* [1970] 1 Q.B. 46, 65; *supra*, pp. 74–75.

[44] *e.g.* Town and Country Planning Act 1971, ss. 242–245.

[45] *Supra*, p. 160.

[46] K. C. Davis, *Administrative Law Treatise* (1958) St. Paul West, iii, p. 388.

[47] For a criticism of the type of reasoning resorted to in *Byrne*'s case see D. Lloyd, "Judicial Review of Expulsion by a Domestic Tribunal" (1952) 15 M.L.R. 413; "Disqualifications Imposed by Trade Associations—Jurisdiction of Court and Natural Justice" (1958) 21 M.L.R. 661; "Natural Justice and the 'Warned Off' Bookmaker" (1963) 26 M.L.R. 412.

[48] *Hill* v. *C. A. Parsons & Co. Ltd.* [1972] Ch. 305, 316.

[49] *e.g. Att.-Gen. (Gambia)* v. *N'Jie* [1961] A.C. 617; *Arsenal Football Club* v. *Ende* [1977] 2 W.L.R. 974; *Turner* v. *Secretary of State for the Environment* (1973) 28 P. & C.R. 123.

[50] For a strict view see *Gregory* v. *Camden Borough Council* [1966] 1 W.L.R. 899. For a generous view see *R.* v. *Thames Magistrates' Courts, ex p. Greenbaum* (1957) 55 L.G.R. 129.

[51] *Remedies in Administrative Law*, Law Commission Report No. 73, Cmnd. 407 (1976).

[52] The Rules of the Supreme Court (Amendment No. 3) 1977, S.I. 1977 No. 1955 which, *inter alia*, introduces a new Order 53.

[53] See further J. Beaton and M. H. Matthews, "Reform of Administrative Law Remedies: Order 53" (1978) 41 M.L.R. 437; Carol Harlow [1978] P.L. 1.

[54] Similarly *Hopkins* v. *Smethwick Local Board of Health* (1890) 24 Q.B.D. 712.

[55] *Taaffe* v. *Downes* (1813) 3 Moo.P.C. 36n.; *Anderson* v. *Gorrie* [1895] 1 Q.B. 688; *Hammond* v. *Howell* (1677) 2 Mod. 219; *Peacock* v. *Bell* (1666) 1 Wms. Saund. 74.

[56] L. A. Sheridan, "The Protection of Justices" (1951) 14 M.L.R. 267; D. Thompson, "Judicial Immunity and the Protection of Justices" (1958) 21 M.L.R. 517.

[57] *Salmond on Torts* (R. F. V. Heuston) (17th ed., 1977) Sweet & Maxwell, p. 409; *Winfield and Jolowicz on Torts* (W. V. H. Rogers) (10th ed., 1975) Sweet & Maxwell, p. 598.

[58] *O'Connor* v. *Isaacs* [1956] 2 Q.B. 288. For a wider test, see *Abbot* v. *Sullivan*

[1952] 1 K.B. 189, 202 *per* Denning L.J.

[59] de Smith, *op. cit.* pp. 96 *et seq.*

[60] de Smith, *op. cit.* p. 296; J. F. Garner "Administrative 'Fraud' and Damages" [1963] P.L. 407.

[61] *Supra*, p. 136.

[62] *John* v. *Rees* [1970] Ch. 345, 402 *per* Megarry J.; *supra*, p. 185.

FURTHER DEVELOPMENTS: UNFAIR TRIAL AND FAIR APPEAL (p. 197)

The decision of the Privy Council, at present briefly reported, *Calvin* v. *Carr* (1979) 123 S.J. 112, contains interesting observations on the question whether a defect in natural justice at one stage in proceedings can be cured by a fair hearing at a later stage. Lord Wilberforce criticises Megarry J.'s dictum in Leary's case as being too wide. There are, he suggests, three types of case; (i) where the rehearing is by the original body or an enlarged form of it; here the second hearing supersedes the first (but see *supra*, pp. 45–47 and cases cited there); (ii) where a party is entitled by the rules of an organisation, such as a trades union, to natural justice at every stage of proceedings, *e.g. Leary*; (iii) where parties accept that they will be bound by a decision which is, in the end, fairly reached whatever defects there may be at any particular stage. This would be the position in cases, such as *Calvin* v. *Carr* itself, which arise out of disputes concerning the powers of domestic tribunals which regulate standards and behaviour in sport. Any defect in procedure on the part of stewards, referees, umpires and similar officials will be remedied by a fair hearing by the appropriate appellate body.

Lord Wilberforce described a decision taken in breach of the rules of natural justice as void but until it was so declared it could have some existence in law and was susceptible of appeal.

CHAPTER 9

CONCLUSION

In the years since *Ridge* v. *Baldwin* was decided, the rules of natural justice have been applied to bodies and tribunals which, before 1964, would not have been thought subject to such controls. Indeed recent decisions and dicta suggest a concern on the part of the courts that litigants may be seeking to push the protection given by these standards of procedural behaviour too far. In *R.* v. *Secretary of State for the Home Department, ex p. Mughal* [1974] Q.B. 313, 325 Lord Denning M.R. said, "The rules of natural justice must not be stretched too far. Only too often the people who have done wrong seek to invoke 'the rules of natural justice' so as to avoid the consequences." With respect, such a ground for caution in extending natural justice should be treated with the greatest suspicion. The justification in many cases for a hearing is, precisely, because the seemingly guilty are revealed to be innocent. Megarry V.-C. has recently urged caution on a different ground; "The concepts of natural justice and the duty to be fair must not be allowed to discredit themselves by making unreasonable requirements and imposing undue burdens"; *McInnes* v. *Onslow Fane* [1978] 3 All E.R. 211, 223.[1] Clearly, it is important not to try to extend natural justice too far. At the same time it is necessary to remember that there remain areas where the courts—or litigants—have not invoked natural justice, for example applications for regional development grants and other forms of government assistance to industry.[2] The assumption that natural justice does not apply to planning applications was mentioned earlier in Chapter 6. In some areas the appearance of judicial intervention has been to some extent at least, deceptive. "Fairness" has supplied a test which, in a number of situations, has fallen far short of what natural justice has, traditionally, been thought to require. Nor should it be overlooked that, as was seen in Chapter 8, the courts are willing, even when they find a breach of natural justice or unfairness, to exercise their discretion and withhold a remedy. Against this background of increasing reliance on natural justice, to an extent which has led the courts to issue warnings against allowing the concept "to run wild" (*Hounslow L.B.C.* v. *Twickenham Garden Developments* [1971] Ch. 233, 258 *per* Megarry J.), it is proposed in this chapter to discuss two questions; first, are there, as Pennycuick V.-C. seemed to think in *Glynn* v. *Keele University* (*supra*, p. 159), situations where natural justice is so obviously inapplicable that there could hardly be argument to the contrary; secondly, how far can and ought the courts to go in giving content to the rules of natural justice.

Perhaps the factor to which most weight has been attached in cases decided in the last few years on the applicability of natural justice is the gravity of the consequences of a decision to the person affected. On this basis Pennycuick V.-C. in *Glynn's* case distinguished between those decisions of university bodies which were subject to natural justice and those not so subject. Even if gravity were the only test of the right to a hearing it would not remove all uncertainty; how serious must consequences be before the courts will interfere? Nonetheless, emphasis on the seriousness of the matter at issue would require that in cases where, in the past, courts have been cautious in interfering, such as the treatment of aliens,[3] a conscious policy decision would in the future have to be made instead of treating the outcome as an inevitable conclusion drawn from premises involving such concepts as "acting judicially," "right" and "privilege." It would then be possible to see the factors which influenced the court and for argument about the weight which should be attached to each factor to proceed rationally. There is clearly something wrong with a method of judicial reasoning which can, for example, argue that the position of an alien seeking an extension of permission to stay in the United Kingdom "is exactly the same as that of a man who takes a lease of a house for three months and wishes to renew it for a further period: the landlord can reject his application out of hand"; *Schmidt* v. *Secretary of State for Home Affairs* [1969] 2 Ch. 149, 173 *per* Widgery L.J.

Where a decision has, objectively considered, serious consequences

—which must include refusal of entry to the United Kingdom, deportation or extradition—other factors should of course be relevant in determining whether the courts can appropriately interfere and, if so, what procedural standards they should require. Thus, apart from other considerations, there is no injustice in allowing a policeman to arrest without a preliminary hearing because of his liability in damages if he has acted unlawfully.[4] Similarly, where a ministerial decision is challenged, the appropriate ground for judicial intervention may be found by reference to unreasonableness or *ultra vires* (in the sense of exercising a power for a purpose not intended by the legislature or of taking into account irrelevant considerations) rather than by trying to imply a right to be heard into the relevant statute. As was seen in Chapters 5 and 6 the nature of a decision is sometimes thought to preclude judicial review. Here again there may be another remedy—damages for breach of contract or in negligence against the professional expert. Judicial control may be possible and appropriate where an expert is obviously behaving capriciously or arbitrarily; *Nagle* v. *Feilden* [1966] 2 Q.B. 633; *McInnes* v. *Onslow-Fane* [1978] 3 All E.R. 211. While the availability of domestic remedies should not necessarily debar a litigant from the courts (*Annamunthodo* v. *Oilfield Workers' T.U.* [1961] A.C. 945; *supra*, p. 195) their presence may render reasonable non-interference with a decision by the courts which, in other circumstances, would have been unreasonable. The distinction between expulsion and non-admission which the courts have drawn is also a proper factor, provided it is given no more than its due weight and is not allowed to be conclusive in determining the existence of a right to a fair hearing. The distinction is justifiable, it is suggested, because expulsion from an organisation inevitably creates suspicion of serious misbehaviour of some kind, according to the rules, beliefs or customs of the group concerned. An individual should have a hearing before his reputation is so damaged. Moreover, because expulsion is usually on the ground of a specific misdemeanour, a right to a hearing is important because it may enable the charge to be rebutted. On the other hand, an application for admission may be refused because a club is full, because of prejudice in the club or for many other reasons which do not reflect on the applicant. Where, however, refusal may prevent an applicant earning a living or has other serious consequences the law clearly should be prepared to intervene. Fuller has drawn a similar distinction in suggesting, and justifying, the use of different procedures to impose penalties and grant awards:

> "Where penalties and deprivations are involved we are operating at the lower levels of human achievement where a defective performance can be recognized, if care is taken, with comparative certainty and formal standards for judging it can be established. At the level where honors and prizes become appropriate we see that there would be little sense, and a good deal of hypocrisy in surrounding a decision that is essentially subjective and intuitive with the procedures appropriate to the trial of a law suit."[5]

Other facts which are clearly relevant, but raise controversial questions about the weight to be attached to them, are national security; *R.* v. *Secretary of State for Home Affairs, ex p. Hosenball* [1977] 1 W.L.R. 766 and the necessity to protect the anonymity of informants in the interest of detecting and suppressing crime; *R.* v. *Gaming Board for Great Britain, ex p. Benaim and Khaida* [1970] 2 Q.B. 417.

Once attention is fixed on the gravity of consequences as the test for the applicability of natural justice, subject to factors such as those discussed in the preceding paragraph, it will be clearly seen that little or, at least, less importance should be attached to such tests as "a duty to act judicially" or the distinction between right and privilege. This approach will also affect discussion of the connection between contract, public policy and natural justice. The drawbacks to making a right to a fair hearing dependent on contract and the conflicting dicta on the possibility of waiving the right by contract were discussed in Chapter 6. In both cases the concern of the courts should be with the importance of the decision in issue to the individual and to the public at large. This approach is to be found in cases such as *Nagle* v. *Feilden* [1966] 2 Q.B. 633 where the Court of Appeal distinguished between social clubs and, on the other hand, associations which exercise "a virtual monopoly in an important field of human activity." How far can such an approach be taken? A newspaper, for instance, may face economic disaster if a large chain of wholesale newsagents refuses to sell it. Ought a firm in a position of monopolistic or near monopolistic power give a hearing to the newspaper owners before deciding not to sell it? There are difficulties, to put it no higher, in the law trying to protect not existing contracts but a man's hope of obtaining a contract. However, it is not unknown for the courts to interfere in such a situation[6] while the Race Relations Act 1976 and the Sex Discrimination Act 1975 amount to statutory recognition of the right not to be denied one's hope of entering into a contract on the grounds of racial origin or sex. If Parliament believes that the number of complaints under the Act will not be too many to handle, then the courts too should not be deterred, if they think natural justice is applicable to the type of case here being discussed, by arguments based on practical convenience and the fear of a multitude of actions.

The case law of the last 14 years has, in extending natural justice to new fields, also emphasised the flexibility—or uncertainty—of the concept. The vagueness of the test of "fairness," the unwillingness even to try to lay down firm rules, can be seen as part of a current judicial attitude clearly expressed in another context by Sachs L.J. in *Holder* v. *Holder* [1968] Ch. 353, 401 when he expressed the hope that: "The rigidity of the shackles imposed by the rule on the discretion of the court may perhaps before long be reconsidered as the courts tend to lean more and more against such rigidity of rules as can cause patent injustice."[7] Natural justice, or fairness, may not even always involve a right to a hearing[8]—and certainly not to an oral hearing. The extent to which a party is entitled to know the evidence against him may vary with the proceedings.[9] The importance of the right to be accompanied by a representative, whether or not legally qualified, has been increasingly recognised although again such a right does not necessarily always form part of natural justice.

It is interesting to speculate whether, in the future, the English courts will be prepared to extend the scope of natural justice to include requirements not so far recognised as forming part of the concept. There are obviously limits to such a process if it is wished to continue to think of the concept, in some sense at least, as consisting of self-evident, elementary principles. However, one rule which might well be thought to fall easily within such a description is that natural justice requires that a party be told of his rights to a hearing which, in appropriate circumstances would include a right to legal representation.[10] There is some English judicial support for this argument. In *Hoggard* v. *Worsborough U.D.C.* [1962] 2 Q.B. 93 a local authority was empowered by statute to make certain payments to a person other than the owner of property if it appeared "to them to be equitable in the circumstances." H took no steps after he was informed by the council that money was available for these payments. The council decided, on the recommendation of a public health inspector, to make the payments to H's tenants. Winn J. held the decision infringed natural justice:

> "Where two parties are in dispute and it is the obligation of some person or body to decide equitably between the competing claims each claim must receive consideration and each claimant must be invited—not merely left to take the initiative if he chooses—to put forward the material ... which he desires to have considered" (at p. 100).

In *Re M.* (*Adoption: Parental Consent*) [1973] 1 Q.B. 108 the Court of Appeal went further, Sachs L.J. saying:

> "legal aid must in serious matters be regarded as something essential for safeguarding the interests of the person concerned ... and for ensuring that justice both is done and appears to be done. There may well arise cases in the future in which a rehearing might have to be ordered simply because a party was not made aware in appropriate terms of the availability of legal advice and aid."

The recognition that natural justice requires that a party is told of his rights provides a ground for criticising the decision of the Privy Council in *University of Ceylon* v. *Fernando* [1960] 1 W.L.R. 223 where it was assumed that natural justice was satisfied if a tribunal allowed a request to cross-examine when a party made such a request; there was no suggestion that he ought to be told of his right. A right to legal aid, referred to in *Re M.* is clearly of importance, particularly in criminal cases. To suggest that it is part of natural justice, however, is to attempt to stretch that concept too far. Such a right cannot be created or enforced by judicial edict; it is no more a natural right than so-called economic rights such as a right to a job.[11] The existence of the "right" is dependent on the availability of government finance. It is in fact at most a desirable goal at which to aim.

There is no doubt of the desirability, as a general rule, of the right of appeal from a decision.[12] However, it cannot be claimed that the English courts have yet recognised such a right as forming part of natural justice. It has long been recognised that practical considerations may dictate the absence of a right of appeal. Thus, to prevent delay and ensure speedy justice, the medieval law merchant often expressly forbade a right of appeal.[13] Pressure of numbers has been advanced by a modern writer as a reason why applicants for university places should not have a right of appeal against refusal.[14] *A fortiori* if there is no natural right of appeal, there can be no right, where there is an express provision for appeal, to insist on putting new evidence before the appellate tribunal where the introduction of new material is prohibited by the document granting the right of appeal; *Brown* v. *A.U.E.W.* [1976] I.C.R. 146.[15]

The desirability of giving reasons for decisions was discussed in Chapter 4. To suggest that natural justice requires the giving of reasons would, at least as the law stands at present, clearly be going too far.

A novel extension of the concept was essayed by Lord Denning M.R. in *R.* v. *Barnsley Metropolitan Borough Council, ex p. Hook* [1976] 1 W.L.R. 1052 when he suggested (at p. 1057) that the imposition of excessive punishment was a breach of natural justice.[16] Such a rule, if recognised, would enable the courts to interfere with any decision which they disliked and goes far beyond any idea of natural justice as a standard for the application of rules. A slightly less sweeping approach which is, perhaps, not an extension of natural justice so much as an extension of the grounds for judicial review is to be found in *Esterman* v. *NALGO* [1974] I.C.R. 625 where Templeman J. held that the court could set aside the decision of a domestic tribunal if satisfied that no tribunal "applying itself correctly as to the law and obeying the principles of natural justice could arrive" at that decision (at p. 632).[17]

Notes

[1] See also *Hounslow L.B.C.* v. *Twickenham Garden Developments* [1971] Ch. 233, 258 *per* Megarry J.; *Norwest Holst Ltd.* v. *Department of Trade* [1978] Ch. 201, 227, *per* Ormrod L.J.

[2] See G. Ganz, *Administrative Procedures* (1974) Sweet & Maxwell, p. 100.

[3] *Supra*, p. 169.

[4] *Cf. Ingraham* v. *Wright* 430 U.S. 651 (1977).

[5] *The Morality of Law* (1964) Yale U.P., p. 31.

[6] *Acrow Automation* v. *Rex Chainbelt Inc.* [1971] 1 W.L.R. 1676; noted P. Raynor (1972) 88 L.Q.R. 177.

[7] See also *Hill* v. *C. A. Parsons* [1972] 1 Ch. 305 and *C. H. Giles & Co Ltd.* v. *Morris* [1972] 1 All E.R. 960 for clear assertions by the courts of an unwillingness to be bound by inflexible rules.

[8] *R.* v. *Aston University Senate, ex p. Roffey* [1969] 2 Q.B. 538, 552 *per* Donaldson J.: *supra*, p. 100.

[9] *R.* v. *Gaming Board for Great Britain, ex p. Benaim and Khaida* [1970] 2 Q.B. 417; *supra*, p. 71.

[10] *Cf. Miranda* v. *Arizona* 384 U.S. 436 (1966); *The State* (*Healy*) v. *Donoghue* [1976] I.R. 325.

[11] See Maurice Cranston, *What are Human Rights?* (1973) Bodley Head, especially Chap. 8.

[12] Particularly where the initial decision is made by a party who, in some sense, may have an interest in the dispute: see *The Citizen and the Administration* (Whyatt Report) (1961) Stevens & Sons, Chap. 4.

[13] W. Mitchell, *An Essay on the Early History of the Law Merchant* (1904) Cambridge U.P., pp. 12 *et seq.*

[14] *Cf.* D. C. Holland, "The Student and the Law" (1969) 22 C.L.P. 61, 64.

[15] Denial of a right of appeal which does exist by virtue of a contract may, of course, be remedied by the courts; *Braithwaite* v. *Electrical Electronic and Telecommunication Union—Plumbing Trades Union* [1969] 2 All E.R. 859.

[16] It has been suggested that *Ex p. Hook* is an example of recourse by a common law court to the principle invoked by the European Court under the name of "Proportionality": L. Neville Brown, "General Principles of Law and the English Legal System", *New Perspectives for a Common Law of Europe* (1978) 171, 183.

[17] See further, Sir Otto Kahn-Freund, *Labour and the Law* (2nd ed., 1977) Stevens & Sons, pp. 187–189.

INDEX

INDEX